Dedicated to the Memory of the
New Zealand Military Historian, James Cowan 1870-1943,
and his successor, William Thomas Parham 1913-1997

THE
COLONIAL
NEW ZEALAND
WARS

Tim Ryan
Bill Parham

Grantham House

New Zealand

ACKNOWLEDGEMENTS

The authors wish to express their gratitude for the help that individuals, libraries and museums gave in respect of the illustrations of this book, especially the following:

Tracey Meech, for undertaking much of the preliminary photographic work.

David Corbett, who gave much advice and help with text and illustrations.

Frances Turton, who kindly allowed reproductions of her fine paintings and drawings.

Nigel Ogle, for his hospitality, photography and illustrations.

Trevor Foy, who loaned weapons from his collection.

Ray Dawson, for making available his unsurpassed fibreglass sculptures of Maori warriors.

John Topham for his maps and diagrams.

Malcolm Thomas who put a great deal of time and effort into his fine line drawings of uniforms and equipment.

Ron Lambert and Don Cimino, Directors of the Taranaki and Wanganui Museums respectively, for their kindness and help in allowing complete access to the collections.

The staff of the Photographic Section of the Alexander Turnbull Library who were helpful over a period of 10 years.

Burton Silver for his advice.

Robin Roddick for his photographic facilities and kind help.

Wally Ruffell for permitting us to draw from his comprehensive writings on weapons and artillery of the wars.

John Gibson, Ann Van Wetering, Claude Poulsen, Rod Allison, Dave Cowe and Anton Van Der Wouden for their assistance with information and illustrations.

Acknowledgments for this revised edition

I wish to acknowledge a debt I owe to my great friend Bill Parham who passed away in 1997. Our collaboration on this book was a productive and very happy one. Bill was a cultured man of integrity, both in his private life and his historical research. He had a love of classical music, a great sense of humour, and I count it a privilege to call him my mentor.

Darryl Hicks for his hospitality and unstinting help.

Brian Scadden for his excellent glass-plate photography.

Kelvin Day for his hospitality and generous help, also Ron Lambert and the other staff members at the Taranaki Museum.

The members of the 65th Re-enactment group for their generous help: Matthew Bonnett, Craig Douglas, Andrew Webb, Dean Hammond and especially Bruce Stewart and Bruce Cairns, without whom the Armed Constabulary reconstructions could not have been done.

The Howick Historical Village for the settings for some of the photographs.

Michael Murrie-Jones for his help with the text.

Jim Glover for his help and hospitality, also Louise Pomare, Vic and Melva Cartwright, Clive Allen, Terry Shattock, Wayne Joseph, Owen Mapp, Rex Hill, Ron Stewart, John Milligan and Barry Northe.

My thanks for their excellent illustrations go to: Brian Conroy, Malcolm Thomas, Sid Marsh, John Belcher and Ernie Thompson for his computer help.

Tim Ryan

First Published 1986, revised edition 2002

GRANTHAM HOUSE PUBLISHING
6/9 Wilkinson Street
Oriental Bay
Wellington
New Zealand

© 1986 Tim Ryan, Bill Parham, revisions 2002 Tim Ryan

ISBN 1 86934 082 5

Typeset by Wordset Enterprises Limited, Wellington.

Designed by Graham Stewart.

Printed in China by Bookprint International Limited of Hong Kong.

CONTENTS

AUTHOR'S NOTE

As a child I can remember my grandfather, who was a veteran of the Boer War and later a Captain during World War I, telling stories of his father (my great grandfather). The Ryan family settled in New Plymouth in 1842 where my great-great-grandfather ran a general store. During the First Taranaki War of 1860-61 the family lived in a fortified house that was loop holed and built into the earthwork defences of the town. At the sound of the signal gun firing (indicating an imminent Maori attack), the women and children would rush to the safety of the Marsland Hill stockade. As a teenager, my great grandfather, George Ryan, was enrolled in the Taranaki Militia and was one of the survivors of the disastrous attack on Te Ngutu-o- te-Manu in 1868.

George Ryan joined the Armed Constabulary in 1870 but did not live to see old age. Whilst crossing a swamp barefooted, he trod on a sharp piece of raupo reed, resulting in a wound that led to his death from blood poisoning, at the age of 40. Only 56 years separate his death from my birth, but during that time New Zealand changed in ways he could not have conceived. The war he fought for land, that he rightly or wrongly considered under-utilised by the Maori, has created a legacy of bitterness that remains to this day. In the opinion of the author, unless ways are found to include detribalised urban Maori in the Treaty settlements, this bitterness will continue to fester and nothing will be settled.

Wiremu te Manewha, chief of the Ngati Raukawa tribe of Otaki. He was an ally of Te Rauparaha, a leader in the fight against the British in 1846. Warriors such as Te Manewha trained in war from boyhood and would not tolerate European encroachment on their land. *Alexander Turnbull Library*

INTRODUCTION

T he negative impact on a Stone Age people caused by the arrival of the first Europeans (who were missionaries, traders, whalers and runaway convicts) was huge. The use of the Bay of Islands by whalers for rest and provisioning brought the twin evils of drink and prostitution, which a handful of missionaries strove to curb. Far more serious was the advent of muskets, which caused an arms race amongst Maori tribes. This created a series of devastating intertribal wars that lasted for more than two decades. It is estimated that the Maori population of New Zealand, in the early 19th century, was between 100,000 and 150,000. Out of this population probably 50,000 to 60,000 people were killed, enslaved or forced to migrate as a result the Maori-versus-Maori inter-tribal musket wars.[1] These wars were the true New Zealand holocaust and not the Anglo/Maori struggle that followed them (as claimed by a member of parliament), which resulted in combined Maori and British casualties of 2,810 killed and 3,050 wounded.

By 1840 the world was on the brink of a tide of migration the like of which had never been known before. In Britain principles for settlement promoted by Edward Gibbon Wakefield attracted both Anglicans and Presbyterians. While some envisaged a transplant of the English class system, a far greater support came from working people, who saw a chance to own land they could never afford at home. With a wave of emigrant ships on the horizon, the British with some reluctance were forced to extend their sphere of government to New Zealand. In 1840 HMS *Herald* brought Captain William Hobson R.N. to negotiate a treaty with the Maori chiefs. The outcome of these negotiations was the Treaty of Waitangi by which certain Maori leaders ceded the sovereignty of New Zealand to the British Government. The meaning of the word sovereignty, which has no equivalent in the Maori language, causes problems to this day.

The New Zealand Company, entering the field early, sent Colonel William Wakefield to acquire as large an acreage as possible. In addition to purchases in the lower North Island, the company 'bought' 30 million acres of the South Island. Unscrupulous speculators from Sydney laid their hands on all the property they could, usually in exchange for guns, tools or drink. For the Maori, permitting the newcomers to make use of land that they themselves did not immediately need was much less burdensome than preparing flax, or growing potatoes and wheat by hand for export. Acquisition often took place with little understanding on either side. Very sketchy translation facilities were partly to blame, but much more so were the completely opposing attitudes to land. The communal system of the Maori knew nothing of an individual's holding land in perpetuity. The newcomer created a farm from the wilderness, to be worked as a business to feed his family and to leave an inheritance for his children. This, although worthy, was far short of the veneration felt by Maori for a possession that formed one of the cornerstones of their way of life. Not understanding the tribal system, a European buyer might pay only some of the supposed owners whose claims were often contested, and this led to such serious disputes as that of Waitara, in Taranaki.

Hobson's replacement as Governor was Robert Fitzroy who had a strong affinity for less advanced people generally, but soon ran into collision with the settlers. Their often exiguous land claims now not only required Crown approval, a fertile cause of argument, but the colonials also resented Fitzroy's handling of a skirmish with some Maori at the Wairau, near Nelson, in which one of Wakefield's brothers died. The outbreak of war with the powerful Ngapuhi tribe in the north was also a factor in Fitzroy's being superseded by Captain George Grey in 1845.

The new arrival, a former governor of South Australia, was destined to carve for himself an indestructible monument in his new country. Grey was a man of brilliant ability, who was genuinely fond of the Maori but was also a man of few scruples and capable of altering the facts to suit his own agenda. He still had to heed the counsels of his ministers for the development of the country, but walked a political tightrope calling for great skill. His reward was often distrust from both sides.

The war in the North of 1845-1846 was not over land, but rather over the vexed matter of sovereignty. Hone Heke and his uncle, Kawiti, bettered the British in engagements in which Imperial soldiers attacked and were repulsed from brilliantly designed Maori Pas. The revisionist historian Professor James Belich[2] asserts that Maori leaders such as Kawiti, who built these Pas, actually invented artillery bunkers and trench warfare. This theory is patently untrue. These Pas grew out of the experience gained in the musket wars. Fortifications with such features had been common in Europe since the invention of gunpowder, many centuries before. He also contends that the war in the North was a small tactical victory but a big strategic defeat for Governor Grey and the British Army. Nothing could be further from the truth. Ngapuhi territory was devastated by factional fighting and Ruapekapeka Pa, which the Ngapuhi leaders had been prepared to defend, had fallen to the British. Within weeks the dissident chiefs surrendered, never to trouble the British Government again.

With a mixture of guile and action Governor Grey defeated uprisings in the Wellington and Wanganui areas, enabling him to turn his hand to the more constructive avenues of peace, until he received the governorship of the Cape Colony in South Africa. The troubles of earlier governors surfaced again for his successor, Colonel Thomas Gore Brown. A land dispute in Taranaki, which arose directly from the dislocations of the inter-tribal musket wars, caused a bitter Maori civil war between land holders and the land sellers. This lasted

A meeting between the chief Mete Kingi and the Rev. Richard Taylor at Putiki, Wanganui, to exchange land deeds. Land sales caused friction between the races, and missionaries often sided with the Government in the alienation of Maori land. *Alexander Turnbull Library*

from 1854 to 1858, resulting in at least 100 casualties. These tensions flared into open revolt which eventually required the services of a British general, Thomas Pratt, before it was quelled. Wiremu Tamehana founded the King Movement which aimed to unite the Maori to end land sales. This further compounded the difficulties of the Government in Auckland.

The situation required the return of Sir George Grey, who soon built up an army, largely of veterans from the Crimea and the Indian Mutiny, which could only have one purpose – the conquest of the North Island were nearly all the Maori were living. In addition to fighting minor campaigns in Taranaki and Tauranga, the army built a military road which gave access to the potentially rich valley of the Waikato River.

Lieutenant-General Duncan Cameron's crossing of the Mangatawhiri stream was New Zealand's Rubicon, committing the Maori to an unsought war against impossible odds. The Waikato and their allies fought a conventional war from fixed defences. These included a series of fortifications that Professor James Belich calls the Paterangi line, which he describes as "quite possibly the most sophisticated set of earthworks built up that time including the formidable fortifications of the Crimean and American Civil Wars". * His statement, like so many regarding the modern Pa, does not stand scrutiny. The earthwork defences and siege lines surrounding Sebastopol and Vicksburg (which were large towns) were on an immensely greater scale than anything built by the Maori. These fortifications included all the features that Professor Belich describes as being a Maori invention. After a heroic resistance at the hastily constructed Orakau Pa, the Kingite tribes were effectively defeated. Millions of acres of their land were confiscated, and they withdrew into what was now to become known as the King Country, never again to challenge the military settlers across the border.

The Hon. Walter Buller crosses the Wanganui River to Putiki to negotiate the formation of a Wanganui Maori Contingent for the South Taranaki Campaign of 1866. The Government often used tribal animosities to divide and rule. *Alexander Turnbull Library*

The British Army's distaste at the settlers' land hunger gave rise to a dispute between the governor and his general Sir Duncan Cameron, who resigned and left the country. The main achievement of his successor, Major-General Chute, was to march his army around the base of Mt Egmont, proving to the Taranaki dissidents that their forests were no longer a safe sanctuary. The British regiments departed, leaving the soldier- settlers of the Forest Rangers and the Militia to hold and develop the Waikato.

Continued unrest led to the formation of the New Zealand Armed Constabulary, a colonial army in all but name. Taranaki was once more aflame under Titokowaru, a better leader than the government colonels, Thomas McDonnell and George Whitmore, who suffered humiliation at his hands in 1868. As if this were not enough, a new guerilla captain, Te Kooti Rikirangi, started a fresh revolt in the densely forested ranges of the Urewera lying between Gisborne and the Bay of Plenty. Titokowaru's fall from grace in the eyes of his followers hastened the end of the South Taranaki campaign.

Whitmore's 1869 invasion of the Urewera started Te Kooti's decline. Thereafter it was cynical Government policy to use the powerful tribes from the East Coast, Rotorua and Wanganui (known as Queenites or Kupapa), supporters of the Government, to continue the pursuit of Te Kooti into the Urewera fastness. The role of the Kupapa tribes is to this day a sensitive issue, and many contemporary activists would have us believe that they were traitors to their race. Many Maori informants were shown in the television series *The New Zealand Wars*. However, not one of them gives the Kupapa tribes' point of view – political correctness is alive and well in New Zealand. Te Kooti followed will-o'-the- wisp tactics for some time until dogged Kupapa pursuit forced him to take refuge in the King Country. Like Titokowaru, his depredations only affected sparsely settled areas of the country, and revisionist assertions that these two Maori leaders almost brought the Government to the brink of capitulation are greatly exaggerated. Te Kooti's retirement from the field of battle signalled the end of the wars, though passive resistance inspired by Te Whiti Rongomai and Tohu Kakahi perplexed the Government for years afterward.

[3]Peter Maxwell, in his book *Frontier,* promotes the theory that the New Zealand Wars were won by neither race, but rather a bond was formed between the settlers and the Maori, who fought on both sides of the conflict, thus becoming fighting friends. In fact, once the bitter struggle ended, the service of Maori loyalist leaders to the Crown was conveniently forgotten by successive cynical settler governments, and many Queenites were pressured, and in some cases forced, to sell the land they had fought and died to retain. Ironically, in many cases the Kupapa Tribes suffered in a simular way to their opponents in the Native Land Court.

As a people, we seem to have little interest in our own past, and the lessons of history are quickly forgotten by succeeding generations. The sites of Battles between Maori and Pakeha, fought by our ancestors for the possession of this land are largely forgotten. This is not a new phenomenon; the baby boomers born in the years immediately after the Second World War were brought up on a plethora of war books and films relating to that struggle. Twenty-five years before that another generation fought a war to end all wars. These two world wars were the most destructive in human history, but how many children in today's schools would have ever heard of the Kaiser or Stalin? The intention of this book is to recreate the past in the hope that it will stimulate the interest of a new generation of New Zealanders in the exciting history of their country.

Tim Ryan 2002

THE MAORI WARRIOR AND WARFARE

In pre-European days, armed conflict was endemic among the Maori, who were a race of warriors. A warrrior (toa) was trained in the arts of war, in suppleness of body, fleetness of foot and skill in the use of all weapons from an early age. He had no time for a heavy weapon, because his most remarkable quality, both in attack and defence, was agility. Neither the bow and arrow nor the sling was used, missile weapons being confined to stones and spears thrown by hand, and the whip-propelled dart. These were not favourite arms, however, for the Maori much preferred hand-to-hand combat.

Before the arrival of the pakeha, causes of war were endless. It was waged to defend territory, or to extend it. Insults, slights or sorcery were fertile sources of strife, so that war, though often suspended for long periods, was never finished, and a tribe or family might wait for generations before a chance for revenge (utu) presented itself.

Perhaps the most common reasons were a desire by tribes or individuals for mana, utu or muru. Mana is impossible to define with a single English word, but can mean authority, control, influence, power, prestige or psychic force. Thus a warrior was born with mana, but could increase or decrease it by his own way of life. Skill in war, wealth, bravery and powerful allies increased mana. Utu means to give satisfaction or payment in the event of a slight or insult, and therefore the Maori code was very much an eye for an eye. It did not matter if the real culprit escaped after, say, a murder, so long as some members of his tribe or family were killed in payment (utu). Muru meant to plunder, and this was an important method of redistributing goods in an economy where there was little surplus. All these elements were later present in the conflict between Maori and European.

In war the tribe (iwi) or sub-tribe (hapu) were led by a chief (ariki), who was generally the first-born male of the leading family. However, in addition

Kingite warriors in war costume, Waikato, 1864. *Alexander Turnbull Library*

5

to the privilege of birth, the mana of the ariki was dependent on his character, bravery, wisdom and natural gifts of leadership.

There was no natural or elected leader of a tribe, for there might be several ariki. If the first-born of the senior family was lacking in military prowess, then a younger brother or a hopeful from a junior branch of the family might assume leadership. These distinctions tended to break down during the later stages of the wars with Europeans, when some tribesmen became disillusioned with their hereditary leaders and so joined Te Kooti, who was not a chief by birth.

A Maori chief was more of a war leader than a commander, and relied more on example than counsel. The fact that such a man could not effectively command made it all the more necessary for him to set an example, since the general absence of military discipline lent importance to his mere presence to ensure victory. It was common for the rank and file to flee if the chiefs leading them were slain, so that even on the brink of victory an attacking force might withdraw for this reason — as at the battle on Moutoa Island in 1864 when Te Moro, a warrior friendly to the Government, killed the Hauhau prophet Matene.

When the Maori individually or collectively took fright, on the loss of a leader or for any other reason, nothing could stem their flight. An old Ngapuhi chief, when talking to F. E. Maning about Hone Heke's war against the British in 1845, gave his opinion:

> One soldier as I have heard say, was shot by another because he had run away. I don't think it is right to do this. When a man feels afraid who is ordinarily of good courage, it is a sign that he will be killed, and he ought to be allowed to go away.[1]

The basic fighting unit of the Maori was the hapu. Their accounts refer to war parties of Hokowhitu (70–100 men), and Rau Hokowhitu (300–400), but it is unlikely that during the 1860s any concentration numbered more than 1,500. Titokowaru, the Ngati Ruanui war chief, had only about 60 warriors at

A sketch by William Strutt of a Maori war dance (peruperu), 1860. It is interesting to note the British weapons and equipment carried by the warriors. *Alexander Turnbull Library*

the start of his campaign, rising to a maximum of 400 after his successes against Government forces. Rewi Maniapoto had some 300 followers at Orakau, but these included women and children. During the 1860s volunteers often came in from outside tribes, giving the Maori forces a semblance of a national front, but the wars were mainly a series of pitched battles in which each tribe made a final desperate stand on its own hereditary domain.

Te Ati Awa at Waitara, Waikato at Rangiriri, Ngatı Maniapoto at Orakau and Ngaiterangi at the Gate Pa all fall into this category.

When white traders and missionaries came to New Zealand in the first years of the nineteenth century, Maori chiefs were quick to see the advantages of the musket and the power it gave over enemies without it. Whereas in pre-European times the fighting had been man to man and pitched battles probably uncommon, the acquisition of muskets by the northern tribes allowed them to set out on wars of destruction, the scale of which was unprecedented.

In the first 30 years of the century, thousands of Maori must have fallen before the firearms of Hongi Hika (uncle of Hone Heke) and Te Rauparaha. Since pakeha settlement was mainly concentrated in the North Auckland area, Hongi Hika's Ngapuhi were well placed to buy guns. Before this development, when Maori society became increasingly disorganised under the impact of an alien culture, there was a season for warfare between November, when the crops were planted, and early autumn, when the crops were harvested. This season was dedicated to Tu, the God of War. The rest of the year belonged to other deities such as Rongo, god of the kumara (sweet potato) and of the pleasures of peace.

Left: Riwhitete Pokai, chief of the Ngapuhi tribe, was prominent in Hone Heke's war. He and his men took the blockhouse at the foot of the flagstaff at Kororareka and shared in all the later fighting. He was wounded by a bayonet thrust at Okaihau. *Auckland Institute and Museum. Right:* A fully tattooed warrior, sketched from life in 1864 by Major-General H. G. Robley, a young officer engaged in the Tauranga campaign. From *Moko or Maori Tattooing*

Before the teachings of Christian missionaries took effect, cannibalism was a regular practice in war. Human flesh eked out the precarious food supply of war parties. This was customary only under those conditions, being rarely adopted in peacetime except on ceremonial occasions. Maoris believed they were securing utu (revenge) and mana (prestige) by eating their enemies.

This practice had almost disappeared when the first large European settlements were established in 1840, and rarely featured in the wars until Titokowaru revived it in 1868. This custom, and the cutting out of the heart of the first enemy slain in battle, was meant to instil fear into the white troops, and undoubtedly increased the ferocity to the conflict.

The taking and preservation of heads was also a long-established Maori custom. The head of a warrior was the most sacred (tapu) part of his body, and because of this the face was heavily decorated with the deeply incised patterns of tattooing (moko). No doubt it was the sacredness of the head which gave rise to the practice of drying and preserving. Those of enemies were so treated in order that they might be mocked and reviled. Later, during the Hauhau phase of the wars, Captain Lloyd's severed head was carried around the country as a prophetic emblem to incite war fever.

When on the warpath, the Maori was seeking mana and not following the path of chivalry on the European model. Nevertheless there were times during the 1860s when Maori conduct was highly ethical, as, for example, was the code of behaviour drawn up by the Ngati Raukawa chief Henare Taratoa before the engagement at Gate Pa in 1864.

These instances of chivalry stemmed from the influence of missionary teaching, and their extent has been much exaggerated in later accounts. Traditionally the Maori was a fierce, vindictive and sometimes treacherous fighter. His chief assets as a warrior were his skill with simple but ingenious arms, his cunning in strategy and tactics, the solidity of his defence works, and lastly, if all else failed, his ferocity in combat. He seldom expected or gave quarter, as was illustrated by the old Ngapuhi chieftain Toenga, who said to Lieutenant-Colonel T. McDonnell:

> You ask if it is not better to save the life of an enemy, when you have rendered him helpless, than to kill him? No it is not better neither is it wise, be first or they will kill you.[2]

During the North Island wars, the Maori relied on their time-honoured tactics of building a pa on the tribal land they wished to defend and inviting the British or Colonial troops to take it. Time had, however, run out for such conservative means. The strategy worked well when both sides relied on the same weapons, but were outmoded with the advent of heavy artillery. Similarly the Maori learned that despite their courage, and because each man fought in his own way, the discipline of the British soldier always prevailed in set-piece battles on open ground.

Once these hard lessons had been learned, the Maori warrior turned to the guerrilla alternative of ambush and surprise raids in which he had always excelled, but by then the odds against victory were too great. The theory of divide and rule was also applied by the Government, who clearly saw the advantage of employing friendly tribes who were often the enemies of 'rebel' Maori and could be relied upon to fight with the skill and ruthlessness of their own countrymen. In many ways the aims of the loyalist Maori (kupapa) were no different from those of their Pai Marire or Hauhau opponents. All wished to ensure the survival of their land and, through the retention of that heritage, the culture which depended upon its possession.

An unknown Maori
photographed in the late
1860s carrying a tupara, or
double-barrelled shotgun.
His cloak is of dogskin.
*Hawke's Bay Art Gallery
and Museum*

In traditional Maori culture, peace-making was usually initiated by those who had been getting the worst of the fighting. This was stated forcibly by a Maori veteran of the Waikato war:

> After our defeat at Rangiriri, overtures of peace were proposed to us; but though we had lost our pa and many men we never sued to the pakeha for peace. To sue for peace is a confession of weakness — an acknowledgement that one is beaten. We invariably treated all these offers with contempt. Numbers of times the pakeha sent heralds of peace to us, proclaimed it (almost without our knowledge) in the Gazette, sent flags of truce to us to treat for peace, just as if they had experienced all the reverses and losses themselves that we had. Why could they not have waited until we made signals to that effect? This persistence irritated us more than our own defeats had. We tore up their Gazette, fired upon their flags of truce, and shot and tomahawked their messengers.[3]

Sir John Fortescue in his history of the British Army wrote of the Maori warrior:

> The British soldier found the Maori on the whole the grandest native enemy that he ever encountered. Gurkhas and Sikhs were formidable before them: Zulus were formidable after them, but all these had copied European discipline. The Maori had his own code of war, the essence of which was a fair fight on a day and place fixed by appointment, which the best and bravest man should win. The British soldier, therefore, held him in deepest respect, not resenting his own little defeats but recognising the noble side of the Maori and forgetting his savagery.[4]

This Maori war trumpet (putara) captured by Captain Newland at Opotiki in 1865 was made from a large tropical shell found in Northland.
McArthur and Co., Auckland

This is a simplistic view of the Maori warrior, but it does contain some truth. The Maori had his own unwritten rules of warfare, which under the influence of the missionaries did include elements of chivalry. If all other methods failed, he preferred a hand-to-hand struggle in which the bravest man won. The British soldier showed a great deal of respect for his opponent, even to the extent that one regiment (the 65th) had a special relationship of friendly rivalry with the foe. This attitude changed after the major Maori defeats in the Waikato and Taranaki because of disillusionment with Christianity and the rise of the Hauhau religion.

The Pai Marire (Good and Peaceful) or 'Hau Hau' movement was initially an attempt to come to terms with the European settlers and their way of life. However, these efforts soon became embittered, so that the Hauhau adherents returned to their traditional fighting methods.

Maori losses in the wars between 1845 and 1872 have been estimated at 2,000 killed and 2,000 wounded. Kupapa casualties were approximately 250 killed. British and Colonial forces lost 560 killed and 1,050 wounded.

Maori war dress

This traditionally consisted of a short kilt or apron-like garment (maro), with a thickly woven war belt into which weapons could be thrust. Shields were never used, although sometimes mats were wrapped around the left arm to ward off blows. Often a warrior would strip off and fight naked for the sake of free movement. Closely woven full-size war cloaks were occasionally worn, often soaked with water before fighting. This was supposed to render them capable of stopping spear thrusts.

The mark of a fighting man was always the characteristic facial tattooing (moko), a pattern of deeply cut spiral lines. Legs, thighs and buttocks were often similarly decorated. Tattooing was such a painful process that it was not begun until manhood. It had no connection with tribal distinction or rank, but was purely decorative.

Frederick Maning described a war party of the 1830s:

> As I have said, the men were all stripped for action, but I also notice that the appearance of nakedness is completely taken away by the tattooing, the colour of the skin, and the arms and equipment. The men in fact look much better than when dressed in their Maori clothing. Every man is without exception covered with tattooing from knees to waist; the face is also covered with dark spiral lines.[5]

Left: Mihaka Tumuakuingi (left) and Te Ewiata in the war dress of the 1860s. *Hocken Library. Right:* The fighting costume of a Maori in the 1860s, showing the thigh tattooing. From *Moko or Maori Tattooing*

By the 1840s the usual item of war dress became the rapaki, or waist mat, usually knee length, which could be a blanket or made of native flax. The rapaki was supported by a flax war girdle, and every man generally had a short-handled tomahawk thrust into it just over the hip or at the small of the back.

By the 1860s European dress had been widely adopted, but warriors sometimes still stripped naked for battle. The use of the blanket was almost universal, and when used for a waist mat the front was sometimes drawn between the legs and secured at the back as a form of loin cloth. Shirts and trousers were commonly worn, and warriors favoured waistcoats as these provided pockets for carrying cartridges and percussion caps.

All who had managed to obtain firearms were equipped with from one to three cartouche or ammunition boxes, worn across the chest or strapped around the waist. These were generally made from a solid block of wood, drilled with two rows of holes to receive the paper cartridges and covered by a leather flap.

The practice of male tattooing had virtually disappeared by this time. Most middle-aged men still bore the moko, but younger warriors often grew beards in place of the tattoo.

Right: A warrior of the 1860s wearing a waist blanket or rapaki of European manufacture. The shoulder belt carries a leather-covered wooden cartouche box, and a tomahawk is thrust into the waist belt. He has a Snider breech-loading carbine, which would have been captured in battle or carried by a friendly (kupapa) tribesman. Next to him stands a chief and warrior of the 1860s dressed in a traditional kahu taniko, or fine flax-fibre cloak, with an ornamental border. He bears a long-handled tomahawk (kakauroa). *Far Right:* A Maori of the 1840s in stripped fighting order. His face is fully tattooed and the hair, worn long, is drawn up into a traditional topknot. He carries a taiaha, a hardwood striking and thrusting weapon, the point of which is adorned with feathers and dog fur. Around his waist he wears a war belt with a tomahawk or patiti thrust into it. *Scupltures in fibreglass by Ray Dawson, 1982*

Weapons

Long and short clubs and wooden spears used for thrusting were the usual weapons. In addition to carrying a long spear or club in his hand, the Maori generally had a short club or patu, made of stone, wood or bone, stuck in his belt. Dexterity and quick footwork were needed for their use.

The white traders brought new arms, trade axes and flint-lock guns, as well as the old triangular bayonet which was later used as a spear point. The axes had no handles, so the Maori fitted their own. The long-handled type was called the kakauroa, and the short tomahawk the patiti. While every European combatant in the wars carried a firearm, many Maori did not. The younger man who had not been able to acquire one had to go into battle equipped with long- or short-handled tomahawks.

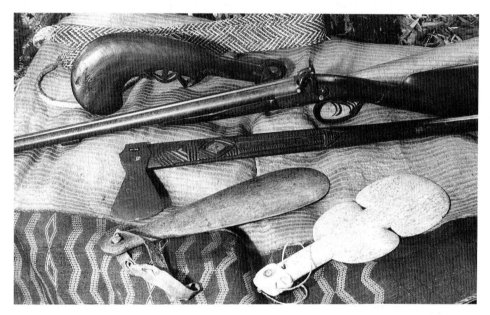

Maori weapons. *From the top: 1. hardwood club (patu wahaika); 2. superior tupara, or double-barrelled percussion shotgun; 3. long-handled tomahawk, or kakauroa; 4. whalebone club, or patu paraoa, with dogskin wrist thong; 5. whalebone club, or kotiate, with flax wrist thong. Taranaki Museum, photographs T. Ryan & N. Ogle*

The Maori called his flint-lock gun a ngutu-parera ('duck bill'), from the shape of the hammer. The other popular firearm was the tupara, or double-barrelled shotgun. At first the latter gave the warrior a slight advantage, for if he was rushed he could get off two shots before his enemy could close and the fighting become hand to hand. The British soon learned when attacking to fall flat on the ground after the first volley, so that the second passed harmlessly over their heads.

Mr W. L. Ruffell, writing in *The Volunteers* (New Zealand Military Historical Society), has pointed out that many of the Maori arms were described as 'Brummagen'. This was a derogatory corruption of the word 'Birmingham', a city noted at that time for turning out cheap and trashy guns for sale to natives in the colonies.

References by some historians to the use of 'Tower' muskets must be taken with a grain of salt. This description in Victorian times implied good workmanship. Knowing this, unscrupulous traders would stamp the word 'Tower' on Brummagen products, deceiving the Maori into believing he was buying a good-quality firearm.

The traders well knew that the Maori would sell his soul for a musket, so they demanded and got exorbitant prices. After making a series of sales these tricksters, who were often seafaring men, would depart smartly for distant parts before customers discovered the fraud. Rarely did these gun runners supply a back-up service in spare parts or ammunition.

Unlike the British soldier, who always had a regular and liberal supply of ammunition, the Maori was obliged to make cartridges from whatever came to hand. Any old paper, powder (including filling from unexploded grenades or shells) and scrap lead were grist to his mill. Sir J. E. Alexander described Maori ammunition:

> Sometimes five nails were tied together, heads and points, also plugs of hard puriri wood coated with tea chest lead. I also heard of bullets cast in the bowls of tobacco pipes, a row of these being laid in the ground and the lead run into them. The means for making rough powder are not wanting in New Zealand, but percussion caps are a great difficulty. When I was in command in Auckland, a Maori came in and offered privately a shopkeeper three hundred pounds in gold for six hundred boxes of caps, the usual selling price of which was eighteen pence. This was a sore temptation but it was resisted.[6]

Many traders were not so scrupulous, and ammunition found its way to the Maori warrior even in wartime. Percussion caps were to be had only on the black market, and were priced accordingly. Often the Maori was forced to use the heads of matches, fitted into boot eyelets. These were a poor substitute for the real thing. Misfires were frequent under the best conditions, and the home-made version was useless in the rain.

When a warrior squeezed the trigger, he was rather lucky if his weapon found its mark. Misfires averaged 15 per cent of all rounds in dry weather, rising to 25 per cent in damp conditions. By the 1860s such faults were very rare in the British soldier's Enfield, since it used waterproof cartridges. Bearing in mind the Brummagen guns and crude ammunition, the results the Maori achieved were truly amazing, for they faced the might of British and Colonial Government forces equipped with the latest small arms and artillery.

A wooden cartouche box, an 1853 pattern Enfield with elaborate Maori carving on the stock, and a whalebone-handled patiti, or tomahawk, displayed on a fine flax cloak covered with kiwi feathers. *Wanganui Museum, photograph T. Ryan*

HONE HEKE'S CHALLENGE

In the late eighteenth century, George III's Ministers decided to solve two problems at a single stroke by peopling empty Australia with felons unwanted in Britain. Outward bound, the convict ships had no space to spare, but the return voyage presented the difficulty of finding something more profitable than ballast to fill the gaping holds.

The land had little to offer, so the captains looked to their own element to provide suitable cargoes. The Southern Ocean was one great untapped whaling ground, and with the petroleum industry yet unborn, the great creatures of the sea could light the lamps of the world for decades to come. So it was that the convict transports carried hunting gear, and were quickly joined in their bloody trade by ships from the ports of New England.

Bases were vital for fresh water and other supplies, as was recreation on dry land for crews after spells of grinding toil — in one case for as long as 11 months without a break. In New Zealand the warm lush shores of the Bay of Islands were most favoured by the whalers. At the little settlement of Kororareka (now Russell) the order of the day was soon rum, women and song.

Kororareka, from a sketch by Captain Clayton, on the morning of 10 March 1845 the day before its destruction by Hone Heke and Kawiti. *Alexander Turnbull Library*

The debauchery of the whalers, along with carnage among the Maori from the increasing use of firearms in their tribal skirmishes, brought pressure from the missionaries and others for an extension of British government from New South Wales. France's interest in the country added an impetus, leading to the appointment of a Resident, James Busby. He was, as the Maori said, 'a man-o'-war without guns' and quite powerless to make much improvement in the state of affairs.

Stronger measures were obviously needed, and in 1840 Captain William Hobson, R.N. arrived in H.M.S. *Herald*. He was appointed Lieutenant-Governor in the same year, and the main achievement of his term of office, cut short by his early death, was to conclude the Treaty of Waitangi with as many Maori chiefs as could be induced to sign. While the Maori gave away their sovereignty, no settler's title to their land would now be secure unless it received Crown assent. Soon afterwards a British Army garrison arrived, originally two companies of the 80th Regiment joined later by another from the 96th.

The signing of the Treaty of Waitangi, 6 February 1840. Hone Heke shakes hands with Governor Hobson at the rear table. A modern reconstruction by L. C. Mitchell. *Treaty House, Waitangi*

Hobson decided that the Bay of Islands was unsuitable for his capital, and so created a new one on the Auckland isthmus. This departure from Kororareka lessened the importance of the dominant local tribe, the Ngapuhi. Far worse, from their point of view, was the new Government practice of levying customs and other dues on the visiting ships. Whaling captains liked the practice no better and promptly sought other bases free of such imposts so that the income enjoyed by the chiefs soon declined.

Hone Heke Pokai, a nephew of Hongi Hika, who with the initial advantage of firearms had decimated tribes to the south, became disenchanted with the pakeha, or white man. Had he not embraced Christianity, spoken in favour of signing the Treaty of Waitangi and presented the tall flagstaff on Maiki Hill behind Kororareka? Now his reward was to see the centre of gravity move to Auckland, leaving the Bay of Islands a sideshow, with its trade vanishing like water in the sand. Events in the south were not lost upon him.

The new governor, Robert FitzRoy, believed that Captain Arthur Wakefield and his companions were largely to blame for the Wairau tragedy and so took no action against the Ngati Toa chief Te Rauparaha, at whose hands the victims had died. Reinforcements who had come from Sydney at the time of the massacre, had returned there.

Meanwhile, one obvious act of protest occurred to Hone Heke. The British colours, symbol of an alien domination he had come to detest, floated from the top of what he still regarded as his flagstaff. For him, to think was to act, and in July 1844 he cut the flagstaff down.

Governors, like their military officers, rarely felt that they had enough troops to guarantee that blessed state, security. The two companies of the 80th Regiment had been dispersed to allay the fears of the settlers at Wellington after the Wairau 'massacre' and to stop a tribal conflict in the Bay of Plenty. After this the troops joined their comrades of the 96th at Auckland.

FitzRoy now sent the latter company to Kororareka. With reinforcements from Sydney, he went to the Bay of Islands in August. Tamati Waka Nene, leader of another section of the Ngapuhi and as much of a statesman in the north as Wiremu Tamehana would prove to be in the Waikato, helped to calm things down, and on his assurance the troops were withdrawn.

Hone Heke replaced the flagstaff, but on reflection and with the prompting of interested parties once again demolished it on 9 January 1845. Back went the men of the 96th to repair the damage, only to see it cut down a third time. The next replacement was sheathed with iron, while blockhouses and other defences were built to protect the flag and the European settlers.

Tamati Waka Nene, chief of the Ngati Hoa tribe. Tamati was one of the first chiefs to sign the Treaty of Waitangi and remained a staunch friend of the British. He led his tribesmen against Hone Heke during the war in the north. *Hawke's Bay Art Gallery and Museum*

Despite these precautions, Hone Heke and his ally Kawiti attacked both the blockhouses and Kororareka on 11 March. The soldiers, with the help of sailors and men of the settlement, held back the Ngapuhi while women and children were taken off to nearby ships. With the fall of Commander Robertson, R.N., Lieutenants Philpotts, R.N. and Barclay decided to abandon the burning village altogether, having lost 19 killed.

FitzRoy's further appeal to Sydney for help was answered by the despatch of the newly arrived 58th (Rutlandshire) Regiment. Upon reaching Auckland the new force under the command of Major Cyprian Bridge was taken over by Lieutenant-Colonel William Hulme with some of his 96th Regiment, and sailed in the transports *Slain's Castle* and *Velocity*.

The ships reached the Bay of Islands on 28 March, finding H.M.S. *North Star* already there. Waka Nene, angered by what he held to be a treacherous

Hone Heke (carrying a musket), his wife Hariata, and his ally Kawiti. A lithograph after J. J. Merrett, 1846. *Rex Nan Kivell Collection, National Library of Australia, Canberra*

attack by his fellow chiefs, had asked for the troops to be sent, and now hailed his pakeha allies. They were treated to their first sight of a Maori Amazon in action, for Waka's wife took an energetic part in a mass haka, or dance, of welcome. It was an accepted practice for women to fight, with reckless bravery, beside their menfolk in battle. Not to be outdone, the British replied with a ceremony of their own. While the band of the 58th Regiment played the National Anthem, the Union Jack was raised on a makeshift staff to reassert Her Majesty's dominion.

Pageantry has its place, but must be backed by more serious action. To open his campaign, Lieutenant-Colonel Hulme meant to deal with a chief called Pomare who was suspected of trying to incite Te Wherowhero, of the Waikato, to rise against Auckland. As there was no wind to carry the ships to Otuihu, there was no alternative to the laborious method of warping or towing by boats.

As some recompense, on arrival the force saw a white flag raised over Pomare's pa, or fortified village. The chief and his family boarded the *North Star* and, as Hulme directed, gave orders for the tribe to surrender their weapons within two hours. The Maori preferred to keep their guns and leave their homes. This was taken as an open invitation to looting by the troops, a regrettable custom followed by both sides throughout the years ahead.

Major Bridge recorded:

I never saw men behave better in my life than the 58th. The 96th on the contrary commenced plundering before the fire began, or before any instructions were received on shore relative to the *Pa* being destroyed; so did many of the Volunteers from Auckland.[1]

The destruction of Pomare's Pa, Otuihu, by detachments of the 58th and 96th Regiments. H.M.S. *North Star* is seen in the foreground. Pomare was detained on board this ship. A painting by Major Cyprian Bridge. *Alexander Turnbull Library*

Pomare. From *Pictures of Old New Zealand*

When the troops left the pa, it suffered the same fate that had befallen Kororareka the previous month.

The colonel proposed to concentrate next on Kawiti's pa, but was advised by the Rev. Henry Williams that he would do better to go to Hone Heke's stronghold at Puketutu instead. The missionary was treading a dangerous path. In the future Maori nationalists would find out that the clergy were not above passing intelligence to the Government during times of unrest, and this was to be a factor in the murder of the Rev. Carl Sylvius Volkner at Opotiki in 1865 (see pp. 125).

Hulme and his men were soon to have their doubts about the new move. After landing at Onewhero Bay, they found what it was like to tramp for hours, heavily laden, along a poor track leading over hills and gullies. Waka had been arrayed in an odd mixture of uniforms, but soon tired of his finery and reverted to his usual blanket, leaving his unlucky wife to carry the discarded clothing.

During the night of 3 May there came a torrential downpour, so that the morning found a very bedraggled force. With both food and ammunition soaked, Hulme made for the Kerikeri mission to dry out for a couple of days. Beginning on 6 May, a difficult march, partly in forest through which a track had to be cut, brought the column to Waka's pa, which was two miles to the north of Puketutu. Here the tribe had put up huts for the soldiers, and hot food and shelter made a most acceptable change after recent discomforts.

At dawn Hulme took Bridge to survey the enemy position, but neither found the prospect pleasing:

> The pa was built on a slight eminence, was square of shape, but zigzagged at the corners in order to bring a crossfire to bear on its assailants. It had three rows of tree-trunk palisades, 15 feet in height, sunk to several feet in the ground, each tree-trunk 5 to 6 inches in diameter, set close together. A mass of stone rubble, collected from volcanic debris strewn about, further strengthened the foundations of the pekerangi (or outer fence). The palisading was carefully caulked with green flax to prevent enemy bullets penetrating the apertures; loopholes were everywhere prepared to facilitate the defence, and to render its storming still more difficult, a deep trench was dug between each of the wooden walls.[2]

As military engineers, the Maori had little to learn, but after the immense labour of building what could sometimes be the equal of an Iron Age hill fort, they rarely bothered about a water supply. While this was not vital in the event of a one-day battle — the norm in tribal wars — it proved a serious weakness when facing a European-style siege.

In the matter of a water supply, Puketutu was not typical, as it stood on the shore of Lake Omapere. Hulme, so far from his base at Auckland and with such indifferent land communications, could not in any case think of a long drawn-out operation. When on the following morning he disposed his force he was only too conscious of the pathetically inadequate means at his command for a softening-up barrage. These consisted of only a dozen naval rockets which, when fired, amused rather than terrorised the Maori.

The attack was to commence on the right, the storming force consisting of the 58th Light Company, a detachment of the 96th, and the balance drawn from marines and sailors. Bridge described their advance:

> They had to cross a narrow ravine between the lake and the left face of the pa under a heavy fire. When half-way over they found themselves opposed by a party occupy-

ing the heights near the opposite sides, so that previous to taking up their separate positions for storming the pa, it became requisite to dislodge this party, who would otherwise have harassed them in their rear. This they did in most gallant style with the loss of only three men, and took possession of a breastwork from which they kept up a fire on the pa as well as the wood in rear of it, into which they had driven the enemy.[3]

Some of Kawiti's followers slipped through the trees to reappear in the rear of the troops. This was a rash thing to do, for the defenders were inviting a devastating experience, as one of them later recalled:

A number of the red tribe who had not joined in the attack on our pa came at our people with a rush with their bayonets fixed to their muskets, yelling horribly, grinding their teeth and cursing. Down went Kawiti's choicest warriors, the ground was strewn with them. Alas, it was a fatal mistake. We never tried that move again. Once was quite enough. But it was wrong of the red tribe to curse us. We were doing no harm; we were merely fighting them.[4]

Their friends in the pa sallied out to help but were driven back, and the battle ended with ineffectual firing by both sides. Hulme felt he could do no more against such a strong position, and led his force back to the coast, having lost 13 men.

Lieutenant Egerton, R.N. (at right of painting) with his Congreve rocket detachment served by sailors of H.M.S. *North Star* during the attack on Puketutu Pa, 8 May 1845. A painting probably by Major Cyprian Bridge. *Alexander Turnbull Library*

The Battle of Puketutu. Hone Heke's sortie from Puketutu Pa is shown at the top right of the picture along with the charge of the 58th Regiment against the Maori who had laid an ambush outside the pa. A painting by Major C. Bridge. *Alexander Turnbull Library*

Major (later Colonel) Cyprian Bridge of the 58th Regiment, from a portrait, *c.* 1860, by an unknown artist. When the regiment returned to England, Bridge became commanding officer of his regiment. His son, Mr H. E. Bridge, settled in New Zealand. *Alexander Turnbull Library*

The colonel left for Auckland in the *North Star,* placing Bridge in charge and with authority to carry out any action which seemed promising. The major quickly set off with a mixed force of his own regiment and friendly Maori (kupapa) to attack a pa up the Waikare River. This was believed to contain much of the plunder taken by the people of the Kapotai, a Ngapuhi sub-tribe, during the sack of Kororareka. When the boats arrived, however, the party found the shore fringed with mangroves, which made landing so difficult that the looters had time to make off almost unscathed with their booty.

Bridge's sortie had been no more successful than the Puketutu venture. Waka sent word that Hone Heke had left the lake and was building a new pa seven miles away. It seemed wise to launch a new attack before the work could be completed. While Bridge considered this invitation, he received orders recalling the troops to Auckland. He took with him a letter from Hone Heke, suggesting in essence that FitzRoy should leave the feuding Ngapuhi factions to settle their own differences.

The governor was not prepared to countenance civil war, nor to leave the loyal Waka in the lurch. The *British Sovereign* brought from Sydney Colonel Henry Despard, along with two companies of the 99th Regiment. A new expedition was despatched, but before it could land at the Bay of Islands Hone Heke decided upon a pre-emptive strike. He pounced upon Waka's pa at the head of 450 warriors. The defence was masterly, fire being held until the last moment. Heke was defeated and wounded as well.

Like many of his men, Colonel Despard had seen service in India and had absorbed the unfortunate habit, all too prevalent among the whites in that country, of looking upon native peoples as more or less a sub-species of humanity. He even regarded Waka in this light. Autocratic and short-tempered, almost his only admirable quality was his aggressive spirit, though even this was marred by the high cost in lives of his bungling. The campaign could hardly have been in the hands of a less suitable man.

Hone Heke prudently retired to nurse his wound, leaving Kawiti to complete the new pa at Ohaeawai, which Despard intended to reach by way of the mission stations at Kerikeri and Waimate. While these were able to ease to some extent the misery of the men in the very wet weather, the position of the missionaries was compromised by their association with military operations.

After the example of Puketutu, the colonel set great store by four guns, which were all but impossible to haul through the quagmire of the track. Bridge commented:

> Before we got them [the men] all housed and I posted the picquets, it was past 4, and I laid down quite exhausted with the hard day's work, having been on my legs from 7 a.m. on the 17th until 4 a.m. on the 18th and wet through without the means or opportunity of changing.[5]

Hone Heke (left) and
Tamati Waka Nene.
Engravings by J. R.
Ashton. *T. Ryan Collection*

The stay at Waimate lasted five days, during which more supplies were brought up. At last the force of over 600 men, with a further strong contingent led by Waka, set out at dawn to cover the seven miles to Ohaeawai. Conditions were such that they did not arrive until dark to make camp in the mud.

The two 6-pounder and two 12-pounder guns hammered the stockade of the pa, but its construction was even stronger than that at Puketutu. The artillery made very little impression, much less a breach. Two assaults were planned but both had to be cancelled, and for several days there was no more than desultory skirmishing. Despard ordered a 32-pounder to be sent from H.M.S. *Hazard*. When it finally came, he himself had a narrow escape when a sudden sortie from the pa routed the men holding what was known as Waka's Hill, used as an observation post.

Bombardment having proved useless, an attack was planned for 3 p.m. on 1 July 1845. The order of battle called for an advance storming party of volunteers from the regiments led by Lieutenant Jack Beatty of the 99th, supported by a first assault formation from the 58th and 99th under Major E. Macpherson, followed by sailors and volunteers from Auckland carrying axes and scaling gear. They were backed up by a second contingent from the same regiments, commanded by Bridge. Lieutenant-Colonel Hulme had 100 men of the 58th and 96th in support, while another 40 from the 58th held Waka's Hill. Despard kept the reserve.

Waka's success in driving off Hone Heke's raid was not lost upon Kawiti. He saw to it that his men did not fire until the soldiers were only 25 yards away, and then the troops were mown down with no hope of retaliation. The attack was pressed with the utmost bravery but was hopeless from the outset. Retreat was sounded after only a few minutes, but even that was long enough for this foolhardy action to have cost 40 lives.

Despard was shaken by losses on this scale and wanted to leave the pa, but was hotly opposed by the friendly chiefs. In the end, Waka persuaded him to wait another two days. The dead were recovered after some delay, and shelling continued as ammunition permitted. Fortunately the enemy left their stronghold at night, and the British destroyed it. Another Maori position at Pakaraka also proved to be deserted and was reduced to prevent further use.

Despard and Hulme returned to Auckland, and the former did not go back to Waimate until 1 September. The Governor was negotiating with the dissidents and withdrew the force to Kororareka. At this point came tidings that FitzRoy was being replaced. He was a high-minded and well-meaning man, but he lacked the support of the settlers which was so essential in the early days of the colony.

An overall view of the British siege lines at Ohaeawai. The pa is at the right of the picture and one of the naval guns is emplaced below the tree. A watercolour by Sergeant John Williams. *Rex Nan Kivell Collection, National Library of Australia, Canberra*

The retaking of Waka's Hill on the morning of 1 July 1845, an incident during the siege of Ohaeawai Pa. A watercolour by Sergeant John Williams. *Rex Nan Kivell Collection, National Library of Australia, Canberra*

'View of the left angle of Heke's Pa at Ohaeawai from a breakwater [stockade] adjoining our right battery.' This painting, by Major Cyprian Bridge, clearly illustrates the heavy stockade which was masked with thick bundles of green flax. The loopholes for musket fire can be seen at the foot of the barrier. *Alexander Turnbull Library*

The repulse of the 58th and 99th Regiments during Colonel Despard's disastrous attack on Ohaeawai Pa, 1 July 1845. Painting by Sergeant John Williams *Hocken Library, University of Otago*

By contrast, his successor, Captain George Grey, proved to be one of the most skilled politicians ever to take the helm in New Zealand. Soldier, explorer and a true man of action who had already gained experience of governorship in South Australia, he lost no time in going to Kororareka to see things for himself. He assured the Maori that they had no reason to fear for their lands, and he gave them 10 days to submit before the war would be renewed. There was no significant response, so Grey told his commander to proceed and returned to his duties in Auckland.

The immediate objective was Kawiti's pa which was known as Ruapekapeka, or the Bat's Nest, sited to the south of the Bay of Islands. Lieutenant-Colonel Robert Wynyard had brought more men of the 58th Regiment from Australia, and when he led the advance guard to Waimio on 22 December, Grey was once again with his troops. With Waka's contingent, Despard had the command of over 1,600 men by the time he finally reached his goal on 27 December.

Ruapekapeka Pa 11 January 1846. Plan by John Topham based on a Royal Navy Officer's survey in 1846.

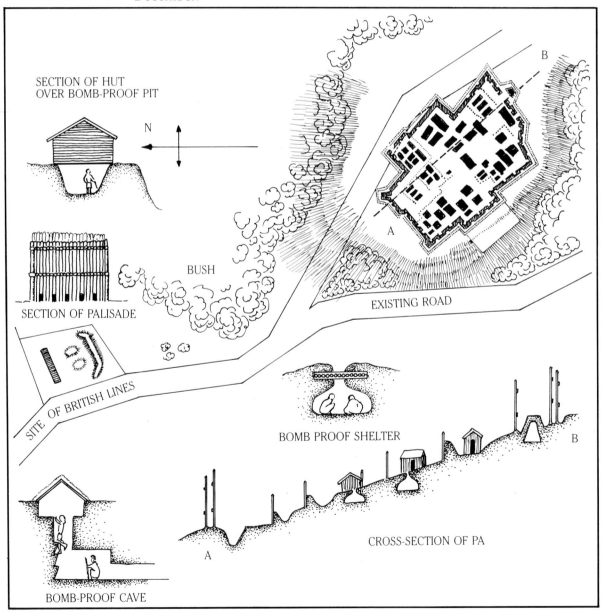

SECTION OF HUT OVER BOMB-PROOF PIT

N

SECTION OF PALISADE

SITE OF BRITISH LINES

BUSH

EXISTING ROAD

BOMB PROOF SHELTER

BOMB-PROOF CAVE

CROSS-SECTION OF PA

Ruapekapeka was by far the strongest fortification the rebels had built. It stood on a ridge, protected by a gully on one side and trees had been felled to form an abatis blocking other approaches. There was more than just the massive palisade; the interior was honeycombed with dug-outs from which the defenders could dominate any ingress through a breach.

Despard's artillery was also correspondingly stronger. He set up three batteries, housing seven guns ranging from 12-pounders to three 32-pounders, with mortars and rockets. Kawiti hoisted his standard emblazoned with the sun, moon and stars, but a single remarkable shot brought down the flagstaff — by no means a happy omen for the superstitious chief. Hone Heke, having recovered from his wound, joined Kawiti on 9 January 1846, bringing another 60 warriors.

By then the defence had been under sustained, if light, fire by the artillery, the pieces being gradually moved closer to the target. An attempt to overrun the breaching battery of two 32-pounders was driven back by Waka. On 10 January the stockade was beginning to crumble under the barrage, and Despard at once wanted to send in his infantry. Waka and his ally Mohi Tawhai vehemently opposed the move, pressing for a delay until the next day when they believed the pa might be abandoned. The colonel finally agreed, but kept the gunners at work all night to make sure that the breaches were still there in the morning.

At daylight on Sunday 11 January, Waka's brother Wiremu took some of his tribe to spy out the land. On reaching a breach, they found the interior apparently deserted and signalled to the soldiers to follow up. Despard, Wynyard and Captain Richard Denny, with 100 men of the 58th, rushed as fast as possible to pour through the breaches.

The pa was not, in fact, entirely empty. Hone Heke and most of the Maori, as practising Christians, had gone into the bush to hold divine service, not expecting the British to desecrate the sabbath with bloodshed. Only Kawiti and a handful of unbelievers remained, enjoying an extra hour's sleep after the noisy night. They were soon fighting for their lives as they were driven from the pa. The tables were now turned with a vengeance, for the defenders faced expert shooting from their own stockade as they tried to reoccupy the pa. After

The siege of Kawiti's pa, Ruapekapeka. The British batteries on the left are firing at the pa on the bush-covered hillside. A painting by Major Cyprian Bridge. *Alexander Turnbull Library*

a struggle lasting four hours it was clearly hopeless, and the Maori left the field.

The rising had been crushed. Hone Heke and Kawiti found themselves cold-shouldered by other chiefs of Ngapuhi who wanted to keep out of trouble. The two sought peace, Waka acting as intermediary. Grey had other problems, and was ready to grant free pardons to be rid of this one. Waka told him: 'You have saved us all.'

Shortly afterwards Waka brought Kawiti to visit the garrison at Victoria (now Waitangi). Private A. Whisker of the 58th watched the officers greeting the rebel, and wrote in his memorandum book with some disgust:

> He walked up to the officers quarters. There he was taken in and treated by them mutch Better than aney of us that fought long and hard and endangered our lives for what they Pleas to call the honour of old England.

Despard left almost at once for New South Wales, to the relief and satisfaction of the troops in New Zealand.

Professor Belich in his book *The New Zealand Wars* (1986) has asserted that the Ngapuhi at Ruapekapeka lured the British into a trap in the bush at the rear of the Pa and there inflicted casualties. This is a modern-day myth, contrary to contemporary accounts that uniformly agree the Pa fell because it was not manned.[6] Both the British and their Maori opponents were attending Sunday religious services that day.[7] It is evident that the fall of Ruapekapeka surprised both sides. In the confusion that followed the occupation, Reverend Burrows' writings[8] reveal that British troops inside the Pa fired on soldiers and sailors who had left their positions in front of the Pa. These men ran around the outside of the fortification in search of loot and were shot by their own men, firing from inside the Pa, causing a number of the casualties that the professor attributes to a non-existent Maori ambush.

Professor Belich also promotes the theory that the Northern War was a victory for the Maori. In fact, Heke's war shattered the North, bringing economic ruin and devastation to the fertile areas of both the pro and anti-British factions of the Ngapuhi.[9] Heke took little part in the war after the battle of Puketutu, having been severely wounded in the thigh in inter-tribal fighting. Only seven days after the fall of Ruapekapeka Heke, Kawiti and Nene had enough of warring and met at the Pa of a neutral chief, Pomare, and agreed to seek peace with the Government. British garrisons continued to occupy Ngapuhi territory, Governor Grey agreed that there should be no land confiscations, and the northern tribes remained aloof from the fighting of the 1860s.[10]

BRITISH CAMPAIGN DRESS IN NEW ZEALAND IN THE 1840s

The British soldier of the 1840s was dressed in the elegant but impractical coatee, which was cut short at the waist in front and had two tails behind. The headdress of the period was the tall cylindrical 'Albert Pot', or shako, named after its inventor, the Prince Consort. This finery was set aside while the men were on campaign in the South Pacific because they received as a free issue only one coatee and pair of trousers a year, together with a new shako every second year, so it was essential that the full dress uniform be preserved with care.

All ranks therefore had another form of clothing, called undress, for daily work. This included a forage cap of dark blue cloth, a plain single-breasted waist-length garment, called a shell or fatigue jacket, dark grey trousers in winter and white duck trousers of strong untwilled linen in summer. Except for his full dress uniform and boots, all items of a soldier's kit were classed as necessaries. Such things as undress clothing, white trousers, shirts, socks, cleaning and eating utensils therefore had to be paid for and maintained by the men themselves.

When the 58th Regiment landed in the Bay of Islands in 1845, they were spared the burden of heavy wooden-framed knapsacks (back packs) which were carried in drays. These packs were said to break a man's health before he was 40 because of the straps which cut into his chest and shoulders. Nevertheless each was hung about with musket, bayonet, a heavy leather ammunition pouch containing 60 rounds, water bottle and a haversack holding five days' biscuit and a further 60 rounds. A greatcoat and blanket were strapped to the back.

An engraving of British soldiers watching a haka, or dance, of Tamati Waka Nene's tribesmen. The campaign dress of the troops, a short red shell jacket, is clearly shown. *Illustrated London News*

The friendly Maori were amazed at the sight of such heavy equipment, and said: 'If we Maoris were loaded up in that way we would be able neither to fight nor run away, great is the patience of the soldier.'[1]

Private Hattaway of the 58th Regiment described the plight of his comrades encamped before Ohaeawai Pa:

The hardships that the men had to endure from incessant rain and insufficient food, produced exhaustion and weakness. They had no change of garments, were ragged tattered and torn, many without boots or tied on their feet with flax, their pants of many colours; blankets and greatcoats reduced in size to repair their continuations. To add to their troubles there were no needles and thread, and the soldiers supplied their wants by means of a piece of wood hardened at the point, and a hole pierced at the other end to carry the flax split to the necessary size.[2]

This private of the 58th Rutlandshire Regiment wears a forage cap of dark blue cloth, with a black band bearing brass regimental numerals. The cap had a pompom or tourie on top which was green in the case of the light company. His waist-length shell jacket is red, with collar and cuffs of the regimental black facings; the brass buttons are embossed with the regimental number. His trousers are of the Oxford mixture of dark grey with a red welt down the outer seam. White linen trousers were worn during the summer. *Drawing by Tim Ryan*

An officer wearing the peaked forage cap, which was also issued to sergeants. The band was of black silk in oak leaf lace. Apart from the cap, the uniform of officers was essentially the same as the men's, including the water canteen and haversack. Captains and subalterns had swords carried by a shoulder belt of white leather bearing the gilt regimental belt plate, those of colonels and majors being suspended from a waist belt. All swords were of the gilt half-basket hilt 1822 pattern, bearing the Queen's cypher and sheathed in a brass scabbard in respect of regimental field officers, black leather scabbards with guilt mountings for other officers and steel scabbards for staff officers. *Drawing by Malcolm Thomas*

The private's accoutrements consisted of two white pipe-clayed shoulder belts, one carrying a black leather ammunition box and the other a 17-inch bayonet, which hung behind the right and left hips respectively. The belts were secured at the point where they crossed on the chest by a rectangular brass plate of the regimental design. A strong canvas haversack was carried suspended from the left hip, and on the right a round light blue water canteen.

In the 1840s there were regiments, including some which served in New Zealand, which were still armed with the old flintlock, or 'Brown Bess', which had been in service for well over 100 years. In 1843 the 58th had received the new 1839 percussion smoothbore musket, a much more reliable weapon. It was 9.6 pounds in weight, and was 4 foot 7 inches long. The rate of fire, in the hands of a trained man, was three rounds a minute, with an effective range of 150–200 yards. *Drawing by Malcolm Thomas*

Te Rauparaha, 1768–1849, war chief of the Ngati Toa tribe. Te Rauparaha's prowess in battle and his remarkable qualities of leadership enabled him to lead his people to the Cook Strait area, where he conquered the local tribes and went on to subdue most of the South Island. His dominance in the Wellington district inevitably led to conflict with the settlers. A drawing by John Bambridge, 1847. *Alexander Turnbull Library*

TROUBLE MOVES SOUTH

When FitzRoy took no action against Te Rauparaha after the Wairau affair the Maori wondered why he had not sought utu, or revenge, as their custom would have demanded. Having escaped scot-free, the doughty warrior and more particularly his nephew Te Rangihaeata created increasing trouble in the Wellington area.

Land deals were being disclaimed and families driven off their farms to seek greater security in the town, although it too was under threat. There were only two companies of soldiers, the 58th and 96th Regiments, to hold the port and try to protect widely scattered settlers in difficult terrain.

Obviously more were needed, so Lieutenant-Colonel Hulme sailed from Auckland with a further five companies drawn from the 58th, 96th and 99th, the convoy including three warships. The fleet's appearance in Port Nicholson relieved a good deal of anxiety among the settlers. A garrison was established in the Hutt Valley, and Major Edward Last was sent by sea to cut off an influx of tribesmen from Wanganui. He took a long time to build a defensive base at Paremata, 13 miles to the north-east of Wellington, and Te Rangihaeata constructed a strong pa to block any British movement. Friendly Maori were set to work on making a road from Wellington to Porirua. Roads such as this, with their rash of stockades and, later, police posts were designed not only for the pacification of the region but also as an aid to surveying and to improving the overland link with other settlements.

Four other men were sleeping in the guard tent and received a volley from their Maori attackers that riddled the tent with shot. Twenty-one-year-old drummer William Allen attempted to sound the alarm on his bugle. When his arm was almost chopped through, he took the bugle in his left hand to carry on until he was hacked to death.[1] Of the other men in the guard tent, two were shot and hacked to death by tomahawk. The other soldier lying under the bodies of his comrades pretended to be dead and thus survived.

A detachment of the 99th Regiment marches past the bank at Wellington. This regiment arrived in Wellington on 3 February 1846 from Sydney, following a previous detachment which took part in the war in the north. An engraving by S. C. Brees. *Alexander Turnbull Library*

His comrades of the 58th, now fully roused, brought rapid fire to bear on the enemy. After a lengthy exchange the troops were on the point of launching a bayonet charge when a mounted patrol of the Hutt Militia arrived to help complete the rout of the raiders, who made off across the river to the shelter of the bush.

After further incidents, Grey decided on a typically bold move — the detention of Te Rauparaha. On 23 July, H.M.S. *Calliope* landed a force of 150 near Porirua. Making a silent approach, they seized the highly indignant old chief from his refuge at the Taupo pa of the Ngati Toa people. Te Rauparaha denied any involvement in his nephew's forays, but suspicion of him remained strong. He was removed to Auckland, where he was detained under a form of open arrest. This action by the Governor was intended to serve as a warning to other dissidents. Te Rauparaha's mana was effectively broken, and he was later allowed to return home after cession of the Wairau by his tribe.

Te Rangihaeata was much affected by this sudden arrest, the more so since, after a vivid dream, he had urged his uncle to live somewhere less exposed to just such a raid. The younger chief now left his position at Pauatahanui and made a stand behind a stockade barring a track which led up a steep hill. The narrow ridge was heavily forested on either side, making any outflanking movement very difficult. After losing Ensign Blackburn and two soldiers, Major Last ruled out any suicidal attack such as that at Ohaeawai. He did no more than keep the rebels under mortar fire until they left their stronghold.

The Maori retired to a spot known as Paeroa, a swampy region which had the advantage of abounding in eels and wildfowl while at the same time being easily defensible. So long as Te Rangihaeata gave up his raiding, the Government was willing to leave him in peace. He was content to remain there until his death in 1856.

Fort Richmond, in the Hutt Valley, was one of a line of strategic posts built as a defence against the disaffected tribes after land disputes in the area. An engraving by S. C. Brees. *Alexander Turnbull Library*

Te Rangihaeata, 1780–1856, chief of the Ngati Toa tribe and a nephew of Te Rauparaha. For most of his life he scorned things European, and after his defeat in 1846 retired to his fortified pa at swamp-surrounded Poroutawhao. At the end of his life he became resigned to co-operation with settlers. A painting by an unknown artist. *Alexander Turnbull Library*

Makahi-Nuku Pa, Hutt Valley. This pa was the headquarters of the chief Taringa-Kuri, who built it on land supposedly purchased by the New Zealand Company. This disputed property became a focal point of Maori resistance in the area. An engraving by S. C. Brees. *Alexander Turnbull Library*

Topine Te Mamaku, chief of the Ngati Haua tribe of the Upper Wanganui. He led his warriors to the Hutt Valley to fight against the British soldiers in 1846 and the following year carried out the attack on the town of Wanganui. An oil painting by G. Lindauer, *Auckland City Art Gallery*

It seemed that no sooner had one outbreak subsided down than another would begin. Hostile elements from the Wanganui district had travelled down the coast to help Te Rangihaeata. Land disputes were once again at issue, and the Wanganui tribes began disturbances in their own territory.

Maori sentiment was divided between those willing to live and let live with the settlers and a faction under Topine te Mamaku determined upon a show of strength. Captain J. H. Laye was sent with two companies of the 58th Regiment to defend the town of Wanganui. He set to work building defences, the principal one being the Rutland Stockade. Some houses were fortified as refuges for local families.

In May 1847 the home of a farmer named James Gilfillan was raided, and though he and his daughter of 16 managed to escape, his wife and three other children were murdered. Friendly Maori captured the five offenders and delivered them up to Laye. A strong taua, or war party, set out to rescue the prisoners, but after a summary trial four of the accused were convicted and hanged before the insurgents arrived. The attack came, but with the help of H.M.S. *Calliope* in the river the garrison was victorious.

Governor Grey himself came up shortly afterwards from Wellington with two companies of the 65th to reinforce the troops already in Wanganui. After some further trouble, Waka Nene and Te Wherowhero helped to restore peace in July, so ending the first phase of the war. As a result, two companies of the 96th and three from the 99th went back to Australia. The 58th remained in New Zealand, being joined by the 65th Regiment.

At the end of 1852, Sir George Grey returned on leave to England. There he was given a new appointment as Governor of Cape Colony. On Grey's departure, Colonel Wynyard of the 58th Regiment acted as administrator, an office he filled until the arrival of the new governor in 1855. He was Colonel Thomas Gore Browne, who had previously been in charge at St Helena.

Tamehana te Rauparaha, son of the Ngati Toa chief Te Rauparaha, visited England in 1851 and noted that the respect accorded to Queen Victoria acted as a catalyst for national unity. He saw no reason why the same principle could not give his own race a sense of nationhood and thus do away with the fratricidal wars which so seriously weakened the Maori's ability to cope with

constant pressure from the white people, whose more sophisticated civilis-
ation gave them in any case a great advantage.

So the King Movement was born, and although Grey had viewed this
development with concern, his forebodings were not shared by his masters in
London. When the Duke of Newcastle, at the Colonial Office, heard that
Potatau te Wherowhero had been chosen as the Maori leader, he felt that
'Potato' could well be left to enjoy his kingly dignity at Ngaruawahia — so long
as he kept the peace.

The attack on Te
Rangihaeata's position at
Horokiri on 6 August 1846
by men of the 58th and
99th Regiments. This
action was Te
Rangihaeata's last stand
before he retired to an
impregnable pa in the
swamps of Horowhenua. A
sketch by A. H.
Messenger. From *The New
Zealand Wars*

Colours presented to the
Taranaki Volunteers at
New Plymouth on 25 June
1861 to commemorate the
Battle of Waireka, the only
battle honour awarded to
a volunteer unit during the
wars. *Drawing by Malcolm
Thomas*

The Taranaki Rifle
Volunteers paraded to
receive their colours on 25
June 1861. The Marsland
stockade appears on the
hill in the background.
Taranaki Museum

THE TARANAKI SAGA BEGINS

Gore Browne, like Despard before him, tended to look upon the Maori as an inferior order of beings. After Grey's sympathetic efforts to help the Maori to advance in such fields as education and agriculture, the new governor's unfortunate attitude could only be seen as a retrograde step at a time when the race was feeling its way towards a new identity.

Good race relations were never more important than at this juncture. The interlude of peace, coupled with a growing prosperity in the South Island which was free of war, attracted an ever-increasing flow of immigrants. On the west of the North Island New Plymouth had been founded by the New Zealand Company. Although the town enjoyed a superb setting, expansion of its surrounding farmlands was confined to a narrow coastal strip between the sea and the heavily timbered foothills of Mount Egmont.

The obvious place to relieve the pent-up pressure of demand lay to the north. The plain across which the Waitara River flowed comprised some of the choicest land on the west coast of the North Island, and in the late '40s Francis Dillon Bell, on behalf of the Government, had bought a tract which still bears his name.

Most tribal conflicts stemmed from territorial disputes, and here the original owners, Te Ati Awa (the Taranaki branch of Ngati Awa), had suffered incursions by the Waikato people. The leading magnate of Te Ati Awa was Te Rangitake, usually known by his Christian designation of Wiremu Kingi, who had helped to prevent Te Rangihaeata from attacking Wellington in 1846. He saw, only too clearly, that the sale of land seriously undermined the basic structure of Maori society by challenging the concept of communal ownership. He set his face against the whole practice as a determined supporter of the King Movement.

Far Left: Colonel Thomas Gore Browne, Governor of New Zealand, 1855–61. An ex-soldier, he had the best of intentions towards the Maori, but lacked understanding. From *Defenders of New Zealand*

Wiremu Kingi te Rangitake, the Te Ati Awa chief who became the focal point of resistance in Taranaki because of the dispute over the sale of his ancestral lands. *Alexander Turnbull Library*

Gore Browne went to what became known as the Waitara Block, of some 600 acres, which the Government hoped to buy. One man, Te Teira, claimed ownership of the block and was prepared to sell, but Kingi, on behalf of the rest of Te Ati Awa, flatly refused and a Maori conference formed a land league to resist sales. Despite this opposition the deal went ahead, but when the unlucky surveyors tried to mark out their subdivisions in February 1860, they were promptly forced off the property and driven back to New Plymouth. There the situation was thought serious enough for martial law to be declared.

The governor went at once to Taranaki, accompanied by Colonel C. E. Gold, the 65th Regiment and some artillery. H.M.S. *Niger* lay off the town to provide further support against a probably imaginary threat. Gore Browne wished to reason with Kingi rather than see blood shed, but the chief, noting the show of force and suspecting a trap, refused to enter into any negotiations.

Gold lost no time in leading nearly all of his command to the scene of the dispute. After finding and destroying a small deserted pa, he came upon a much stronger one, Te Kohia, or the 'L' pa, held by a chief called Hapurona. Mr Parris, the Native Commissioner, attempted to avert the confrontation, but the dissidents would not listen to him.

Three guns, two 24-pounders and a 12-pounder, with the assistance of a naval rocket tube, opened fire on 17 March 1860. When the range closed sufficiently, shooting became general on both sides. The barrage at close range was too much for some of the defenders who as they retreated were charged by mounted Volunteers.

More daring elements still held the pa when night fell, the Maori firing from time to time to remind their enemies that the defence remained undefeated. Early next morning the guns moved in to force a breach, but when the bombardment lifted and the men of the 65th came to the palisade they found, as so often happened, that their opponents had gone.

The pattern of events was changing. Hone Heke had sacked and burned a well-established small town of Kororareka. Te Rangihaeata had not tried to repeat the experiment at Wellington, and the descent on Wanganui was plainly a failure. Now the British Army was being used to enforce a dubious land deal. The message was not lost upon the settlers, much less upon their leaders. In the years ahead they would look not to buying land but confiscating it as a result of conquest — despite the fact that the troops were meant to protect them and not to rob the Maori.

Gold might have won the opening round, but he was left with little leisure to celebrate. The hitherto quiescent tribes living to the south of New Plymouth now showed their solidarity with Kingi by harrying their pakeha neighbours. The little town became choked with refugees, and the men joined hastily formed volunteer units. Among these recruits was one Harry Atkinson, destined for greatness later in life.

On 27 March five pakeha were murdered close to the town, and Gold sent out a two-pronged expedition to bring in the remaining families. Lieutenant-Colonel G. F. Murray led a company of the 65th, with a handful of marines and sailors, along the road south to engage the Maori. The second arm, drawn from the Taranaki Militia and Rifle Volunteers, was to follow the shore, collecting the settlers and rejoining the troops at the Waireka stream.

The plan underestimated the Maori opposition. They saw clearly enough that the disciplined and trained redcoats must be handled with caution, but they cared little for the amateur units playing at soldiers. At the Waireka, the defenders swept down from a pa at Kaipopo and hemmed in the would-be rescuers, who were soon fighting desperately. Fortunately there were a few

Major (later Sir) Harry Atkinson became Premier in 1876. From *Defenders of New Zealand*

Te Hapurona, Te Ati Awa war chief and Kingi's general during the first Taranaki war. He led the defenders of Te Arei (The Barrier) Pa. *Alexander Turnbull Library*

Rewi Manga Maniapoto.
An oil painting by
Gottfried Lindauer.

veterans among them who kept their heads, and on hearing the firing Murray sent a small detachment to help. However, the commander was under orders to be back to town by sunset, and incredibly he withdrew, leaving the scratch volunteer force to its fate.

This might have been a hard one had not Francis Mace, who was to emerge among the most gallant figures of the wars, eluded the Maori and ridden post-haste to raise the alarm in New Plymouth. At once Captain Peter Cracroft, commanding H.M.S. *Niger,* landed reinforcements, and with Mace to guide them the naval party went as fast as they could to Kaipopo Pa. The captain of-fered £10 to the man who brought down the enemy battle flags. Leading Seaman William Odgers hacked his way through the foe to win both the prize and, later, the Victoria Cross. The action was fought hand to hand, cutlass against tomahawk, and drew off the attack from the hard-pressed Volunteers. Back in the town, Cracroft was deservedly the hero of the hour, both Gold and Murray suffering much criticism.

Modern historians allege that when the naval party stormed Kaipopo Pa, it was empty except for an old man. This is contrary to the sworn evidence given by Captain Cracroft at the inquiry into the action. He stated that his party sustained four wounded who had their legs tomahawked whilst escalading the Pa. Captain Cracroft also stated that he personally counted sixteen Maori dead inside the Pa after the storming, and several more were lying on the road outside.[1]

Reinforcements began to arrive for both sides. Rewi Maniapoto, who became perhaps the best-known of the Maori stalwarts, brought a taua (war party) from the Waikato via the Mokau River. Gold received another six companies from the 12th and 40th Regiments in Australia and the assistance of three warships, *Cordelia, Pelorus* and *Victoria.*

Right: Lieutenant Cain of the Taranaki Militia. *Far Right:* An unknown officer of the Taranaki Rifle Volunteers. *Taranaki Museum*

The 65th Regiment on parade at New Plymouth, March 1861. The troops wear dress uniforms, including the white duck trousers adopted in the summer months.
Alexander Turnbull Library

Major Nelson set out from Waitara, taking the men of the 40th and a mixed naval force to hold the disputed block and to carry the fight to the tribesmen if opportunity served. He had with him Captain Beauchamp-Seymour of H.M.S. *Pelorus*. The two men had only recently arrived in New Zealand, and with no experience of local campaigning they probably found passive garrison duty little to their taste.

Wiremu Kingi had fortified a ridge known as Puketakauere in very difficult country. Nelson launched a rash assault on an almost impregnable position on 27 June. His two 24-pounders began the action, but without inflicting any evident damage. When the centre column launched a frontal attack it met a murderous fire from rifle pits and trenches. Although the Navy fought courageously, the thrust failed. The flanking formations fared even worse. The troops found themselves trying to scale steep slopes rising from swampy gullies and impeded by thick undergrowth. They were forced to withdraw, leaving behind many wounded who were at once killed where they lay. Nelson had expected Gold to come up with the 65th in support, but upon reaching a flooded river the colonel returned to his base. His action gave rise to controversy in the press, each side blaming the other for the heavy casualties of 30 killed and 34 wounded.

On receiving news of this serious reverse, Major-General Thomas Pratt, General Officer Commanding Australia, decided to go to New Zealand and take command in person. He was well qualified to do so, having seen action in several widely separated wars. In July he sent off the remainder of the 40th Regiment and sailed to New Plymouth. By then some of the women and children had been shipped away to Nelson to ease pressure in the beleaguered town.

By September, Pratt felt able to take the offensive with a strong force of the 12th and 65th. He went to Puketakauere, then fortunately abandoned; after taking and levelling three other pa, he returned. A few days later he sent Major Hutchins on a sweep to Tataraimaka, with similar results.

Beginning to get the measure of his opponents, Pratt set out again on 9 October with 1,000 men from the 12th and 65th to the Kaihihi River. His object was to engage three pa, built with all the ingenuity the Maori could summon. It was here that the general showed his quality as a leader careful of soldiers' lives. Not for him the hopeless frontal attacks; these were replaced by driving saps right up to the palisade. The defenders were much discomfited by this new approach, and retired with little fighting.

Just as Pratt could have supposed that he had the situation in hand, he heard that, following the death of the Maori King Potatau, his young son Tawhiao had assumed leadership of the King Movement. The latter had allowed, or been unable to prevent, Waikato warriors going south to join in the fighting. With characteristic determination, the general tackled the new threat by setting in motion a pincer movement, leading one column himself from New Plymouth while Colonel Mould brought the other from Waitara.

The Waikato reinforcements for Wiremu Kingi and Hapurona had mustered at Mahoetahi, and Pratt found that his quick response brought its own reward. The pa was old and in a poor state of repair, and the Maori had not yet had time to put the defences in order. Dropping his usual caution, Pratt did not wait for Mould's arrival, but despatched his Volunteers on a flanking movement while two companies of the 65th attacked on the front. They were already fighting inside the pa when their comrades came up from Waitara, and this further blow drove the Waikato off into the forest. Despite the change of tactics, British casualties were very light considering the hand-to-hand fighting.

A boundary post in Taranaki, erected by the chief Katatore to mark the limits of European land at Bell Block. A watercolour by William Strutt.
Alexander Turnbull Library

British artillery in action at the siege of Te Arei. An engraving by Frank Mahoney. From *Picturesque Atlas of Australasia*

This salutary drubbing of the Waikato raised fears in Auckland that the tribe might seek utu, or revenge, for the dead by raiding the lightly held capital from their northern boundary. The harassed Gore Browne ordered Pratt to bring troops to bolster its defence. The directive was obeyed, but it was a wasted journey, for the Waikato did not mean to desert Taranaki after a single reverse. When a battalion of the 14th Regiment landed at Auckland from the British Isles at the end of November, the general took his troops, experienced in local fighting, back to Taranaki.

The indefatigable Kingi soon had his land league adherents hard at work building more strongpoints on the lines of Puketakauere. He had beaten Nelson there with little trouble, and would now put Pratt to the test at Matarikoriko, Huirangi and Te Arei.

This time Pratt operated from Waitara, so shortening his line of communication. He started by throwing up a redoubt about half a mile short of Matarikoriko. On 30 December the Maori, under a flag of truce, pointed out that as it was Sunday there should be no fighting. This was agreed, and the garrison spent the day at their ease while the troops continued to dig. The pa was abandoned that night.

Moving forward, the hard-working British began the process all over again at Huirangi. By 23 January 1861 the Maori realised that they were unlikely to win by waiting until the sap reached their very defences. The alternative, to launch a counter-attack against a superior enemy, was little better, but rather than retreat again without a struggle the defenders turned out at dawn to rush the most advanced redoubt covering the work.

They were not early enough to catch the soldiers asleep and came under fire from the 40th, soon to be joined by two companies of the 65th and some of the 12th. Lieutenant-Colonel Wyatt directed his men with such skill that the Waikato soon learned, as the Ngapuhi had done, that they were no match in the open for regimental discipline and training. Their retreat was hastened by artillery fire. The sappers were finally successful when, 50 yards short of their target, the defenders fell back to Te Arei.

This was the scene of Te Arei Pa, the crux of the campaign:

> It could be seen from the redoubts, and native report had it that it was the strongest and best defended pa in the country. It certainly was a well-selected situation; in the first place, between our position and the very thick bush, there was a mile of perfectly level ground from which the fern had been removed, and just on the border of the dense bush, there were numbers of well-constructed rifle pits, covered over and quite invisible, which extended for about a mile. Behind the pits there was a dense bush, so thick with undergrowth that but for some paths, eighteen inches wide, made by the natives, there was no means of penetrating it, except by cutting down the underwood. Round the pa, which stood on a considerable rise, there was a cleared space, and more rifle pits. The river Waitara, with steep banks, almost cliffs, protected the position on the right and left, and at the rear there was more thick bush.[1]

Kingi no doubt knew that his remorseless adversary would resort to the spade rather than the sword, and did all he could to combat this technique. The rifle pits commanding the open ground took the first shock, and though the 65th suffered casualties in skirmishing against them on 10 February, they gained a low hill which dominated the whole system and built a redoubt to secure their advantage.

The Waikato, finding the rifle pits untenable, exchanged them for the dense bush through which the artillery was being brought forward with great difficulty. This was the type of ground which suited the Maori, and though they inflicted losses, it seemed that nothing could halt Pratt's slow but irresistible advance.

The sappers started work on 14 February, and by 11 March were only 200 yards from the pa. The Maori asked for a truce, and there was a breathing spell of three days. They then tried night attacks, but the only noteworthy result was an heroic defensive action by Colour-Sergeant John Lucas of the 40th Regiment, for which he was awarded the Victoria Cross.

A truce was negotiated, and though the Government agreed to an inquiry into the rights and wrongs of the Waitara land deal, the move was made useless by a delay. A newly honoured Sir Thomas Pratt returned to his post in

General Pratt's siege works at Te Arei Pa, Taranaki, March 1861. Plan by John Topham based on a Royal Engineer's survey.

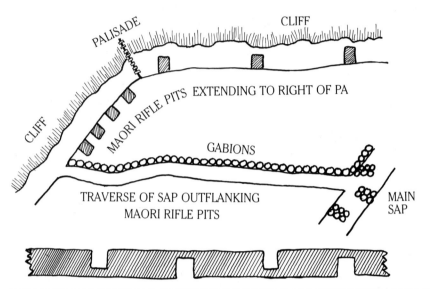

CROSS SECTION OF BRITISH SAP

ELEVATION OF BRITISH SAP SHOWING TRAVERSES TO PREVENT ENFILADING FIRE

British trenches (sap) at the siege of Te Arei.
Taranaki Museum

Australia, and Major-General Duncan Cameron took over command in New Zealand. Once again Kingi was not a party to the settlement, for he left with the Waikato when they went home. The peace would prove to be but an interval between wars.

The Regimental Band of the 18th Royal Irish Regiment, Waikato 1863. The men are dressed in blue serge 'jumpers' (based on the India-pattern 'frocks'), issued to them on their arrival in New Zealand. *Hawkes Bay Art Gallery and Museum*

BRITISH ARMY DRESS AND EQUIPMENT IN NEW ZEALAND, 1860–70

The Crimean and Indian Mutiny campaigns of the 1850s had a profound effect on British uniforms. The two wars showed the impracticability of fighting in tight-fitting and uncomfortable dress clothing. In 1855 the swallow-tail coatee and tall shako were abolished and replaced by a loose-fitting tunic and the lower, so-called French, shako.

During the Indian Mutiny of 1857–59, khaki uniforms were first adopted on a wide scale. However, once the Mutiny had ended, the British Army reverted to the traditional red coats which continued to be worn on active service until 1888.

Contemporary illustrations and photographs show that dress uniforms conforming to the regulations of 1830, 1844, 1855 and 1861 were often worn in New Zealand for ceremonial or garrison duties. In 1860 the dark blue campaign uniform was adopted. This was a radical departure from the usual red, and was brought in mainly because of problems of supply. Colonel J. E. Alexander describes these in his book *Incidents of the Maori War* (1863):

Colonel J. E. Alexander.
Alexander Turnbull Library

> Troops were now frequently paraded and inspected, and the skirts of the men's great coats were cut off to enable them to wear them in skirmishing in the bush and scrub. This plan I did not think well of, and afterwards when preparing some of the 14th Regiment for fighting, I gave them blue smocks over which the great coat was worn, neatly rolled horse-collar fashion, and ready for the evening's bivouac; a man cannot sleep well if his legs are not covered with the skirts of his coat.

The colonel describes in the same book the harsh realities of campaigning in New Zealand:

> Tearing their way through the high fern and scrub, and impeded with their great coats, which with their trousers were soon in rags, and plunging in the swampy ground to the knees, scattered and divided by the fern which was up to their chins whilst they held up their heavy pouches.

The blue smock or jumper became the standard issue for all troops stationed in New Zealand, as Lieutenant-Colonel G. Le M. Gretton describes in *The Campaigns and History of the Royal Irish Regiment* (1902):

> The battalion received their campaigning kit: officers and men were provided with blue serge 'jumpers', haversacks, water bottles and pannikins; all ranks carried a blanket and waterproof sheet slung over the left shoulder; the men were armed with Enfield rifles and bayonets.

The absence of supplies of red serge cloth caused the adoption of a uniform which was much better adapted to rugged conditions of fighting in the New Zealand bush.

Right: This corporal of the 65th Regiment wears a dark blue serge jumper of a lighter colour than the navy blue trousers, which had a red welt down the outer seam. The headdress was the pork pie infantry forage cap, dark green for light infantry and dark blue for line regiments. The brass light company bugle badge surmounts the regimental number on the cap. The tourie, or tuft, on the forage cap was red for battalion companies, green for light companies and white for grenadier companies.

Far Right: The soldier wears a grey greatcoat rolled over his shoulder. Suspended from this is a 'D'-shaped mess tin. His waist belt is of white leather, with a regimental pattern brass locket carrying a bayonet frog on the left hip. The expense ammunition box is attached to the front of the belt as shown in figure 1. The improved 1850 pattern white leather cross-belt is worn over the left shoulder, from which an ammunition box hangs on the right hip. The haversack of white canvas was slung over the right shoulder and rested on the left hip.

Right: Detail of the cap pouch suspended from the cross-belt.
Far right: The 'Italian' pattern, wooden canteen was hung on a brown leather strap over the left shoulder. It was painted blue-grey and was often marked B^O for Board of Ordinance prior to 1854. After the reorganisation of 1854 the marking was changed to W^D which stood for War Department.

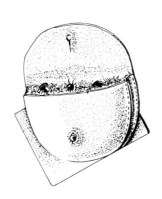

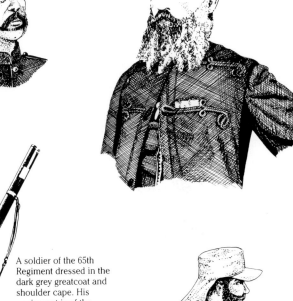

Left: This officer wears the dark blue waist-length patrol jacket with black cords across the front and a black Austrian knot on each cuff. His leather-peaked forage cap, bearing the regimental number, was of blue cloth with a black silk oak leaf band and button.

Far Left: An officer's blue cloth pill-box forage cap, with gold oak leaf band and button. Most officers during this period wore either the patrol jacket or the jumper of other ranks. Often swords were discarded, and revolvers only were worn in shoulder-holster fashion.

A soldier of the 65th Regiment dressed in the dark grey greatcoat and shoulder cape. His equipment is of the standard infantry pattern as described in figures 1 and 2. The expense ammunition pouch suspended from his white leather waist belt follows the later pattern.

Left: A white cloth cover, with neck curtain attached, is worn over this soldier's leather-peaked forage cap. The headdress was worn in New Zealand during the summer from about 1865, and is similar to that worn in India. The greatcoat is rolled in a waterproof oilskin sheet and carried over the usual equipment shown in earlier illustrations.

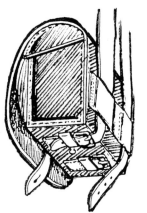

Far Left: Detail of the ammunition box suspended from the 1850 pattern white leather cross-belt. *Drawing by Tim Ryan*

Sir George Grey, 1812–98, served two terms as Governor: from 1845–53 and 1861–68. Later from 1877–79, he was Prime Minister. He was a mixture of philanthropist, visionary and man of action, but was also autocratic and egotistical, being unable to recognise his own mistakes. He developed an understanding of the Maori people, however, and was largely respected by them, despite his failings. *Hawke's Bay Art Gallery and Museum*

Far Right: General Sir Duncan Cameron, 1808–88, was a veteran of the Crimean War, when he commanded the Highland Brigade at Balaclava. A soldier of the old school, his rigid sense of responsibility brought him into conflict with Governor Grey and led to his resignation. From *Defenders of New Zealand*

Tawhiao te Wherowhero, 1825–94, the second Maori King. After succeeding to leadership of the King Movement in 1860, he took little positive part in deciding policy but allowed his council to make decisions. He urged his commanders to follow guerrilla tactics, but they insisted on putting their faith in fortifications. All his life Tawhiao was a steadfastly independent representative of his people. From *Picturesque Atlas of Australasia*

Far Right: Hori Ngakapa te Whanaunga, Ngati Paoa chief, who was one of the leaders of the attack on a British escort at Martin's farm and later at Pukekohe East Church stockade. Hori fought at Rangiriri and escaped by swimming across the lagoon. *Iles photograph, Alexander Turnbull Library*

CHAPTER 7

THE ADVANCE ON RANGIRIRI

Gore Browne was convinced that the Waikato meant to attack Auckland, so General Cameron concentrated all his forces save the 57th, which remained in Taranaki, at Otahuhu camp. The governor was being pulled in two directions, his Ministers as ever seeking more land while Wiremu Tamehana, Chief of the Ngatihaua, argued the King cause with much ability.

A call to the Maori to submit and take an oath of allegiance produced little response. The governor seemed to be convinced that renewed fighting was inevitable, and when the Wellington settlers pointed out that they were without means of defending themselves, the veteran of a campaign in Afghanistan replied with little sympathy: 'War is not made with rose-water.'

Gore Browne found that the parliamentary majority on which he was relying melted away in those days before closely knit parties. London came to look upon him as another FitzRoy, and chose the same solution as in 1845. Sir George Grey was brought back to Auckland from Capetown to take over from Gore Browne, who left for easier conditions in Tasmania.

Although on his arrival the country was at peace, Grey was under no illusion that the problem was going to be any simpler to solve than that in the '40s. The defeat of the Waikato in Taranaki had stiffened the King opposition. The strength of Cameron's force was still growing, but even more threatening in Maori eyes was the building of an extension of the Great South Road from Drury to Pokeno, where the Queen's Redoubt was raised.

The Government was under pressure to find room in the Auckland area for a tide of would-be farmer immigrants and unsuccessful gold diggers from the Coromandel field. Most suitable land had been taken up, and families were driven to such expedients as trying to hack farms from the heavily timbered Hunua, where giant trees could be as much as 11 feet in diameter. Envious eyes turned to the potentially rich fern-clad Waikato.

Although Grey and others tried to get Wiremu Tamehana to take part in the inquiry on the Waitara problem, nothing came of their approaches. The chief complained of liquor being smuggled into the Waikato, and John E. Gorst was sent there to act as a magistrate. In this capacity he failed, being without means of asserting his authority in the Maori community. Instead he took charge of an industrial school financed by the Government, and started up a newspaper, *Te Pihoihoi Mokemoke,* in opposition to the Kingite journal, *Te Hokioi.* Gorst's activities at Te Awamutu included passing intelligence reports, and it is scarcely surprising that he was evicted by Rewi Maniapoto.

In January 1863 the governor went, almost alone, to see the leading Kingite chiefs at Ngaruawahia. On their side, the Maori restated the aims of the King Movement and refused permission for steamers to use the Waikato River. In answer to a question as to his intentions, Grey said of Tawhiao:

> I shall not fight against him with the sword, but I shall dig round him until he falls of his own accord.[1]

On his empty-handed return to Auckland, trouble erupted again in Taranaki. During Kingi's rising, the farmers on the Tataraimaka block, about 15 miles south of New Plymouth, had been driven out with the loss of their homes. In March Lieutenant-Colonel Warre took the 57th Regiment to build a redoubt at Poutoko in order to give some sort of security to the settlers trying to remake their lives. Shortly afterwards Grey and Cameron went to assess the position for themselves and promptly ordered reinforcements from Auckland. With four companies of the 65th and 70th, and Captain Mercer's Royal Artillery battery, Cameron established a second redoubt on 4 April.

The Maori did not try conclusions with either column, but on 4 May ambushed a small party of the 57th which was escorting a prisoner to New Plymouth. At the Wairau stream Lieutenant Tragett, Dr Hope and all their men except for Private Kelly were killed. Although the latter was wounded, he managed to reach St Patrick's Redoubt to raise the alarm.

The Taranaki and Ngati Ruanui should have persisted with these hit-and-run operations, but instead reverted to building a pa, the old option which had already proven so vulnerable to British attack. They chose a site which could scarcely have been more ill-advised, near the mouth of the river. Cameron made his move early in June, bringing into play the combined fire power of his Royal Artillery battery and the guns of H.M.S. *Eclipse.* Before the defenders could recover from the bombardment, the 57th swept all before them in a bayonet charge.

It was, however, a hollow victory, since the general had to return north with all his troops except the 57th. Warre was kept under constant threat by marauding bands, and suffered a concerted attack when reinforcing St Patrick's Redoubt on 2 October 1863. Majors Butler and Shortt were heavily engaged in the open, while Lieutenant Mills had all he could do to beat off an attempt to take the fort. A contingent of the Militia, commanded by Captain Atkinson, took part in the action, and Captain Mace once again behaved with exemplary bravery by bringing up fresh ammunition under heavy fire. The premier distinctions went to Ensign John Down and Drummer Dudley Stagpool of the 57th, who won the Victoria Cross for saving one of the wounded.

Captain F. J. Mace. From
Defenders of New Zealand

While Taranaki might be a perennial nuisance, it was a long way from the main centres and for the present at least was no more than a sideshow. By contrast, the territory nominally held by the Maori King was the key to opening up the North Island, for the great river passing through it from Lake Taupo to the sea provided the natural and only practicable highway. No road building or land sales were permitted. If hostilities broke out the central position of the Waikato Maori gave them the advantage of interior lines, and they could draw in peripheral tribes to help.

Grey followed a trail well worn by New Zealand governors when he demanded another 3,000 troops. The War Office duly supplied these from the 18th, 43rd, 50th and 68th Regiments which included many veterans of the Indian Mutiny. A half-caste interpreter named Fulloon sent in a report which claimed that a two-pronged assault on Auckland was planned by the southern tribes. One party would cross the Manukau Harbour to come in from the west while the second thrust north from the Hunua forests, to attack simultaneously at dawn. Even if ever seriously considered, the project was abandoned, probably because of the difficulty of co-ordinating such an ambitious night operation.

In its place, the Maori harried and burned the homesteads of settlers in the Hunua and Pukekohe districts. In one of these raids, on 22 July, James Hunt, a bushman was killed when cutting timber with three other men on the edge of the bush. Captain Clare turned out his small Militia detachment from Papakura, and was hard pressed by 40 or 50 Maori until Captain Ring brought 100 men from the Kirikiri Redoubt. Even then the augmented force was almost surrounded as more Maori streamed out of the forest, and the tide was turned only by the arrival of Captain Rait leading a cavalry contingent.

The attack on Pukekohe East Church stockade on 1 September 1863 by a war party of 200 Waikato tribesmen. A drawing by A. H. Messenger. From *The New Zealand Wars and Pioneering Period*

The following month brought an even more desperate skirmish at Pukekohe. Settlers from Cornwall and Scotland had sent their families into Drury and Auckland as Maori raids became more frequent, the men remaining to look after their farms as best they could. The wooden Presbyterian church at Pukekohe East was put into a state of defence to provide a refuge against attack. Logs and tree trunks were embedded 10 feet from the building to form a stockade seven feet high, though as yet it stood no more than about five feet. The farmers formed themselves into the Forest Rifle Volunteers under Sergeant Perry.

In the middle of August a youngster named Scott had been killed, and on the 31st his father and three other men were tending farm animals when raiders struck. Two ran at once to the church, but Scott and Elijah Roose were cut off and went to ground in the bush which came uncomfortably close to the defences. The Maori did not intend to give up, and when night fell they lit fires which would show up the fugitives if they made a dash for the stockade. Their luck changed when heavy rain put out the flames and the two joined their comrades. Two others, Messrs Comrie and J. B. Roose, had been to visit their families at Drury, and on returning found the church encircled. They turned in their tracks and galloped back to get help.

Perry's situation looked far from bright. He mustered only 17 men to hold off something like 200, who had plenty of cover in the bush and behind tree stumps even closer. The defence relied on old-fashioned muzzle-loading rifles, and if volleys were fired attackers might overrun the post during reloading. The sergeant therefore ordered his men to fix bayonets which, protruding through the stockade, could be clearly seen by the enemy, and to fire only when an opponent showed himself. In this way the sight of the bayonets deterred a charge, and ammunition was saved.

Perry's acumen proved its worth, for the defenders had to rely on their own efforts for six hours before Lieutenant Grierson and soldiers of the 70th arrived from Ramarama. By then some were almost out of ammunition. Captains Inman and Saltmarshe brought men of the 18th and 65th to end the action. The Maori suffered numerous casualties, and it seemed incredible that the only hurt suffered by Perry's band was a single man struck by a flying splinter of wood.

The Government's intentions were placed beyond doubt by the appearance of newspaper advertisements in Australia and Otago. These called for a new corps of Militiamen to follow up an Army advance and, as soldier-settlers, to hold and farm occupied territory. Fortune's favourites on the goldfields were few, and unlucky diggers provided many of the best men in the four regiments that were formed.

The 65th Regiment crossed the Waikato River at Tuakau to throw up the strong Alexandra Redoubt to command the waterway. The 12th, 14th and 70th breached the tacit frontier of the Mangatawhiri, and on 17 July were in action against Maori holding a hill position at Koheroa. Cameron actually led his troops in person, perhaps inspiring the bayonet charge to carry the day.

Every mile Cameron advanced beyond his headquarters at Queen's Redoubt inevitably compounded the problem of bringing forward supplies. At least the river could help, and a water transport corps was formed to man two shallow-draught steamers, the *Avon* and *Pioneer*. These vessels were intended to serve both as transports for men and supplies, and as gunboats providing supporting fire in actions against enemy pa along the banks.

Alexandra Redoubt, at Tuakau, Waikato, was built by the 65th Regiment on a strategic bluff 300 feet above the Waikato River. A detachment of Forest Rangers is shown moving upstream in captured canoes.
Illustrated London News

The river gunboat *Pioneer*, specially built in Sydney for the New Zealand Government. A paddle-steamer of 300 tons, she drew only three feet of water when fully loaded. The vessel was 140 feet long, and was armed with a 12-pounder Armstrong gun in each of the two iron turrets. *Illustrated London News*

The gunboat *Pioneer* bombards the Maori entrenchments at Mere Mere in 1863. *Illustrated London News*

Traffic along the Great South Road was still vulnerable to ambush from the forest section near Drury. To some extent this threat was countered by felling and burning a swath for 10 miles of its length. To prevent the Maori from infiltrating behind the troops, a chain of redoubts was built from Miranda, on the Firth of Thames, to Pokeno.

To flush out the guerrillas, the Government decided to apply the lessons learned in Taranaki by Atkinson's Bush Rangers. During the first week of August 1863 the following advertisement appeared in the *Daily Southern Cross:*

NOTICE
TO MILITIAMEN AND OTHERS

ACTIVE YOUNG MEN, having some experience of New Zealand Forests, may now confer a benefit upon the Colony, and also ensure a comparatively free and exciting life for themselves, by JOINING A CORPS OF FOREST VOLUNTEERS, now being enrolled in this province to act as the Taranaki Volunteers have acted in striking terror into the marauding natives, by operations not in the power of ordinary troops.

By joining the Corps the routine of Militia life may be got rid of and a body of active and pleasant comrades ensured.

Only men of good character wanted.

For further information apply to the office of the Daily Southern Cross, O'Connell Street, Auckland.

A young Papakura farmer of Yorkshire origin, William Jackson, came forward to lead what soon became known as the Forest Rangers. At an interview with Governor Grey and Thomas Russell, the Defence Minister, he made it clear that he was moved not by patriotism but by the all-pervading land hunger of the Europeans:

By following up the Natives, I run a great risk of being killed, and your Excellency must not think I wish to show any disrespect to you if I speak rather plain, as I think a fair understanding now will save a great deal of unpleasantness afterwards. You say you will give me land; I may therefore tell you that it is not for the pay, neither am I anxious to get a name, but if I get through, I shall expect a lump of good land.[2]

The governor answered:

We do not wish to bind ourselves too tight, but I will give you not merely a lump, but a large slice in the choicest part of the Waikato; I will settle you down in Rangiawhia [sic].[1]

Confiscation was obviously intended when the war was won, which he expected to be in three months.

Jackson enrolled William McGregor Hay as ensign and John Mackintosh Roberts as sergeant in No. 1 Company. Being able to offer a private eight shillings a day — more than three times the pay of the Militia — there were plenty of recruits. For a base Jackson chose the 'Traveller's Rest', an odd mixture of inn, store and farmhouse which had been boarded up breast high with heavy planks to give it something of the appearance of a blockhouse.

As the Forest Rangers began combing the bush, they were joined on their second venture by a remarkable character who had roamed the world before becoming war correspondent for the *Daily Southern Cross*, the Auckland morning paper. He was Gustavus Ferdinand Von Tempsky, who came from a

German military family of Polish descent. After service in the Royal Prussian Army, he had led a party of colonists to the Mosquito Coast of Nicaragua, where he met his future wife.

The unhealthy climate had decimated the colony, and after a spell of leading Mosquito Indians against the Spaniards, Von Tempsky joined the gold rush to California, but with indifferent success. He returned to Nicaragua after an epic two-year journey on horseback through Mexico, Guatemala and Costa Rica. Marrying Emelia Ross Bell, 'Von' worked with her father and brother cutting and shipping mahogany before going to Scotland and then Australia. While gold prospecting in Victoria, he tried unsuccessfully to join what became the Burke and Wills exploring expedition.

The Coromandel goldfield beckoned Von Tempsky, now with a family of three children, to New Zealand to work as a digger and local correspondent for the *Daily Southern Cross.* When the war started, he attempted to form a Militia company, but failed largely on account of his German nationality, unpopular at the time, and so came to report on the Forest Rangers.

Left: Major Gustavus Ferdinand Von Tempsky. *Alexander Turnbull Library*

Far Left (top): Pouch badge of the Forest Rangers. *Drawing by F. Turton*

Far Left (below): Captain (later Major) William Jackson, who formed and commanded No. 1 Company, Forest Rangers, 1863–64. From *Defenders of New Zealand*

The sweep through the bush was an arduous one. The heavily forested, broken country would have tested newly raised troops even in good weather, and they were dogged by heavy rain. The undergrowth entangled the movements of men carrying weapons, ammunition, food and blankets. At night they had to sleep in the open, Von Tempsky being one of three people trying to get some shelter in a deserted boar's lair under a log which was hardly big enough for two.

Corporal William Johns recounted:

> It was the rum that kept us alive. We had so much wet, hard work, swimming and fording rivers and creeks, and camping without fires. When we camped in the bush on the enemy's trail it was often unsafe to light a fire for cooking or warmth, because we never knew when we might have a volley poured into us. So we just lay down as we were, wet and cold, and we'd have been dead without the rum. [4]

After passing a deserted enemy camp, the Rangers heard a Maori encouraging his fellows:

> Ah! If we had the pakeha before use now, would we not give it to them![5]

This painting by J. McDonald gives a good impression of bush fighting during the Waikato campaign. *Taranaki Museum*

He was acclaimed with shouts of 'Come on, Come on!' As Jackson's company crept forward to oblige, one man accidentally discharged the cap of his weapon, and no contact was made. Food ran short, and on emerging from the bush at Drury all hands sought a meal at the nearest hotel.

Jackson had seen enough to realise that his new friend knew more than any

of them about bushcraft, learned long ago from the Mosquito Indians. The captain had another interview with Grey, as a result of which Von Tempsky was given British nationality and a commission as a supernumary ensign in the Forest Rangers. This was the first step in a career which was to become part of New Zealand folklore.

A couple of weeks later the Rangers had their first brush with the rebels, and Von Tempsky gave a vivid description of the action:

> We mustered about fifty men, including fifteen Mauku Rifles, under Lt Lusk. From the Lower Mauku, where the stockade of the settlement was erected, the houses of the settlers straggle along a wooded ridge running south; at about a mile and a half another ridge joins the former at a right angle, dotted with another set of settlers' houses, amongst them a little church with a white steeple, now made bullet-proof and garrisoned by settlers and Militia. At the eastern end of that settlement the native village of Patumahoe commences; It had been abandoned long ago by the natives who had joined the cause of the fighting tribes. South of this about a mile or two lies the farm of Messrs. Lusk and Hill. We visited the house, and there at last we found fresh tracks. We followed them like sleuth-hounds. They led through the corner of a large paddock, then entered the bush by a well-beaten path. We were about a mile from the paddock when we heard three, four, five, six shots fired, evidently in the paddock. We turned and hastened back. It was reported from the rear that the Maoris could be heard shouting to one another. Jackson and Lusk decided that the party should divide, a process I did not believe in but had to assent to. One party, under our ensign, Hay, and guided by Mr Hill, were to look up the Maoris in our rear, as it was thought that there would be found the strongest number of enemies; thirty men, all Forest Rangers, were allotted to that party. The

Williamson's Clearing, Waikato, 1863, showing the military road under construction by General Cameron's troops. *C. J. Urquhart Album, Alexander Turnbull Library*

remaining twenty, under Jackson, Lusk and myself, proceeded towards the paddock. . . .

We had just scattered a bit when another shot was fired, towards the south-west corner of the paddock. There was no mistake in this; there were the Maoris, and they intended to draw us on. We pleased them to a certain extent, but not exactly the way they wanted us to go — across the open paddock right on to the dense bush where the shot was fired. We made for the bush immediately opposite to us and followed its cover along the edge towards the direction of the shot. We knew that at every step now we might come upon the Maoris, and I can assure you we kept a sharp lookout all round us; but we saw nothing; nothing moved except what we moved.

Thus we marched on. Where the deuce are the Maoris? Down comes a volley with a vengeance. The powder-smoke is blown into our faces; I rub my eyes — I can hardly see for the saltpetre-fumes in them. 'Give it to them boys, right and left!' and away crack our carbines and rifles. Over the din, the clatter and spatter of shots, you can hear the high-pitched voice of a Maori chanting an incantation. Our carbines answer. Ah, you hear a change of key now — you hear those two or three fellows singing 'Miserere Domine' — and such a Miserere — that one fellow in particular must have been hit in the spine, for his yells are abominable. Are none of our men hit? I cannot see one down yet — they are all behind trees, and blazing away for the very life of them. . . .

At last, while the fire of our opponents had grown slacker, for very good reasons, a party was sent from our right flank to cut them off. We were to charge when the cheer of this party was heard. We rushed with frantic valour into the bush. The bush was calmer than ever. We traverse and jump from tree to tree. Strange is this bush fighting — mysterious: blue smoke, green leaves, perhaps a black head: cries, defiant, soul-rending, you hear perhaps — yes, you can hear them talking next door to you, coolly, familiarly, but you see nothing — nothing tangible to grasp, to wrestle with. . . .

We returned to Mauku laden with spoil and intoxicated with our victory. The Forest Rangers and Mauku Rifles had fleshed their arms at last, and that is no small matter with young soldiers. In casualties Alfred Speedy, son of Major Speedy, was shot through the cap, W. Worthington through the trousers, and Mr Wheeler through the coat. This from a volley at 20 to 15 yards. Too much powder, ye Maoris![6]

Skirmishes similar to this were widespread to the south of Auckland, involving not only the Rangers but also the 18th, 65th and 70th Regiments. Cameron did not intend to move against the next major obstacle to his advance until the rest of the 12th landed from Australia and he could satisfy himself that all was ready.

Time hung heavily on the hands of a young officer, Thomas McDonnell, who was attached to Lieutenant-Colonel Nixon's Moveable Column. A friend of Von Tempsky's from Coromandel days, he conceived a madcap plan to go to a strong enemy position at Paparata on a one-man spying expedition. McDonnell asked Von to help him get the necessary permission, to which the latter agreed so long as they both went on the venture:

We started together in search of Colonel Nixon, and laid the matter before him.

For a long time he would hear nothing of it, and withheld his consent to speak to the General, pleasantly remarking that we were too valuable officers to lose.

He said that Sir Duncan [Cameron] would never give his permission, that he had reconnoitred the place before with a large body of troops, and had thought it best to let it alone for the present. After much persuasion the fine old fellow promised to see about it next morning, but gave it as his opinion that the General would not allow us to risk our lives. I thought differently, and that any information about Paparata would be very acceptable, as he wanted information.

Far Left: Lieutenant (later Major) D. H. Lusk was a settler and surveyor who formed and led the Forest Rifles early in the Waikato War. *Alexander Turnbull Library*

Left: Captain (later Lieutenant-Colonel) Thomas McDonnell was probably the most experienced Colonial soldier of the wars. He fought in 40 separate engagements, being wounded four times. He was awarded the New Zealand Cross many years after the wars ended. *Alexander Turnbull Library*

Next morning Von Tempsky and I were requested to attend at headquarters at 1 p.m., when, introduced by our Colonel, we met the chief, who told us the heads of the information he wished for, and kindly gave his permission for us to go, and wished us a safe return. We received a letter to the officer who commanded at the next post, Colonel H., of the 12th Regt, to allow us to pass, and early the following morning we started. . . .

In a short time we came to the branch track leading in the direction of Paparata, now about seven miles distant. The country was quite level up to it, with the exception of a few small gullies. A very large swamp was to our left hand, backed by a high wooded range intersected with deep ravines running into the swamp. To our right was the road we had just come along, the Waikato river, and the enemy's position at Meremere. Before us lay Paparata.

The path we were now on was scarcely discernible it being very dark; and at times we could scarcely tell if we were off or on the track, but by keeping the night air on our left cheek, and stooping down now and again to feel for the road, we moved slowly along. Any tree or dark object was carefully approached, lest it should prove an enemy. Our object was to avoid a meeting, if possible, for many reasons, and we did not know but that we might fall in with scouts sent to shoot natives, and pick up information. . . .

Presently we heard voices approaching, so we retraced our steps till we could get to one side and allow the natives to pass us, but we had not gone far when we heard other voices approaching in what had been our rear.

'We are for it now,' I whispered to Von Tempsky, and it struck us both we had been seen by scouts as we had passed over the razor-backed ridge before mentioned, and that we were in rather a mess, and were being hunted. One chance seemed open — to leave the path and strike for the narrow belt of forest. This we did, and went a short distance and sat down to rest for a while. The two parties of natives met nearly opposite to where we were seated, muttered a few words too indistinct for us to understand, and then they moved off in the direction we had been going. . . .

We now heard a horseman approaching, and presently a native galloped past on a grey horse. A brute of a dog yelped at his heels. The dog stopped close to where we lay. He evidently scented mischief, and was trying to attract attention to it; but at last he obeyed a shout from his master and made after him, a great relief to us.

It was now light enough to distinguish objects more plainly. The flax we found ourselves hidden in was about four feet high. This was all the shelter we had, and to our disgust, we found it would be impossible to gain the forest without being seen by the natives, some of whom were on the alert. Our position was such that we required to use the greatest caution lest we should be discovered. We were in a small piece of flax swamp that stood in the centre of a level bit of country, showing a very different aspect from what it had appeared to be as we had marched on it by night.

I stood upright to get a good view of the position, when Von Tempsky gave me a tug. I turned, and he pointed silently to a native standing about twenty paces from us holding a bright double-barrelled gun in his hands. I at once threw myself down on the ground; fortunately he had not seen us.

After the sun had risen we took another view. Good heavens! we were almost in the centre of the natives, and on two sides of us and about 500 or 600 yards off were newly-dug rifle pits and some earthworks, and new roughly-made whares.

'After the natives have had their breakfast,' whispered Von Tempsky, 'they will find us out old fellow.'

'Very likely,' I replied; 'some horrid old hag will be coming to cut flax and discover us hidden here; of course she will yell out her discovery; other natives will come up and we will be tomahawked.'

We resolved, should we be discovered, to fire right and left and make a dash for it as well as we could. Many queer thoughts came over me. Poor Von Tempsky, I could see, was thinking of his wife and little ones. I blamed myself for bringing him. It did not at that time matter so much for myself. I had no one to care for me. Having arrived at the conclusion we were in what the Yankees term a 'considerable fix', we determined to make the best of it, and commenced our breakfast of biscuit, two cakes of chocolate, and a tin of kippered herrings, and prepared for what might happen. . . .

We dared not stir, and at times our very breath seemed suspended, our nerves were strung to the uttermost, and several times I was on the point of rushing out and having the suspense over. Anything was better, so it seemed, to silent endurance. The wind now proving our best friend, continued to rise and soon increased to a gale, and rain fell in torrents continuing without intermission all day, and to this change in the weather, thank God, we owe our lives.

The little hollow where we lay commenced to fill with water, which soon rose five or six inches. The high wind beat down the flax so that we could not sit upright, but had to lie on our sides in the water, keeping ourselves dry as best we could. It was trying work, for twelve long hours we were forced to keep this position, every moment expecting to be found out. At last the day passed away into night, and the rain ceased. We tried to resume our sitting posture, but were so cramped we could hardly effect this; after chafing our limbs as well as we could, we prepared for our return. We had run the risk, but had gained a considerable part of our object, and had a tolerably correct estimate of the enemy's strength, and from speeches we had heard we collected a certain amount of information needless to repeat. . . .

The next day we returned to Queen's Redoubt and headquarters, reporting ourselves and the result of our trip to the General, who was pleased to thank us for the service, by letter, and in G.O. Our dear old Colonel was delighted to see us safe back, and threw his cap up and cheered; indeed our welcome back to camp was very flattering to us.[7]

Both men were promoted to captain. The original company of the Forest Rangers had been enlisted for a period of three months, but its record was felt to justify not only its retention but also the addition of a second company. Captain Von Tempsky was given the new command, with John Roberts as his subaltern.

Cameron waited over three months for a flotilla to be built and collected so that he could take maximum advantage of the river in operations against the next strongpoint. This, at Meremere, promised to be much harder to reduce than Koheroa, and the general intended to make full use of artillery. The *Avon,* under the command of Captain Hunt, gave the defenders a taste of what to expect when, early in August, her Armstrong guns and rockets were brought into play.

By late October the two steamers were augmented by four old hoop-ironed barges for troop carrying, grandly named H.M.S. *Ant* and similar insect-prompted titles. Ashore, the soldiers built a redoubt to house a 40-pounder Armstrong on the edge of the Whangamarino swamp. On 29 and 30 October the bombardment opened up in earnest, with the general and his staff aboard *Pioneer* to assess its effectiveness. The big gun was firing short-fuse shells which burst in the air over the trenches, while those from the ships exploded on impact. The results of the barrage exceeded all hopes, for when the infantry scaled the bluff they found the pa completely deserted, the defenders having retired to avoid being outflanked.

The general made Meremere his advanced base for the next move. The Kingites had fortified a hill dominating the low, swampy country between the river and Lake Waikare. Early on 20 November a combined advance by land and water set out to take Rangiriri, a name long to be remembered by both sides.

The repulse of the Royal Navy storming party at Rangiriri on 20 November 1863. A sketch by Major C. Heaphy, V.C. *Alexander Turnbull Library*

Cameron had yet to learn that in taking most enemy pa it was not necessary to incur heavy casualties. Far from profiting by Pratt's example, he meant to launch a pincer movement against a position that was to prove far stronger than expected. The force numbered about 1,300 men drawn from the 12th, 14th, 40th and 65th Regiments, with artillery and engineer support and a naval party of sailors and marines.

Cameron led the main contingent, which marched from Meremere and reached Rangiriri at 3 p.m. The defences appeared to consist of a long line of trenches, with rifle pits to cover any approach from the river. While waiting for the *Avon* and *Pioneer* to bring their complement ashore to attack in the rear, two 12-pounder Armstrong guns shelled the entrenchment but were inadequate to breach the defence.

A high wind and currents delayed landing from the ships and barges, and as the afternoon slipped away Cameron sent in his frontal attack without waiting for the support of the flanking party. At first all went well. The troops carried the outlying part of the trenches and overran the rifle pits, but they were then confronted by a strong redoubt which had previously been hidden by the configuration of the hill.

From its ditch a parapet reared about 20 feet upwards, and the scaling ladders were too short to reach the top. The defenders, in excellent cover, raked the helpless troops below. The 65th were driven back, to be replaced by 36 men of the Royal Artillery led by Captain Henry Mercer, who also had to give ground when he fell wounded. A last determined effort by Commander Mayne, R.N., leading his sailors and marines, met with no better fate. Cameron was forced to call a halt to stem the rapidly mounting casualties and, belatedly, he ordered a sap to be started.

The second attempted assault on Rangiriri by Captain Mercer and 36 men of the Royal Artillery. Mercer was killed and the attack failed. *Taranaki Museum*

Views of the Central Redoubt at Rangiriri after the surrender on 21 November 1863. The engraving shows the camera used to take the photograph of the same scene, from the same vantage point. *Illustrated London News* and *Spencer Collection, Hawke's Bay Art Gallery and Museum*

Captain Henry Mercer, Royal Artillery, killed at Rangiriri on 20 November 1863. From *Defenders of New Zealand*

The troops landing in the rear found the Maori escaping and opened fire. Their retreat cut off, shooting by the rest of the garrison allowed the besiegers little sleep that night. This prodigal waste of ammunition compelled a surrender early the next day, when 183 prisoners were taken. The victory was dearly bought, with over 130 casualties. The injuries of some, including the gallant Mercer, proved to be beyond the primitive medical facilities of the time. As was usually the case, Maori losses were unknown, since the dead and wounded were carried away by their comrades.

The vanquished of Rangiriri were taken to Auckland, and at the insistence of Grey's Ministers were imprisoned in the coal hulk *Marion*. The governor did his best to alleviate their suffering, and the captives were eventually taken to Kawau Island in the Hauraki Gulf. They escaped from the island, and took refuge among the Ngapuhi.

A Royal Artillery sergeant major, Wanganui 1866. He wears a dark blue forage cap with gold braid and grenade, a dark blue patrol jacket braided with black and gold-on-red insignia on the shoulders, and dark blue trousers with a red welt down the outer seams. *Alexander Turnbull Library*

CHAPTER 8

BRITISH ARTILLERY IN NEW ZEALAND, 1845–66

The first detachment of regular artillerymen arrived in New Zealand in November 1845. These were 15 men of the Honourable East India Company Artillery from the ship *Elphinstone*. Prior to this, all artillery in action against Puketutu and Ohaeawai Pa had been served by gunners of the Royal Navy.

The British attack on Ruapekapeka Pa was particularly arduous. Three naval 32-pounder guns, one 18-pounder, two 12-pounder howitzers, one 6-pounder brass gun, four mortars and two rocket tubes were hauled through 15 miles of roadless hills, forests, swamps and streams. The march of combined naval and military forces was a feat of pioneering.

It was necessary to make roads, fell bush, bridge streams and to use block and tackle to move the guns over rough ground and up steep hills. The men were compelled to carry, in addition to their arms and equipment, boxes containing either a 24- or 32-pound shell. The advance on Ruapekapeka took more than a month, but the walls of the pa were breached after a 24-hour bombardment.

A detachment of the Royal Artillery was sent from Australia in 1847, and took part in the action at St Johns Wood, Wanganui.

All the artillery used in these engagements consisted of smooth-bore muzzle loaders, which were essentially unchanged from the weapons used in the Napoleonic wars of 30 years before. When the first Taranaki war broke out in 1860, the guns used against Te Kohia Pa at Waitara were basically the same as those of 1845.

Five main types of projectiles were used in the smooth-bore muzzle loaders during the New Zealand wars:

1. Round shot were solid cast-iron spheres, the weight of which defined the size and classification of the pieces from which they were fired. These were used for one purpose — to breach the walls of fortified pa. Throughout the whole smooth-bore period 70 to 80 per cent of the ammunition held in the field was of this type, so clearly great reliance was placed on it.

2. Shrapnel shell was invented by Henry Shrapnel, R.A. in 1784. It consisted of a hollow iron ball filled with bullets and with a bursting charge which was ignited by a time fuse set to explode the projectile at a point on the trajectory from which the balls would cover the most ground and at the same time be lethal when they struck. The flash from the propellant charge ignited the fuse.

4. Case, or canister, shot consisted of a tin case filled with iron balls. When fired the case broke open at the muzzle, the balls spreading out like the charge from a shotgun.

5. A common shell was a hollow iron-cast sphere filled with gunpowder and with a time fuse which was ignited by the firing of the charge. It burst either in the air to 'search' trenches or earthworks, or on the ground to destroy fortified positions. In the field it was fired only by howitzers and mortars.

6. Carcase was a hollow iron sphere into which a hot incendiary mixture had been poured and allowed to set. The ball was pierced by a number of holes through which the flash from the propellant set fire to the contents, which were very difficult to put out. Carcase was used on one or two occasions to burn the fern and scrub around Maori positions, but without much success.

The effectiveness of artillery against Maori pa altered radically when, in March 1861, Captain Mercer brought into use in Taranaki a battery consisting of three rifled breech-loading 12-pounder Armstrong guns. For months General Pratt had been bombarding Te Arei with smooth-bore artillery, which did little damage because the defenders were well protected in bombproof rua, or dug-outs.

When the Armstrongs were brought into action, the shells penetrated the rua and burst inside. After sustaining three days of this type of shelling the Maori sued for peace. Mercer had been anxious to ascertain the effect of 12-pounder shellfire, and after the battle he was reported as being fully convinced of the decided superiority of rifled ordnance over smooth-bored. The amazing fact is that after rifled breech-loading guns had been proved in colonial campaigns such as those in New Zealand the British Army in 1870 elected to return to muzzle-loading artillery. This came about because the British military hierarchy was extremely resistant to change and unable or unwilling to cope with the few mechanical problems the revolutionary Armstrongs presented. It was not until the 1890s that the breech-loader was finally reintroduced into the British Army.

The Armstrong gun used a unique segment shell made up of a central cylinder containing a bursting charge surrounded by a number of cast-iron segments, the whole being covered up to the shoulder by a lead sheathing. Upon firing, the projectile was forced into the bore, the lead filling up the grooves of the rifling to make a gas-tight fit.

A metal time or concussion fuse was screwed into the nose of the shell. It could be set to burst the projectile on trajectory as with shrapnel, or set at zero to burst it in the muzzle, producing the same effect as case or canister. Alternatively it could be set to explode on impact. In addition to segment, solid projectiles — that is, shot and common shell — were used.

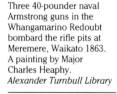

Three 40-pounder naval Armstrong guns in the Whangamarino Redoubt bombard the rifle pits at Meremere, Waikato 1863. A painting by Major Charles Heaphy.
Alexander Turnbull Library

Forty-pounder Armstrong siege guns of the Royal Artillery in Australia before their shipment to New Zealand. *B. Cresset*

When the Waikato war broke out the Royal Artillery, equipped mainly with 6- and 12-pounder Armstrong guns, again took the field. Two 40-pounder Armstrong siege pieces were used against the Maori entrenchments at Meremere, but because of their lack of mobility, such heavy guns were used only once more, during the action at the Gate Pa. The two 40-pounders used there were not, however, the same as those used at Meremere: they were naval guns.

The difficulties of the gunners on campaign were vividly described by Lieutenant A. F. Pickard, V.C., R.A.:

About the end of July a night march was made to some native settlements about 15 miles from Koheroa, where a large body of Kingites were reported to be located. The track was not well known, and no wheeled conveyances had ever before travelled on it. Two 12-pr. Armstrongs, drawn by bullocks and carrying several fascines and planks for bridge making purposes, accompanied the force, which started at about 9.30 p.m. The night was very dark and the track was so narrow and slippery that, when about three miles from camp, one gun upset down the side of a steep ridge; it was, after some difficulty, brought up again on the track and, one wheel having been broken, the gun was left behind with an escort, and soon a second wheel was brought from camp by running it along on a tent pole run through the nave of the wheel. In several places the bullocks had to be taken out and the guns drawn by hand. The other gun continued with the column which, finding the natives had left their settlements and retired to the bush, returned to Koheroa the following day.[1]

At the battle of Rangiriri three Armstrongs plus the gunboats *Avon* and *Pioneer* bombarded the pa for nearly two hours. The solid earthworks (there were no palisades) suffered very little damage, but many casualties were inflicted on the Maori crowded in the trenches. This shelling did not prevent the defenders from repulsing two separate assaults by the Army and the Naval Brigade and a suicidal attack by men of the Royal Artillery armed with swords and revolvers. The pa fell the next day when the garrison ran out of ammunition.

After Rangiriri the guns went forward to Ngaruawahia by flat-bottomed boats. Two 12-pounders bombarded Paterangi Pa, but on 21 February 1864 General Cameron outflanked this post and marched on Rangiaowhia with three 6-pounder Armstrongs drawn by two horses each.

General Cameron, leaning against the centre of the gun carriage wheel, with a member of his staff and Royal Artillery men at sunrise on the morning of the attack at the Gate Pa, 29 April 1864. *Alexander Turnbull Library*

The Maori entrenchments at nearby Hairini Hill were taken the next day, with the guns firing very effectively over the heads of the advancing troops. After two unsuccessful assaults without artillery support, a 6-pounder Armstrong was used against Orakau to little effect. It would appear that Cameron had not learned the lesson of how essential this covering fire had proved at Hairini.

When fighting broke out at Tauranga the general, impressed by Maori resistance at Orakau, assembled for use at Gate Pa a mighty artillery force — the largest concentration ever used against a Maori fortification. Included were two 8-inch mortars, six Coehorn mortars, three 6-pounder Armstrongs, two 24-pounder howitzers, two 40-pounder naval Armstrongs and a monstrous 110-pounder naval Armstrong mounted on a cumbersome ship's traversing platform.

These extraordinarily heavy batteries of 15 guns opened fire on a weakly constructed pa defended by 250 warriors soon after daybreak and continued until 4 p.m. By 3 p.m. the 110-pounder had fired 100 rounds — all that had been brought ashore — but much of it was wasted in trying to hit a flagstaff that was thought to be in the centre of the pa but was in fact sited on the crest some 50 yards to the rear.

Some of the overs landed amongst the 68th Regiment at the back of the pa, and the gunners consistently misjudged the depth of their target, causing many of the shells to burst beyond the rear fence. All this fire did little damage apart from breaching the flimsy palisade which was mostly for show anyway. When the final attack went in, the British were bloodily repulsed by an enemy protected by bombproof dug-outs and virtually unharmed by the artillery 'preparation'.

This battle was the last to feature artillery in large numbers. Cameron was to take two 6-pounder Armstrongs with him on his west coast campaign, but these saw little use.

During General Chute's advance through Taranaki in 1866, three of these guns were used very effectively against Otapawa Pa when it was stormed by Imperial troops. It was a herculean task to transport these pieces through the trackless bush, the men having to cut their way through with hatchets and billhooks, not to mention crossing innumerable gullies and small rivers swollen by heavy rain. Chute's march was virtually the last campaign of the British Army in New Zealand, although detachments of artillery remained in some garrisons until 1870.

It is interesting to note that when the British Army decided to return to muzzle-loading guns the Ordnance Select Committee reported in 1865:

> The many-grooved system of rifling, with lead coated projectiles and complicated breech-loading arrangements, is far inferior for the general purpose of war to the muzzle-loading systems, and has the disadvantage of being more expensive in both cost and ammunition. Muzzle-loading guns are far superior to breech-loaders in simplicity of construction and efficiency in this respect for active service. They can be worked with perfect ease and abundant rapidity.

All of these statements, except that on cost, were disproved during the New Zealand wars. The fault was not with the breech-loading system of the Armstrong but with those officers who could not come to terms with the new technology. The die-hards won. This is illustrated by a conversation between Sir Andrew Noble, an advocate of rifled guns, and a senior artillery officer whom Sir Andrew was trying to convince of the superior accuracy of breech-loading guns. Sir Andrew drew a diagram showing that the shot from a rifled weapon fell into a much smaller area than those of the smooth-bore. The eminent gunner was not shaken:

A detachment of New Zealand Armed Constabulary artillerymen at Tauranga in 1870 with 6-pounder Armstrong guns inherited from the Royal Artillery. Their R.A. instructor stands beside the limber at the right. *National Museum*

> That only proves what I have already maintained, that our smooth-bore is the best in the world. With your new-fangled gun firing at me I've only to keep outside that small area and I shan't be touched, but with the smooth-bore firing at me I'm not safe anywhere.[2]

Above: The 4.4-inch Coehorn mortar, which fired an 8½-pound shell, was used extensively in sieges both by the Royal Artillery and the colonial forces, notably by the latter at Ngatapa in 1868. The barrel was fixed at a constant angle of 45 degrees and the range was gauged by careful measurement of the powder in each charge. For example, 3 oz 12 dr of powder gave a range at 45 degrees of 600 yards. The fuse of the exploding charge of the shell was ignited by the muzzle flash when the mortar was fired. The weapon's high trajectory allowed common shell to be fired over ramparts and into trenches. Mortar shells were often used as hand grenades, as at Rangiriri. Carriage was usually by cart.

Below: A cross-section of a 12-pounder Armstrong gun. This clearly shows the built-up method of construction, which was obtained by heating the outer tubes and allowing these to shrink on to the inner tube upon cooling. The breach mechanism comprised two main parts: a breech block or vent piece (A), and a breech screw operated by a weighted crank handle on its rear end (B). The block moved vertically in a slot cut in the breech end of the piece (C). It was lifted out bodily for loading and replaced for firing. This block incorporated a vent into which was inserted a friction tube with a lanyard attached. When the lanyard was pulled, it caused a flash in the friction tube which ignited the propellant charge (D). Both the charge and shell were loaded through the hollow breech screw, which was then tightened against the 'vent piece' or breech block to prevent it from blowing out. *Drawings by Malcolm Thomas*

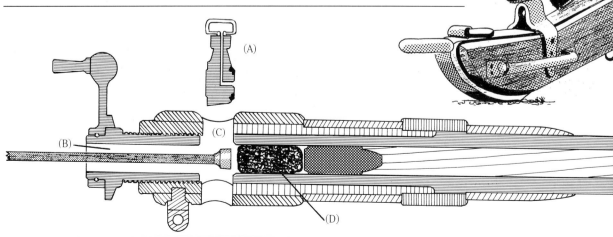

A 12-pounder rifled breech-loading Armstrong gun of 1860. The accuracy of this piece was quite revolutionary in its day, for tests showed it to be more accurate at two miles' range than the smooth-bore at a quarter of that distance. The rifling consisted of 38 shallow grooves, with a twist of one turn in 38 calibres. The carriage was fitted with an elevating gear in the form of a screw and with a traversing gear, the latter being unique in field artillery of the Armstrong era. The axle-tree boxes contained shells and charges, including the obligatory case shot to be used only in defence of the gun itself. The carriage was painted grey overall. *Drawing by Malcolm Thomas*

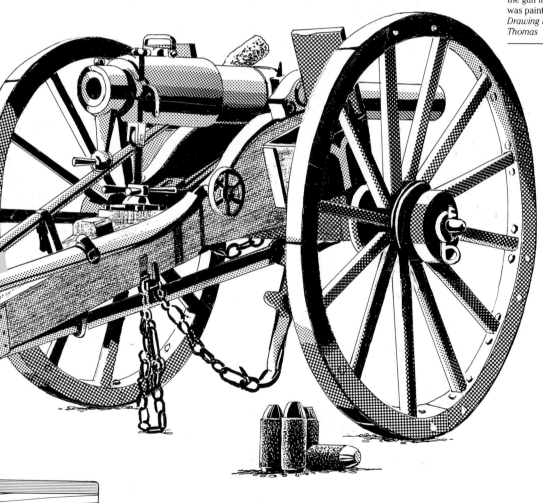

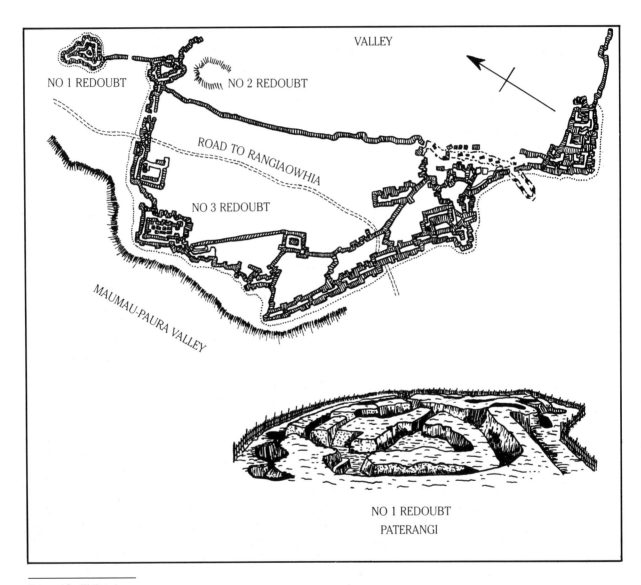

VALLEY

NO 1 REDOUBT

NO 2 REDOUBT

ROAD TO RANGIAOWHIA

NO 3 REDOUBT

MAUMAU-PAURA VALLEY

NO 1 REDOUBT

PATERANGI

Paterangi Pa, Waikato in
1864. Plan by John Topham
based on a survey by
Captain E. Brooke R.E. in
1864. This extremely strong
pa was never attacked by
the British Army, instead it
was outflanked and
consequently abandoned
by the Maoris.

COURAGE IS NOT ENOUGH

Although the victory of Rangiriri had been costly, it opened up the entire Waikato Valley to the British advance. Another Maori stand might well have been expected where the hills shut in the gorge at Taupiri, but Cameron was allowed to march unhindered to King Tawhiao's capital at Ngaruawahia, his warriors fell back to positions in the Waipa Valley well to the south.

The King's palace was used as the guardroom, while the Army camped in the potato fields nearby. The 43rd and 68th Regiments arrived in Auckland, freeing the 50th to join Cameron. The Forest Rangers were also sent south from the Hunua, and henceforth acted as commandos.

Early in January 1864 Cameron was ready to move on:

> The Waikato at this time was alive with small craft. Little river steamers panted up-stream, sometimes towing barges filled with soldiers. Slim gunboats attracted the admiring gaze of friendly natives, whose canoes crowded the river, carrying stores to the British camps.
>
> For miles and miles now there was an unbroken stream of soldiers, bullock-drays, artillery, packhorses and orderlies meandering over the plains and fern ridges of the sacred Maori delta (junction of the Waikato, or Horotiu, and Waipa Rivers at Ngaruawahia). Yellow clouds of dust hovered along our road, to the great disparagement of our faces, sight and clear speech.[1]

The Maori had chosen two hills at Pikopiko and Paterangi to fortify, and the British camped at Te Rore, close to the latter position. The general was in no

Paterangi Pa after it was evacuated in 1864, looking south from No. 3 Redoubt which is on the right of the photograph. The figures give some idea of the immensity of the fortress. *Spencer Album, Hawke's Bay Art Gallery and Museum*

Von Tempsky's painting of the skirmish at Waiari. He is directing the fight, sword in hand. *Auckland Institute and Museum*

hurry to show his hand, and while waiting for the arrival of his heavy stores an Armstrong battery kept the Maori on the alert.

Action was not entirely one-sided. About a mile south of Paterangi, at Waiari, there was a loop in the Mangapiko, and the narrow neck of land it enclosed had long since been fortified with ditches. The site was now overgrown with heavy manuka scrub, and a large pool here was used by the troops for bathing. On the afternoon of 11 February, men from the 40th and 50th Regiments came to bathe and were soon under fire from a strong body of Maori hidden in the undergrowth. The sound of shooting brought up Lieutenant-Colonel Sir Henry Havelock, V.C., at the head of 200 men of the 40th and Forest Rangers. A desperate hand-to-hand struggle in the scrub ensued until, when darkness came on, the troops were ordered back to camp. Both sides suffered significant losses in the encounter.

Its most noteworthy feature was the rescue of a wounded man of the 40th by Captain Charles Heaphy, who had come to the country as the New Zealand Company's draughtsman in the *Tory* as long ago as 1839. A Volunteer officer, he often acted as a guide, and after two others had been killed while trying to bring in the fallen corporal he, with great coolness, succeeded where they had failed, although hit by five shots in the process. Heaphy was recommended for the Victoria Cross, but because the award was for the regular forces only, it took three years, and considerable pressure from the governor, before he eventually received the medal.

Later that month Cameron decided that the easiest way to reduce the two pa was to cut off the food supplies. These were drawn from the large village of Rangiaowhia, situated on some of the best land in the Waikato. Leaving forces to cover Pikopiko and Paterangi, a column of cavalry and infantry from the regiments and colonists made a night sortie under strict silence on 20 February. Progress was slower than had been hoped, and it was broad daylight before the village, straggling along a ridge between the Anglican and Roman Catholic churches, came in sight.

To take advantage of what surprise might still be possible, the Colonial

Defence Force Cavalry galloped ahead and exchanged fire with Maori in the whare (houses). Horses were of little use in these conditions, and two Maori-speaking officers, Captain T. McDonnell and Ensign William G. Mair, called out to the defenders to surrender. These appeals were ignored, and resistance crystallised on one particular house. Colonel Marmaduke Nixon fell mortally wounded along with a sergeant and another soldier. Eventually the place caught fire, and 30 years later the tragic end to the heroic stand was still vivid in McDonnell's mind:

Colonel Marmaduke Nixon. From *Defenders of New Zealand*

> Volley after volley was poured into the hut, and we concluded that all had been killed inside, when a naked little child, about four years old, darted out of the burning whare, and rushed first to one side and then to the other, its large brown eyes dilated with terror as it dashed about, trying to escape, like a wild bird. Several shots were fired, but the men, in their excitement, did not know what they were firing at. At last, seeing that escape was impossible, and being exhausted, the child sank down on its knees by a young bush, as if appealing for its protection, and, covering its eyes with its baby hands, sat panting. Mr Mair wrapped it in a greatcoat, and the men put biscuits before it. The child gazed from one to another, trying every now and then to repress a deep sob. At last it looked shyly at the food, and presently commenced to eat heartily.
>
> Another rush from the burning house, and a man came out. Many shots were fired, and I and Von Tempsky could hear the thud of balls as they struck him. He staggered and reeled, and the firing ceased. The Maori lifted his head and gave one earnest look around, as if bidding us a mournful farewell, then taking up the corner of the half-burned blanket he had on, he covered his face and lay down and died.[2]

The fight at Rangiaowhia, 21 February 1864. Colonel M. Nixon falls mortally wounded at the door of the whare at the left. *Auckland Public Library*

The remains of the occupants of that fatal hut were charred beyond recognition. Kereopa's claim that these included his two daughters could there-

fore not be refuted when he tried to justify his role as the instigator of the ritual murder of the Rev. Volkner the next year. A further charge that divine service was being held in the whare seems unfounded, both because of the early hour and the existence of two churches in the settlement.

The fact that Bishop Augustus Selwyn rode with Cameron's force was condemned by the Waikàto Maori, even though his intention was humanitarian. Sunday had been chosen by the British to make what seemed a cowardly attack on women and children in an open settlement. How could actions like these accord with the teachings of Christianity? The desire had been to spare life as much as possible rather than to storm the fighting pa, but the whole affair fell far below Maori conceptions of fair play.

The next day Lieutenant-Colonel Waddy, facing Paterangi, found the garrison was departing, and Havelock's opposition at Pikopiko also melted away. The Maori moved to the top of Hairini Hill, near Rangiaowhia, where they prepared a ditch and parapet for battle.

This time Cameron was willing to oblige, and ordered an immediate assault by the 50th, 65th and 70th with the Forest Rangers. One of the latter described the action:

> It was as pretty a bit of hot firing as I have ever seen. The Armstrongs were sending their shells screeching over us, and the Maori bullets were cutting down the fern near me with as even a swathe almost as you could cut it with a slash-hook. We were lying within 300 yards of the enemy. At last the 'Charge' was sounded, and away we went, the whole of us, we Rangers making for the Maoris' right flank, and the 50th Regt, on our right, for the centre. With a great cheer the 50th swept splendidly up to the parapet with bayonets at the charge. We on their left stormed the Maori line on even terms with them; we had no bayonets, but used our revolvers for close-quarters work.[3]

The defenders broke ranks under the impetus of the charge, falling back to a nearby swamp and making for Maungatautari. The general moved his headquarters forward to Pukerimu in the eastern Waikato, renaming it Cambridge in honour of the Commander-in-Chief, the Duke of Cambridge.

A British attack had driven Rewi Maniapoto from his home at Kihikihi, and he now prepared to make a final stand at Orakau, close to Brigadier-General Carey's base at Te Awamutu. He set a scratch contingent of Maori drawn mainly from the east of the North Island who had not yet tried conclusions with the invader to build the inevitable pa in a food-growing area.

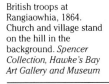

British troops at Rangiaowhia, 1864. Church and village stand on the hill in the background. *Spencer Collection, Hawke's Bay Art Gallery and Museum*

Rewi Manga Maniapoto,
1815–94, war chief of the
Ngati Maniapoto tribe and
defender of Orakau Pa.
*Hawke's Bay Art Gallery
and Museum*

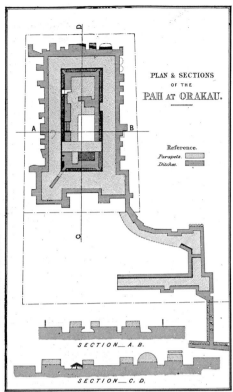

Plan of Orakau Pa. From
War in New Zealand

The British siege of
Orakau Pa, 1 April 1864,
showing the sap which
commenced in the peach
grove at the right of the
picture. *Illustrated London
News*

Carey did not hesitate to reply to this latest challenge, and Lieutenant John Roberts described the opening phase of the battle:

> On the first day my twenty Rangers had the honour of being on the left of the Imperial Corps under Capt Ring (18th Royal Irish) in the advance on the pa. I remember that although we Rangers marched in single file out through the high manuka and scrub on the bullock track from Kihikihi to Orakau, the Imperial men marched in fours, in close order, and I could not help thinking it was very foolish in such a favourable place for ambuscades. As we approached the pa we passed through some very high flax and scrub, and we could see a large peach grove ahead. We extended in skirmishing order, in our position on the left, and advanced to within about 70 yards. We could hardly believe it was the main position at first.
>
> Suddenly, as we advanced, the whole west face of the pa, the front we were approaching, opened fire. Puffs of smoke and gun flashes ran along the front of the entrenchment and back again, the rain of bullets from the Maori tuparas (double-barrelled guns) came over our heads. We were hunting down cover in an instant.
>
> We lay down on the edge of the cultivation and went to work as hard as we could with our long knives, each man digging a shallow shelter for himself and throwing up the earth in front; the bullets were coming over thick that day.[4]

'Retire' was sounded, and the assault party was reinforced by another company of the 40th Regiment. Though some of the Rangers reached the ditch, the second wave fared no better than the first and Ring was hit fatally. Captain Baker, of the Staff, called for volunteers to try a third time, but Carey was forced to give up the attempt to take the position. He settled down for a siege, and started a sap.

Cameron sent a further 200 men on 1 April, and the Maori also received reinforcements. The Forest Rangers were holding the sector where the latter might try to break through for a link-up with the defenders. Von Tempsky wrote:

> About 12 o'clock we began to see natives trooping along the ranges to the east, and making for the forest between us and Rangiaowhia. Their numbers increased at every moment. I was stationed in a hollow where the main road from the pa crossed a swamp and led up an adjoining ridge, on which stood a large weatherboard house. I had previously put a picket near that house, as the view from it commanded the very point of the forest now that reinforcements were gathering.
>
> The natives in the pa had seen the arrival of succour as well as we had, and repeated cheers and volleys announced their appreciation of the sight. From the forest responsive cheers soon established a sympathetic intercourse between the two separated bodies, and I must confess that as far as I was concerned at least the enthusiasm was all on their side. Some Maori trumpeter in the pa commenced one of those high-pitched shouts, half-song, half-scream, that travel distinctly over long distances, particularly from range to range. He was giving the reinforcements some instructions. I have never been able to find out what they were, though we had plenty of interpreters with us. I went to the picket with reinforcements, and extended a line of skirmishers along the brow of the hill in the tea-tree scrub. There was open ground between us and the line of forest in which the reinforcements were, and they had to cross that opening if they wanted to come to us.
>
> About this time the natives in the pa commenced a war dance. Of course, we could see nothing of it, but we could hear it — the measured chant — the time-keeping yell — the snort and roar — the hiss and scream — the growl and bellowing — all coming from three hundred throats in measured cadence, working up their fury into a state of maniacal, demoniacal frenzy, till the stamping of their feet actually shook the ground.

There was soon an echo in the forest of this pandemoniacal concert. Another chorus of 300 or 400 throats made the woods tremble with their wrath of lung and the thundering stamp of feet. Twice it subsided, and skirmishers appeared, firing lustily into us. I must confess there was something impressive in these two savage hordes linking their spirits over this distance into a bond of wrathful aid, lashing one another's fury into a higher heat by each succeeding yell echoing responsive in each breast. Yet when the result of all this volcanic wrath broke against us, when the simple crack of our carbines sent line after line of their skirmishers back into the bush, then the third war dance to get up steam became almost a laughable affair.[5]

Cameron came from Pukerimu and could not help admiring the Maori's desperate stand — 'rare plucked 'uns', as he put it. As usual, the pa was without a water supply, only a few calabashes for the wounded having been brought in through the British lines at night when sentries looked the other way. By now the thirst of the able-bodied was such that they could not swallow food.

The general was becoming thoroughly disenchanted with the campaign. Far from protecting the settlers, as had initially been the case in Taranaki and as was the supposed reason for his troops' presence in the country, they were clearly being used to conquer territory and to rob the Maori of their ancestral lands. Ever since Rangiriri he had tried to minimise casualties, and now he wanted to spare the defenders from a probable blood bath. Ensign William Mair was sent to the head of the sap with a flag of truce and spoke to his hard-pressed foes:

Friends, listen! This is the word of the General. Great is his admiration of your bravery. Stop! Let the fighting cease; come out to us that your bodies may be saved.[6]

Ensign (later Major) William Mair. From *Defenders of New Zealand*

Hauraki rejecting General Cameron's peace terms at Orakau. *A. H. Messenger*

The chiefs discussed the offer, but only one favoured acceptance. The obdurate Rewi had little difficulty in securing rejection, expressed as the most famous defiance in New Zealand history:

Friend, we shall fight against you for ever and ever![7]

In later years Rewi himself was credited with having been the speaker, but Mair, who came to know him well, firmly denied this claim. A further plea to allow the women and children to leave was also refused, and the ensign narrowly escaped a shot as he dropped back into cover.

One reason for the continued resistance stemmed from Rangiriri, for on 3 May 1864 Grey wrote to the Duke of Newcastle:

The natives distinctly state that the reason why they would not accept the terms offered to them by General Cameron at Orakau was because they feared they would all be taken to Auckland, as the prisoners were from Rangiriri, and perhaps never be liberated.

Supplies in the pa were now very low, and having turned down the possibility of surrender Rewi was left with no alternative but to break out. The point chosen was that held fairly lightly by the 40th Regiment, and the troops were astounded to see:

. . . a solid column, the women, the children, and the great chiefs in the centre, and they marched out as cool and as steady as if they had been going to church.

The Maori actually reached the front line before the troops opened fire. The pace soon quickened as the refugees headed for swamp and scrub. Their escape was headed off by Lieutenant Rait's Royal Artillery troopers and the Defence Force Cavalry, permitting the Forest Rangers to come up. Roberts told of an episode that haunted the rest of his days:

There was one Maori, after we crossed the river, who kept us off for a long time by turning and kneeling down every now and again and presenting his gun at us. We fired, but did not hit him at first. He did not return our fire. He was gaining time to enable some of his older people to get away. At last I and another man shot him, and I shall never forget how sorry we were when we went up and found that his gun was empty. He had been presenting an unloaded gun at us all the time. We were terribly grieved to think we had killed so brave a man. Of course we would have spared him had we known he hadn't a shot left.[8]

Maori losses were the heaviest experienced in this campaign. Cameron had expected to have to deal with another strong position at Maungatautari, dominating his post at Pukerimu, but found this deserted.

The Waikato war had ended, and the Government Ministers presented their initial demand for land to be confiscated. This called for one million acres in the Horotiu and Waipa Basins, and a further 600,000 in Taranaki. These gentlemen wished, they said, to 'avoid any charge that a war of conquest had been waged'. If this was their idea of moderation, it was as well they were not greedy.

Ensign William Mair receives the reply to his plea to allow the women and children to leave the pa. *Taranaki Museum*

The charge of the Defence Force Cavalry at the Battle of Orakau. From *Picturesque Atlas of Australasia*

A Maori pa, painted by Major G. F. Von Tempsky, gives a good impression of a fortification of the 1860s. The light stockade resembles that at the Gate Pa, serving not as a barrier but as an obstacle — as barbed wire was used in later times. Other defensive elements shown include internal and external rifle pits, covered ways and dug-outs.
Auckland Institute and Museum

A view of an ordinary pa surrounded by potato plantations. This painting, attributed to Major Cyprian Bridge, depicts the outer stockade and gate of the 1840s. The loopholes for musket fire appear at the foot of the palisade, behind which rifle pits would be sited. Flanking angles in the stockade facilitated a cross-fire along the face of the pa.
Alexander Turnbull Library

THE MAORI PA

Because of constant intertribal warfare, the pre-European Maori was a master of the art of fortification. The traditional pa, or fortified village, was usually built on a scarped or trenched hill or ridge, often surrounded by palisades. Weapons were limited to those of a short flight nature (the bow and sling were unknown), hence the fighting was frequently hand-to-hand. A man standing 100 feet from a besieged pa could do so in complete safety.

The advent of muskets obtained from European traders rendered hilltop pa untenable. People moved down from the hills to flat land and constructed new pa, often on the banks of a stream or lake providing a permanent water supply. Hills afforded cover for a stealthy approach by an enemy and might dominate the traditional pa. When a fortification was built on the flat, cover was in some cases unobtainable, so giving the garrison a distinct advantage over the attackers who had to advance across open ground.

The gunfighters' pa generally had two stockades, the outer screen being erected about 30 inches in front of the main fence. A trench was sunk behind the inner stockade and the earth thrown up to form an inner parapet. The pickets of the outer screen did not reach the ground so that the defenders could thrust their muskets through the uprights of the main fence and under the screen.

During the 1860s some pa were built without any stockades. This occurred either because of a lack of timber in the area or because of a time factor. Sometimes the ramparts and trenches were considered to be of such strength that palisades were not needed, as at Rangiriri.

The Maori was almost as conservative as the British when it came to the tactics of warfare. It had been his custom for centuries to construct a fortified pa, usually a masterpiece of military engineering, and then invite the enemy to take it. When both sides were armed with the same weapons, battles in the open were just a matter of fighting until one side or the other gave in. During his conflict with the British, the Maori applied the same basic tactics.

Pa warfare should theoretically have suited the British admirably, for the arts of fortification and siegecraft were among the few military subjects taught at the Royal Military Academy, Woolwich and the Royal Military College, Sandhurst. The Royal Artillery could stand off out of musket range and knock down the works with impunity, since the Maori had no artillery with which to reply.

British commanders, however, persisted both in the 1840s and the 1860s to make suicidal frontal attacks on Maori fortifications, the strength of which they constantly underestimated. The ineptitude of British officers invariably allowed their enemies to escape 'out of the back door' via carefully prepared routes.

During the Taranaki wars, one or two discerning chiefs soon came to realise that it was a waste of time to build a pa only to have it demolished by gunfire to which their forces could not reply and which would inevitably lead to evacuation. They also learned, through bitter experience, that despite the unquestioned valour of their men, they were no match for regular British troops in set-piece battles in open country. Some leaders advocated guerrilla tactics, but it seems that few agreed with them. Like their British opponents, they insisted in persevering with the time-honoured methods of their race.

The Maori chief Hapurona, who commanded the garrison at Te Arei Pa in Taranaki, was the first leader to come under the fire of 12-pounder Armstrong field guns, the shells from which penetrated the Maori rua, or dug-outs, and burst inside, causing heavy casualties. After three days of this punishment, the defenders sued for peace.

Hapurona later stated that, if the war was renewed, his men would resort to ambushes and the shooting of unarmed persons to make up for the lack of artillery. He realised that he could achieve more by fighting from the bush, where man to man the Maori warrior was better suited to a guerrilla struggle than the British soldier.

In the late 1860s the war chiefs Titokowaru and Te Kooti widely followed a similar doctrine of guerrilla warfare and achieved some success, but by this stage time had run out for their cause. Had all Maori leaders acted on Hapurona's advice they could have inflicted many more casualties on the pakeha, at little cost to themselves, but the traditional codes of warfare prevailed, bringing about inevitable defeat.

The following descriptions of four fortified Pa, taken from contemporary accounts, illustrate the genius of Maori field engineers such as Kawiti, builder of Ruapekapeka.

This engraving purports to illustrate the assault on Rangiriri in 1863. There were, however, no stockades at that pa, the 21-foot-high parapet being the main defence. The picture gives a much better impression of attempts to storm pa held by Hone Heke and Kawiti in the 1840s. From *Picturesque Atlas of Australasia*

Ruapekapeka Pa, Bay of Islands district, 1846

Colonel Despard wrote the following account of this pa, attacked by British troops in the 1840s:

> The pa itself was an oblong square, with projecting works on each face, and at two of the angles, so as to form a flanking fire in every direction. . . . The first range of stockade was about 10 ft high, composed of either whole trees of the puriri wood, the hardest and toughest wood known in New Zealand, or of split timbers of the same wood, sunk in the ground from 2 ft to 3 ft deep, and placed close to each other. Many of the former were from 12 in to 15 in in diameter, and loopholed close to the ground. Within this stockade on two faces, at 3 ft distance, was another stockade, equally strong, also loopholed close to the ground, corresponding with those in front; and within that again there was a ditch 5 ft deep, and the same breadth, with an embankment of earth on the inner side, behind which a man could lie and fire through the loopholes of both fences. On the other faces the ditch was between the two stockade fences. The ditch was divided, at every 5 ft or 6 ft by traverses, leaving a small opening passage, not opposite each other, but alternate on either side. The ground in the interior was excavated in many places to afford shelter to the garrison from cannon shot. Some of these excavations were entered from the ditch, and others were thatched over to keep out the wet.

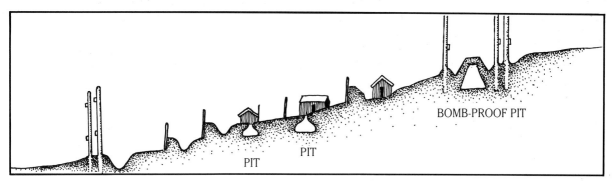

Cross section of Ruapekapeka Pa, Bay of Islands, 11 January 1846. Plan by John Topham based on a Royal Navy Officer's survey in 1846.

Dr Thomson's description of the same pa is as follows:

> Ruapekapeka pa measured 170 yds by 70 yds, and was much broken into flanks. It had two rows of palisades 3 ft apart, composed of timbers 12 in to 20 in in diameter, and 15 ft out of the ground; there was a ditch between the palisades, and the earth was thrown behind to form an inner parapet. In principle it resembled Ohaewai, but was much stronger. Within the pa the enemy numbered 500. . . . English engineers said a breach should have been made in the palisades of Ruapekapeka by exploding gunpowder close to them, as was done in bursting the gate at Ghuznee, but Ghuznee gate was one piece of workmanship, the Ruapekapeka were three independent works. From an inspection of Ruapekapeka, the troops saw that an assault would have been attended with severe loss, and it was universally admitted that the natives were becoming masters in the science of fortification. . . . In an English fort the ditch is deep, and outside the defences; in a New Zealand pa the ditch is shallow, and inside the palisade. In an English fort the ditch is made to obstruct the enemy; in a New Zealand pa the ditch is made to cover the defenders, who stand in it to fire at the besiegers.

The British troops opened fire on the above pa with three 32-pounders, one 18-pounder, two 12-pounders and seven brass guns and rocket tubes. At the end of 10 days the troops took this pa by assault — after the enemy had obligingly vacated it.

Manutahi Pa, Taranaki, 1861.

The remarkable skill displayed by the Maori in the construction of stockaded entrenchments is particularly well illustrated in a description given by an early Taranaki settler, George Robinson, to the historian James Cowan.

The front palisading reached across from bush to bush, perhaps 100 to 120 feet in length, the ends being carried well into the bush and blocked and screened with branches and native briar (*tataramoa*). The supports of the front palisade (as also the others) were of tree-boles about 12 inches in diameter, sunk deeply and firmly into the ground about 10 feet apart and projecting above the ground to a height of 12 to 14 feet. To these were lashed horizontally, with supplejack and rata-vine, at heights of about 3 feet 6 inches and 10 feet from the ground, heavy split rails (the Maoris before the war possessed axes, saws, wedges, spades, etc), and to these, vertically and fairly close together, were lashed other split rails, the tops about the height of the posts, and the butts reaching to about 1 foot above the ground. Behind this palisading was a trench 8 feet deep by 10 feet wide at the top and 6 feet wide at the bottom; behind this again was a second palisade similar in design and strength to the front one. Behind this, firing galleries or passages had been dug parallel with the front. The galleries were about 5 feet deep by 3 feet wide — not dug in one straight line, but with blocks or traverses about every 20 feet to provide against the effect of a bursting shell. These galleries were roofed over with logs on which were placed saplings and fern, well trampled down. The whole was covered with the earth from the trenches and galleries; this covering was from 3 to 4 feet deep. The front galleries or firing-trenches extended the full length of the pa. Loopholes were left under the log covering (about on a level with the outer front) through which the Maoris could fire on the advancing foe without themselves being seen or being in danger. From the firing-galleries passages went back to a central passage in the pa (covered in the same manner as the others), which in turn led by a covered way to the gully and stream in the bush, by which passage the Maoris could escape in case of defeat, or could be reinforced during the fighting. The sides and rear of the pa had single palisading only, inside the trench, as the Maoris did not expect any assault on those sides. In front of the pa for a distance of about 300 yards all fern had been broken down or removed; so for that distance no cover was afforded the advancing enemy and the defenders could see them and fire at them from the loopholes. The twelve months' war experience had taught the Maoris two things: (1) that the military always made frontal attacks; (2) that no soldier would willingly enter the bush, or could make his way through it should he be taken there, being easily entangled amongst the dense scrub and the supplejacks and other vines. The heaviest field-gun used by the troops at that time was the 24 lb howitzer, throwing solid shot or shell. Either of these striking the vertical palisading would simply cut the piece struck, and, as it was tied in three places, the ends would swing back again, leaving the palisade apparently as before. Should a shot strike a post it might smash it down, but rarely did so. (At Puke-ta-kauere in 1860 I saw the artillery, at 300 yards and under, fire at the palisading for over an hour without doing any appreciable damage). Artillery fire usually commenced at about 80 yards from a pa, and was taken closer. Should a shot strike the palisading, the effect would be as I have described. Should the aim be low, and the ball strike the ground in front of the pa, it would ricochet over it. The chances were more than a hundred to one against a ball or shell entering a loophole through which the Maoris fired; they were screened by the two palisades, though the vertical rails, not coming within a foot of the ground, did not obstruct the Maoris' view of the enemy nor interfere with their firing. Assuming the outer palisade was broken down, the assaulting-party would have to face the trench and inner palisade, and were these overcome and the enemy got into the pa, they would see nothing but a bare earth surface. The Maoris could not be got at, but would escape by the covered way into the gully and bush, where they would not be followed. The only effective way of dealing with such forts was by the use of heavy Coehorn mortars, which threw a shell at a high angle, descending vertically after describing a parabolic curve. Up to the date of this pa, however, such guns were not available.

Cross section of Manutahi Pa, Taranaki, 1861. Plan by John Topham based on a sketch plan by G. F. Robinson, who was a Government road engineer in Taranaki.

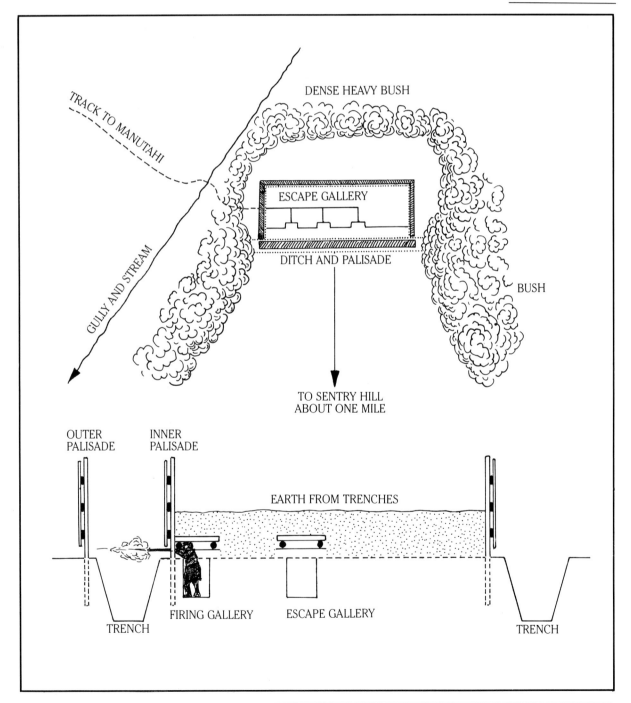

Rangiriri, 1863

The following notes on the Maori earthworks at Rangiriri were made by Major Charles Heaphy, V.C.

To stop the advance of General Cameron the natives chose a narrow strip of dry land lying between the Waikato River and a series of deep swamps and lagoons. The main road lay along this, going from left to right across the sketch. Across this road they built a bastion connected by a long curtain and ditch with the river and the swamp. The ditch, which was dry, was too wide to cross without planks, and the parapet too high (21 ft) to climb without ladders. No such appliances were with the attacking party. About 220 natives held the bastion and traverses about it. They were attacked by a portion of the 65th Regiment who got on to the parapet of the curtain, but were unable to take the bastion. A detail of the Royal Artillery men (36 men) with their carbines then assaulted it. They got close up to the bastion and their commanding officer was mortally wounded and lay close to the rear of the bastion, but they were obliged to retire.

About 90 men of the Naval Brigade then advanced. They got into the ditch, but all attempts to capture the bastion failed. A midshipman, the most advanced, was killed in a covered way that led from the ditch into the interior of the bastion. Though foiled, the sailors did not altogether retire; they scooped out holes and caves in the counterscarp and so sheltered themselves from the enfilading fire from the bastion, and thus remained in close proximity to it all night, occasionally throwing hand grenades amongst the natives.

During the night the assailants made a partial mine under the near face of the bastion, and at daylight on seeing a cask of powder being brought to blow them up, the natives hoisted a white flag and surrendered, 183 in number. Thirty-six natives had been killed.

Two nine-pounder Armstrong guns throwing shells at the bastion made no practical impression on it. A naval six-pounder and two gunboats also fired into it without effect.

The place is interesting as showing how natives can improvise earthworks that will successfully resist the sudden rush of disciplined troops unsupplied with ladders and planks, and without breaching artillery.

The Rangiriri pa, that withstood two assaults by British troops, is thus described by Maj Gen Alexander:

The enemy's works consisted of a line of high parapet and double ditch, extending between the Waikato river and Lake Waikare, the centre of this line being strengthened by a square redoubt of very formidable construction, its ditch being 12 ft wide, and the height from the bottom of the ditch to the top of the parapet 18 ft. The strength of this work was not known before the attack, as its profile could not be seen from the river or the ground in front. Behind the left centre of this main line, and at right angles to it, there was a strong interior line of rifle pits facing the river, and obstructing the advance of the troops from that direction. About 500 yards behind the front position was a high ridge, the summit of which was fortified by rifle pits.

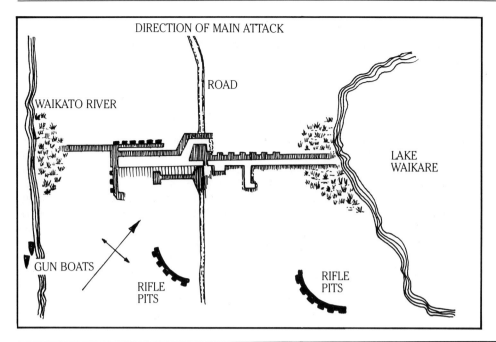

DIRECTION OF MAIN ATTACK

ROAD

WAIKATO RIVER

LAKE WAIKARE

GUN BOATS

RIFLE PITS

RIFLE PITS

Rangiriri Pa, Waikato, 20th November 1863. Plan by John Topham based on survey and drawings by Charles Heaphy.

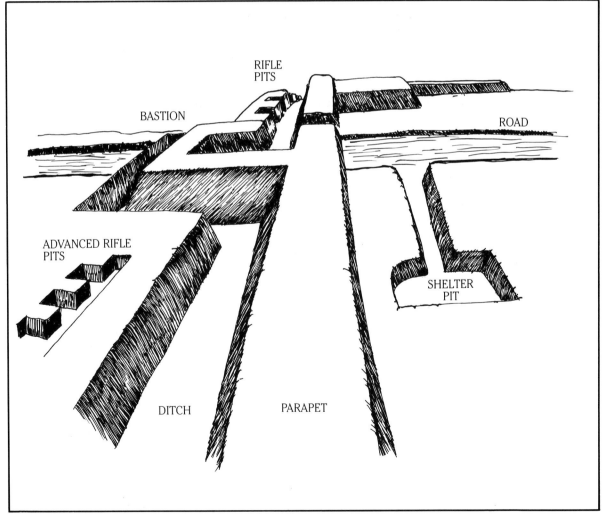

RIFLE PITS

BASTION

ROAD

ADVANCED RIFLE PITS

SHELTER PIT

DITCH

PARAPET

Tauranga-Ika Pa, 1869

Kimble Bent, a deserter from the British 57th Regiment, described the war chief Titokowaru's pa at Waitotara to James Cowan:

> It was of large size, fully defended with palisading, trenches, parapet and rifle pits. It was between two and three chains in extreme length at the rear, with a somewhat narrower front. . . . Two rows of palisades, high and strong, were erected around the position; the posts, solid tree trunks between the larger stockade posts were filled in with saplings set upright close together, and fastened by cross rails and supplejack ties; these saplings did not rest on the ground, but hung a few inches above it, so that between them and the ground a space was left for the fire of the defending musketeers, who were enabled to pour volleys from their trenches behind the war fence on any approaching enemy with perfect safety to themselves. Behind the inner stockading was a parapet about 6 ft high and 4 ft wide, formed of the earth thrown out of the trenches. The interior of the pa was pitted everywhere with trenches and covered ways, so that in the event of attack, the defenders could literally take to the earth like rabbits, and live underground secure from rifle fire, and even from artillery. The place was a network of trenches with connecting passages, roofed over with timber, raupo, reeds and earth. To any assault that could be delivered by the Government forces then available, the fort was practically impregnable.
>
> At one angle of the pa the Hauhau garrison erected a roughly timbered watchtower about 35 ft in height. . . . There were two gateways in the rear stockading, giving access to the bush.

Bent states that the item used as a gate or door to close the narrow entrance to a pa was a kind of hurdle consisting of two stout stakes on which was built a frame closely interlaced with supplejack vines. When not in use this stood up against the palisade close at hand, so that it could readily be placed in position and there lashed.

Professor James Belich contends, in his revisionist book *The New Zealand Wars* (1986), that the Maori invented modern trench warfare and therefore influenced the conduct of the First World War. This flawed theory ignores the fact that underground bunkers for protection against artillery fire, positions linked with communication trenches, and interlocking fields of fire had been present on a grand scale in European siege warfare since the 16th century. If one wishes to find a direct 19th century parallel with the horrors of the 1914-1918 war, one need go no further than the siege of Sebastopol. The prolonged trench warfare of the Crimean War was on a scale not seen until the horrors of the Western Front and mirrored all aspects of that conflict, including the mud of a winter campaign, suicidal frontal attacks against bunkers, and artillery positions. In contrast, the New Zealand Wars were a minor, colonial struggle that had all but been forgotten by that generation of Boer War Cavalry generals who directed the course of World War I.[1]

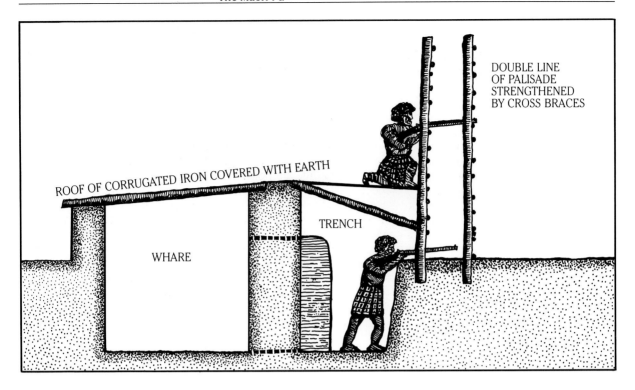

DOUBLE LINE
OF PALISADE
STRENGTHENED
BY CROSS BRACES

ROOF OF CORRUGATED IRON COVERED WITH EARTH

WHARE

TRENCH

Cross sections of
Taurangaika Pa, 1869. Plan
by John Topham after J.
Buchanan.

Cross section of palisade
and trench of Taurangaika
Pa, Waitotara, 3rd February
1869. Plan by John Topham
after J. Buchanan,
Government surveyor.

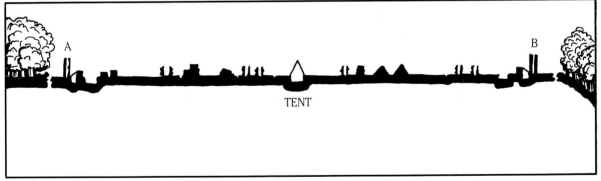

A

B

TENT

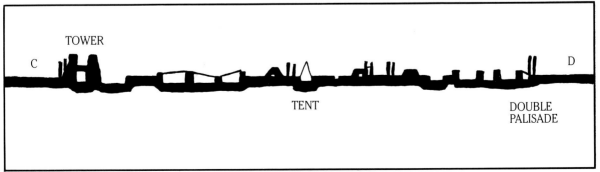

TOWER

C

D

TENT

DOUBLE
PALISADE

Plan of the Taurangaika
Pa, Waitotara

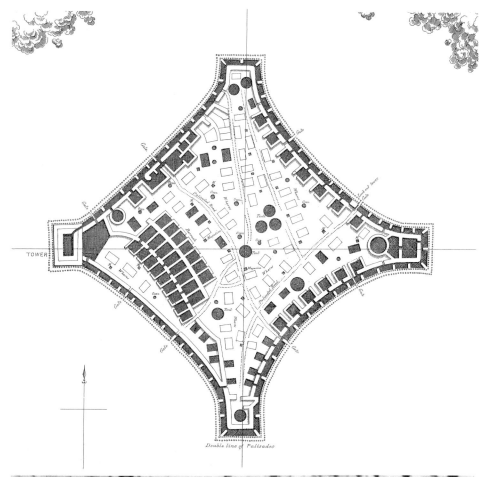

TOWER

Double line of Palisades

Wiremu Tamehana
(Tarapipi Te Waharoa),
1802–66, chief of the Ngati
Haua. Called the
Kingmaker, he was a
courageous diplomat who
worked tirelessly to
reconcile the two races.
He failed and died a
broken man. *Alexander
Turnbull Library*

CHAPTER 11

BATTLES AT THE BAY

Rewi had been the general of the Maori cause, gallant if unsuccessful against impossible odds. Wiremu Tamehana, the architect of the King movement, was a politician of a quality to fence with the subtle Grey himself. His part in the campaign had been to try to rally support for Tawhiao from other tribes which might be at risk.

The response was mixed. Unrest still growled in Taranaki, but probably the critical factor from Grey's point of view was the attitude of two powerful tribes which, had they thrown in their lot with the Waikato, could have made life a good deal more difficult for the Government.

The original malcontents, the Ngapuhi, had lived in peace for nearly two decades, and saw no reason to risk alienation of their lands by going to the aid of Waikato, who had been lukewarm in Hone Heke's day. Even more important were the Arawa, who lived in the country lying between Maketu and the Rotorua lakes. These people were to prove such remarkably steadfast Queenites as to earn the sobriquet 'Loyal Arawa', and their part in the later phase of the wars was about to begin.

The bulk of the defenders of Orakau were drawn from the Urewera and from the Ngati Raukawa of the eastern Waikato. Tamehana's appeal was also heeded by the people of the East Cape littoral who, in February 1864, assembled at Te Awa-o-te-Atua (Matata), centrally placed on the Bay of Plenty coastline. The Arawa territory of the Kaituna Valley barred the way to the

The war dance (peruperu) performed by the Ngaiterangi before the soldiers and settlers at Tauranga. Lieutenant H. G. Robley, the artist, sketches in the foreground.
Illustrated London News

beleaguered Rewi, and a request from the East Coast forces for permission to pass was at once declined.

The Civil Commissioners, Messrs T. H. Smith at Maketu and H. T. Clarke in Tauranga, urged the Government to send help, without which there was a serious risk that the Arawa might be overwhelmed and the way opened. Major Colville was sent to Maketu with 200 men of the 43rd Regiment who built a redoubt named in his honour.

In a skirmish at Ngauhu on Lake Rotoiti early in March, the Arawa drove back a probing force, which retired to Matata. On 21 April the eastern tribes reached the Waihi estuary lying east of Maketu. They achieved such complete surprise that Colville himself, who was duck shooting there with two of his men, was all but captured or killed.

Returning to Maketu, the major sent Captain Smith with a party to drive the invaders back across the ford. The warriors had already returned of their own volition to the eastern side, where they dug in on the sandhills. The next day passed with much long-range but ineffectual firing across the mouth of the lagoon, but that night the attackers again crossed to the west bank and took up a position from which to menace the Maketu garrison.

On 26 April Colville was reinforced by the arrival of H.M.S. *Falcon* and the colonial vessel *Sandfly*, the latter equipped with Armstrong guns. The combined fire from the fort and offlying ships drove the eastern tribes back once more across the estuary. Captain McDonnell and the Forest Rangers, with Te Pokiha and his warriors set out in pursuit, soon to be joined by 300 inland Arawa. The eastern tribes now made the fatal mistake of retreating along the

Below: Te Konapu, a warrior of the Arawa tribe of Maketu, Bay of Plenty. *Alexander Turnbull Library*

Below Right: Hamiora Tu, chief of the Ngaiterangi tribe of Tauranga. An oil painting by Gottfried Lindauer

beach, where they were completely exposed to shelling from the warships steaming close inshore.

The Arawa pursued their foes along the narrow corridor between the hills and the sea towards Matata, the running battle being known as Kaokaoroa. The insurgents sought the haven of their distant homes, leaving the recently arrived 43rd and 68th encamped on the site of modern Tauranga, where the names of the regiments, Monmouth and Durham, are still to be found.

The next act in this drama was more reminiscent of an invitation to some medieval jousting tourney in the days of chivalry than a grim struggle for land. The dominant people of what is today the smiling farmland surrounding Tauranga, then largely swamp, were the Ngaiterangi. Those who had fought for Waikato had now returned. Rawiri Puhirake proposed to Lieutenant-Colonel Greer a trial of arms, observing rules much on the lines of the Geneva Convention, and pointed out that a track had been formed leading to his pa for the colonel's convenience.

Greer's orders forbade him to accept the challenge, and having had no response the chief sent a further missive. If the suggested battlefield was too far away, he would build a new pa much nearer to suit the troops. So came into being a new position at the base of the peninsula on which the camp stood. The track leading inland was closed by a gate at the boundary between the mission and Maori lands, and this was to provide the name for an encounter almost as famous as Orakau — Gate Pa.

Having broken the resistance of the Waikato people, who turned their backs on Grey in the fastnesses of hill and gorge south of Mount Pirongia, Cameron went to Te Papa, as Tauranga was then known, to deal with the new defiance. He was taking no chances. By mid April he had mustered 1,700 men with unusually strong artillery support to confront a mere 300 Ngaiterangi. It was like using a sledgehammer to crack an egg.

Lieutenant (later Major-General) H. G. Robley's sketch of the defences at the Gate Pa, 30 April 1864. *Auckland Institute and Museum*

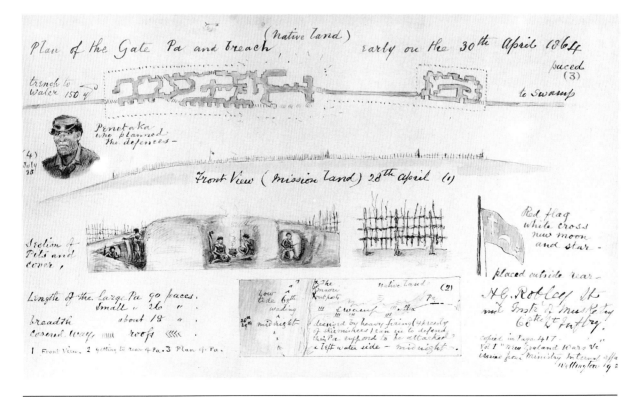

The Rev. A. N. Brown and his wife entertained nine officers to dinner on the evening of 28 April 1864, the meal being followed by communion. Twenty-four hours later all but one of the guests, Assistant-Surgeon William Manley, would be dead or mortally wounded. For the present, Greer used the night to lead the 68th in an encircling movement, so that by 3 a.m. they were in a position to block any retreat from the pa. In the event, this deployment cost Cameron dear.

Captain Hamilton, of H.M.S. *Esk*, killed at the Battle of Gate Pa on 29 April 1864. *Alexander Turnbull Library*

At 7 a.m. the artillery opened up a barrage which lasted well into the afternoon, but some of the 68th had to shift their ground because of overshooting. The pa was so small, about 70 yards by 30, that one of the rebels afterwards said that many of the British casualties were caused by their comrades' small arms fire passing right over the site to the attacking force on the other side. The system of trenches and dug-outs within the pa gave plenty of shelter, though part of the defences had to be abandoned because of enfilading by Armstrong 6-pounders.

By 4 p.m. the palisade had been breached for an attack by 300 men drawn equally from the 43rd and a naval brigade. Lieutenant-Colonel Booth and Commander Hay led the assault, which carried the breach, but as they thrust through the troops came under a heavy fire which decimated their officers. Hand-to-hand fighting developed, and Captain Jenkins of H.M.S. *Miranda* found himself in the melee armed only with his brass telescope. He laid about with it doughtily enough to escape from his predicament.

The Maori were driven back, and had the way been open would have left the field. However, finding their escape cut off by the 68th, they turned about. The frontal party, now largely leaderless, seemed to assume their enemy had been reinforced, so that they in their turn retreated pell mell. Lieutenant Garland of the 43rd, with seven of his men, tried to stop the rout, but it was hopeless.

The last soldier on the field was Manley, attending a badly wounded man. By the time he had finished his work he was surrounded, but being armed (as was usual at the time), he fought his way out. The assistant-surgeon's Victoria Cross was richly won, and he later achieved the unusual distinction of being decorated by both sides for his services in the Franco-Prussian War of 1870.

Above: Lieutenant H. G. Robley's depiction of hand-to-hand fighting in the attack on the Maori trenches at the Gate Pa. *National Museum. Left:* A scene in the pits at the Gate Pa early on 30 April 1864. This painting by Lieutenant H. G. Robley shows the interior of the earthworks about the centre of the position. The dead and wounded had not yet been taken away. *National Museum. Below Left:* The rear fence of the Gate Pa, showing clearly the slight nature of the Maori palisade. British dead lay beyond the rear of the pa, some soldiers or sailors having charged right through the position. A painting by Lieutenant H. G. Robley. *National Museum*

Cameron dug in nearby, and the troops endured a night of heavy rain. At dawn probing parties found the Maori had escaped in small detachments through the darkness, but not before tending Lieutenant-Colonel Booth and other wounded. Someone had brought them water in no man's land — a brave and humane act. The credit was claimed by a woman named Heni te Kirikaramu who, with her husband, later kept the 'Travellers' Rest' at Maketu, but there is a possibility that Henare Wiremu Taratoa, by then dead, was the real Samaritan of Gate Pa.

The Gate Pa garrison included one woman, Heni te Kirikaramu, who fetched water at great risk to herself and tended the mortally wounded Lieutenant-Colonel Booth of the 43rd Regiment. *Above Right:* Henare Taratoa, who drafted the humane order to protect unarmed or wounded men and respect the dead. He was killed at Te Ranga. *Hawke's Bay Art Gallery and Museum*

Casualties were heavy after the close encounter, and Cameron's losses totalled 120 killed and wounded. Bearing in mind his immense superiority in trained men and artillery, the defeat must rank high in the record of disasters to British arms over the centuries. Nor was the general personally able to expunge his humiliation, for after redoubts were thrown up at the Gate Pa and nearby Judea to cover Te Papa, his presence was again required in the south. He sailed south with most of his troops, leaving Greer once more in command.

The victors of Gate Pa could not rest upon their laurels. The weakened garrison offered a tempting target, and Rawiri set his tribe to work on new defences, cutting the track leading south at Te Ranga. This time Greer's instructions had been reversed. At all costs he was to prevent any repetition of the recent inglorious episode, and on 21 June the colonel started out to nip this latest affront in the bud.

His original force of 594 men from the 43rd and 68th Regiments was judged insufficient to cope with an enemy of about the same number holding a fortified position, and Greer sent for all those left at Te Papa. The advance party kept up a steady fire on the Ngaiterangi until the reinforcements arrived. The Regulars, joined by some of the 1st Waikato Regiment then advanced in a frontal attack. Two companies of the 43rd closed in on the right flank, and Major Shuttleworth committed the reserve.

This time the troops made no mistake, and the names of Captain F. A. Smith and Sergeant John Murray were added to the growing list of Victoria Cross winners. The Maori suffered even more grievously than the British had at the Gate Pa. Their own trenches were used for a mass burial of 107 dead, including both Puhirake and Taratoa. The Ngaiterangi had had enough, and in July surrendered to the Government. For a time at least peace returned to the Bay of Plenty.

Hori Ngatai, orator, at the surrender of the Ngaiterangi tribe to Colonel Greer at Te Papa, Tauranga, 25 July 1864. A painting by Lieutenant H. G. Robley. *National Museum*

Weapons and equipment:
Taranaki Militia officer's
sword; Adams revolver,
holster, cap and tunic;
Volunteer two-band and
three-band 1853 Enfield
rifles. *N. Ogle, T. Ryan*

NEW ZEALAND MILITIA, VOLUNTEERS AND SETTLER COMPANIES

New Zealand Militia

The Militia Act of 1845 first established a citizen force to defend the lives and property of settlers in New Zealand. This Militia was essentially a home force. Service was limited to within 25 miles of the local police office. The Act provided that all able-bodied men between the ages of 18 and 65 held themselves ready for service, and should train for 28 days annually.

During 1845–46 small detachments of Militia volunteered to serve as pioneers during the war in the north. The Wellington Militia was also involved in skirmishing in the Hutt Valley and at Porirua during the troubles of 1846.

The year 1855 saw the New Plymouth Militia gazetted because of the disturbances in that district. It became the Taranaki Militia in 1858 upon establishment of the province. This unit saw much service during the wars of the 1860s, notably at the Battle of Waireka, and earned the first battle honour won by a New Zealand formation.

Other Militia units raised included Napier (1859), Wairarapa (1860), Wanganui (1860) and Rangitikei (1864). The amending Act of 1858 provided for Militiamen to find substitutes at their own expense. As the threat of war receded, service became unpopular, and an increasing number of the able-bodied purchased substitutes for between £5 and £10.

Volunteer units

Volunteering gave immunity from Militia service, the opportunity to elect officers and a choice of uniform, assisted by a capitation allowance from the Government. The most famous volunteer unit was the Forest Rangers; others included the Taranaki Rifle Volunteers, Taranaki Bush Rangers and the Wanganui Rifle Volunteers. Men were usually enrolled for three months of active service, often at high rates of pay.

Military settler companies

The Government of New Zealand recruited bodies of Military Settlers, whose role was not only to take part in the fighting but also subsequently to settle in the frontier areas. This idea was first tried in 1847–48, when four settlements of British ex-regulars called 'Fencibles' (from the word defensible) were established near Auckland.

In 1863 more than 2,500 men were recruited in Australia and Otago to establish four regiments of Waikato Militia. It was intended that these men should be granted confiscated land after serving for three years and become settlers after the war. Most of these volunteers were single, but 1,000 wives and children were passengers in the 11 ships chartered by the Government.

These regiments took part in a number of actions during the Waikato war, notably Titi Hill-Mauku (1863), Orakau, Gate Pa and Te Ranga (1864). Many of the Militia elected to serve in the Imperial Commissariat Corps, working as clerks, storekeepers, pioneers, bullock drivers, butchers and boatmen.

Once active service in the field was over, farms were laid out as close as possible to the towns established around defensive stockades. Land was allotted according to the rank of the settler, the scale being:

Major	400 acres
Captain	300 acres
Subaltern/Surgeon	250 acres
Sergeant	80 acres
Corporal	60 acres
Private	50 acres

Similar units were established in Wanganui, Hawke's Bay and Taranaki, where 10 companies of Military Settlers recruited in Melbourne and Otago were assigned land. Many men never farmed their allotments, but either sold as soon as they were able or purchased substitutes.

By 1869 many of the Militia companies had been disbanded, and their role was taken over by the Armed Constabulary. The Waikato units were dissolved in 1867 and became part of the 4th Battalion Auckland Militia.

Below: Major T. J. Galloway, (left) who arrived in New Zealand in 1861 as Colonel of the 70th Regiment. He was appointed Commander of Militia and Volunteers in the Province of Auckland on 22 July 1863. He wears a dark blue frock coat according to infantry regulations of the time. On the right his staff officer, Major Tighe, is dressed in a dark blue patrol jacket of the infantry. *Painting by F. Turton*

Left: A corporal of the Wellington Veteran Corps, 1866, (left) wearing a red Garibaldi style jumper with black braiding, a dark blue peaked forage cap and navy blue trousers. On the right, a private of the Auckland Militia, 1845, in full marching order. He has a blue pork pie forage cap with red tourie, blue shirt and dark blue trousers. *Painting by F. Turton*

New Zealand Militia and Volunteer uniforms:
1. 1845 early Volunteer outfitted in grey or blue shirt and dark grey trousers supplied by the 58th Regiment.
2. 1858 Auckland Militiaman dressed in standard grey infantry greatcoat, with Balmoral bonnet.
3. 1863 Volunteer of 1st Waikato Regiment on the way to Drury. His uniform includes the blue jumper and standard British equipment, with the infantry knapsack and rolled greatcoat on top.
4. 1863 An NCO of the 1st *Waikato Regiment, dressed in a blue frock* coat, blue trousers with red welt at the seams, and pill-box forage cap of the standard pattern.
5. 1868 Auckland Militiaman in full marching order, with knapsack and rolled greatcoat. He wears a grey shirt, dark blue trousers and Balmoral bonnet. *Drawings by F. Turton*

Right: Te Ua Haumene, founder of the Pai Marire ('Good and Peaceful') religion, which set out as a method of coming to terms with European culture. A painting by C. F. Lindauer. *Auckland City Art Gallery*

Below: The 57th (West Middlesex) Regiment storms the Maori pa at Katikara, Taranaki. *Illustrated London News*

BIRTH OF THE HAUHAU

Trouble always seemed to start in Taranaki. Even while Orakau and Gate Pa had yet to be fought, the murder of a settler named Patterson all too close to New Plymouth signalled a fresh outbreak.

When Cameron returned to Auckland after his successful foray on the Katikara, he left Lieutenant-Colonel Warre to conduct a holding operation. The colonel had men of his own 57th, supplemented by Atkinson's Bush Rangers and 600 Taranaki Military Settlers. By March 1864 he was given permission to change from merely maintaining a presence with flying columns, which had been as much as he was allowed apart from static defence. The Maori were active at Kaitake, and Cameron was prepared to sanction a showdown there.

Although the preliminary reconnaissance cost the life of one soldier and five other casualties, Warre meant to leave as little as possible to chance when he mounted his assault on 24 March. Atkinson's men, together with Volunteers under Captain Corbett, were given time to make their way through heavy bush and rugged country to encircle the pa. Captain Martin of the Artillery set his gunners to work with such effect that not only was the palisade smashed but the whare were also set on fire.

The smoke masked the frontal attack made by three companies of the 57th, while another, with one from the 70th, joined the colonists in a general movement. The defenders quickly saw that their stand was hopeless and fled into the bush. However, it soon became obvious how little this smart victory had achieved.

Only two weeks later Captain T. W. J. Lloyd took a mixed party of the 57th and Volunteers to comb the area with the purpose of destroying crops which would sustain the rebels. Part of his force was resting at Te Ahuahu when a sudden onslaught of Maori from good cover resulted in the deaths of Lloyd and seven of his men. The incident, though minor in itself, took on a much greater significance as the first real demonstration of a new cult.

The association of Bishop Selwyn and the clergy with hostile military operations, plus the unending reverses, drove many Christian converts among the Maori to the conclusion that God fought only for the pakeha. The King movement had failed to save the lands of the Waikato, and nationalists cast round for a new force to stem the British advance.

Its prophet was Te Ua Haumene, who propounded a new religion he called Pai Marire. A mission-educated Maori, he had an encyclopaedic knowledge of the Bible. He now married biblical and old Maori religious beliefs and devised new rituals which centred on a tall pole called a niu. His followers would circle around it, their prayers and chants punctuated by shouts of 'Hau! Hau!' When these calls were first heard by British troops under attack they supposed the converts were imitating the bark of a dog. The name Pai Marire ('good and gentle') gave way to 'Hauhauism'.

Bishop George Augustus Selwyn. From *Defenders of New Zealand*

The ambush of Captain Lloyd and a small combined party of the 57th Regiment and Military Settlers at Te Ahuahu on 6 April 1864. A painting by Major Von Tempsky. *Auckland Institute and Museum*

Other elements of the religion changed too, for Te Ua was used by extremists for their own purposes, the nationalist aspects being seized upon to revive some warlike practices of pre-European times. The concept of utu — payment, or revenge — came back in full measure, along with the practice of decapitating foes, whose heads were then dried. This was the lot of Lloyd and his dead comrades. The captain's head, indeed, became a religious trophy. The Angel Gabriel was claimed to have instructed the victors to carry this symbol throughout the North Island, raising a multitude of followers who would irresistibly reclaim all the lost lands and utterly destroy the white race.

The Taranaki tribes could scarcely wait to carry the holy war to the enemy and chose a small redoubt north of New Plymouth known as Sentry Hill, manned by a detachment of the 57th under Captain Shortt. Led by Hepanaia, the Maori had been told that by holding up one hand and chanting a few words they would be immune to hostile bullets. The attackers simply marched forward, making no attempt to take advantage of cover. The soldiers could hardly credit the sight, but when the Hauhau were as close as Shortt wished, a concentrated fire was poured into them, killing possibly as many as 50. One of the wounded, Titokowaru, lost an eye; he was destined to play a leading role in the resistance over the next few years.

If the charm to ward off bullets had failed (although it was to be tried again in the future), perhaps the general uprising would fare better. Matene Rangitauira set out with Captain Lloyd's head for Pipiriki, in the upper reaches of the Wanganui River, where his people lived. The new faith, with its insistence on utu, struck a responsive chord among those who had lost relatives in the Taranaki fighting.

Matene and his new recruits set off downstream, bent upon fire and pillage at Wanganui, but the Ngati Hau and other tribes, through whose territory the taua would have to pass, would neither join them nor allow passage.

The situation could be resolved in only one way — by the ordeal of battle. By agreement this took place on the island of Moutoa, a traditional venue for such conflicts. On 14 May the Hauhau landed from their canoes to demonstrate to the unbelievers the overwhelming power of their creed. At first their inspired morale seemed as though it must carry the day. Some of the defenders, under Tamehana te Aewa, were driven like chaff before the wind to the northern tip of the island. There, by a herculean effort despite a painful wound, the chief rallied his men to stem the rout.

Their allies from the other end of Moutoa, led by Haimona Hiroti, took the Hauhau in the rear, and it was now the latter's turn to be cornered. Forced down the beach, they sought refuge in the water. Matene, swimming to the bank, was seized as he landed and clubbed to death. His followers returned whence they came, but the second fiasco did no more than the first to shake belief in the miracles of Pai Marire.

Tamehana te Aewa. From *Defenders of New Zealand*

A Hauhau war dance (peruperu). *Hawke's Bay Art Gallery and Museum*

A Pai Marire or Hauhau niu pole. The first niu pole was a mast taken from the wrecked steamer *Lord Worsley*, which ran aground near Cape Egmont in 1862. By 1865 a niu stood in nearly every large village from Taranaki to the Bay of Plenty, excepting the Arawa country.

Some poles were up to 70 or 80 feet high. They were rigged like a ship's mast, and often decorated with carvings. The top of the pole might carry the representation of a bird, rupe or dove, while carved knobs in the form of a beckoning hand might adorn the yards or cross-trees. The knobs were called Rura and Riki, the names of Te Ua's two gods.

Flags were hoisted on halliards running through blocks on the yardarms. It was thought that spirits descended these ropes to the people below. The Riki or war flag is shown at the left, a long red pennant with a white cross. Beneath it is a large handsome flag, black with a white cross at the inner margin and a blue fly, the whole surrounded by a narrow scarlet border. The third is another red pennant with a white St Andrews Cross.

These flags were described by Lieutenant H. Meade (who barely escaped with his life) on a pole he saw at Tataroa in 1865. The ensign shown on the right is white, with the word 'Aotearoa' and a cross in red. It is symbolically in ascendance over a Union Jack. *Drawing by N. Ogle*

WAR FLAGS OF THE MAORI

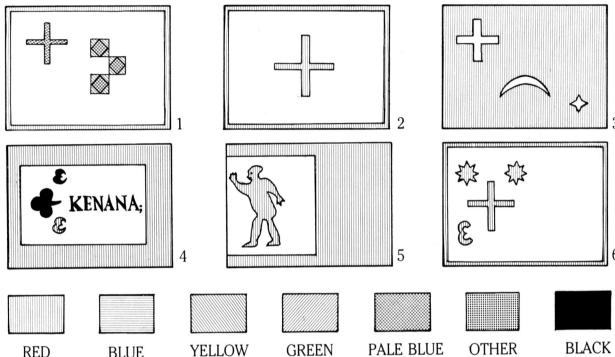

CHAPTER 14

RED   BLUE   YELLOW   GREEN   PALE BLUE   OTHER   BLACK

The Maori warrior greatly venerated his war flags. He recognised that the Union Jack symbolised British dominion. In rejecting the Treaty of Waitangi, from which that power was derived, the tribes banded together to form the King Movement, and sought a similar mana for their own monarch.

When Te Wherowhero accepted the kingship in 1857, he emphasised his position as the leader of his people by flying flags bearing the words Kingi (King) and Niu Tireni (New Zealand). The King's flag flew at his residence and preceded him on visits to other tribes which recognised his authority. When a king died the flag was buried with him, and a new one was made for his successor. This was strictly sacred (tapu) and kept by a special custodian.

Many Kingite flags were made especially for recruiting purposes. These were carried by parties visiting other areas of the country to enlist warriors or support for the cause.

The Pai Marire (Hauhau) Movement believed that the British flag possessed mana of itself, and was thus a particular manifestation of divine power. The prophet Te Ua also held that Europeans worshipped a terrible war deity, to whom the British Army did homage around the flagstaff every morning and evening. It is little wonder, therefore, that the Hauhau attached so much importance to their flags and niu pole ceremonies. The Hauhau usually flew three flags from such poles: Riki for war, Ruru for peace, and a personal standard of the prophet or priest who presided over the ceremony. The relative positions of Riki and Ruru indicated if the meeting was peaceful or warlike.

1. The King flag hoisted at Ngaruawahia for Tawhiao's accession in 1861. The blue and yellow devices represent the three main islands of New Zealand.
2. A Kingite recruiting flag carried by a party which visited Poverty Bay in 1864.
3. The war flag of the Ngaiterangi tribe flown at the Battle of Gate Pa in 1864. The star is believed to signify the Star of Bethlehem.
4. Te Ua's personal standard (10 feet by 3 feet 6 inches) bore the legend 'Kenana' (Canaan), showing that he identified the Maori with the Jews.
5. The standard of the Hauhau movement was the largest flag flown during the wars. It measured 23 by 12 feet, and bore a life-size figure of Te Matairenga, a god of war, challenging the enemy to fight.
6. Patara, one of the five disciples of the Pai Marire movement, possessed the flag Rura or pacifier, which represented the Angel Michael. *Drawings by Malcolm Thomas*

7. The flag presented to the friendly Wanganui tribe after their victory over the Hauhau at Moutoa Island in 1864.

8. A Hauhau flag hoisted at Papatapu, on the Waitotara River, in 1868.

9. The flag of Titokowaru, the Ngati Ruahine guerrilla leader, in his campaign against Whitmore.

10. The personal flag of Kereopa, one of Te Ua's five apostles, and executioner of the Rev. Volkner.

11. The Maori leader Te Kooti had a number of flags, the most famous of which was Te Wepu (The Whip). The huge bright-red silken pennant, 52 feet long, was originally made by Catholic nuns for a friendly tribe. It was captured by Te Kooti in 1868, and fell into the hands of Captain G. Mair after he defeated the guerrilla leader in 1870. It was embroidered with the devices of a crescent moon, a cross, Taranaki mountain (Egmont), a bleeding heart symbolising the sufferings of the Maori people and their determination to die for their land, and the Star of Bethlehem. *Drawings by Malcolm Thomas*

7

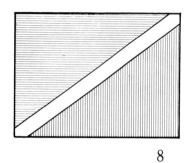

8

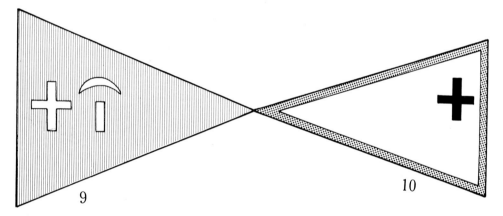

9

10

11

THE LAME SEAGULL'S MARCH

Nrew Plymouth and Wanganui had been selected as sites for settlements by the New Zealand Company a quarter of a century earlier, yet after all that time nobody could feel absolutely secure in either place, and still less on the farmlands for which the towns existed. The emergence of the Hauhau intensified the danger to the whole coastal strip between the two towns, to which settlement was virtually confined.

General Cameron called at New Plymouth en route to Wanganui, to talk over plans with Warre. He was ordered to enforce security between the two ports, and so make confiscation a practical proposition. The Waikato campaign, starting by protecting settlers in South Auckland, had ended with land-grabbing on a large scale. The rising in the Bay of Plenty opened the way to further retaliation of the same kind, and now the process was to move south.

The general had for too long seen his men killed so that the Government could dispossess the Maori people of their birthright. He looked upon the whole affair as iniquitous, and laid the blame at the door of the devious Grey. Relations between the two became chillier with each passing month, and for his part Cameron embarked on a go-slow policy.

In January 1865 a force drawn from the 18th, 50th and 57th Regiments left Wanganui and marched west as far as Nukumaru. The Ngati Ruanui denied the right of the Government to the Waitotara block, and had drawn the support of other dissidents from as far away as Taranaki and Waikato. Nukumaru stood on the disputed land, and the general incautiously pitched his camp near the bush.

The counter attack at Nukumaru by mounted men of the Military Train, or transport corps. A painting by Major Von Tempsky. *Auckland Institute and Museum*

A party from the 18th, under Captain Shaw, were soon in action as they approached the forest and fell back to take cover in a ditch. Seeing that one of his men lay wounded, Shaw and three volunteers went to the rescue of their comrade, earning the captain the Victoria Cross. The shooting alerted reinforcements, who drove off the ambush.

On the following afternoon, outposts manned by the 18th and 50th led by Captain Noblett came under a heavier attack by the Hauhau, the troops being driven back by weight of numbers. During the next couple of hours the Maori skirmished on the very edge of the camp itself, with significant casualties on both sides until, like their friends the day before, the attackers retired to Weraroa Pa.

Grey was concerned that, unlike earlier engagements, the Maori had gone over to the offensive both at Sentry Hill and Nukumaru. He wanted the bolt-hole at Weraroa closed to the Hauhau but Cameron did not relish the task, for as Lieutenant-Colonel Gamble wrote:

> The pa is on a commanding ground within the bush. It is protected on either side by a deep wooded ravine, and in its rear by a steep precipice, which at that point forms the left bank of the Waitotara River. On its left bank the bush is interminable, and the country so broken as to forbid the possibility of military operations in that direction. Under any circumstances the capture of this position by a European force would involve heavy loss of life.[1]

Like so many military commanders, the general claimed that his force was too small for the work it was asked to perform, in this case to take Weraroa and open up the coastal lands.

The political scene had taken on a new aspect. Tired of what he saw as British obstruction, the new Premier, the Hon. F. A. Weld, advocated the departure of the British Army Regulars and the adoption of self-reliance by the colonists. Von Tempsky had preferred to remain on service rather than settle on his land, and took a company of Forest Rangers and Militia, who held similar views, to Wanganui. This unit engaged the Maori near Kakaramea on 13 May, and Weld made much of the colonials hunting the enemy in the bush while Cameron crawled along the coast at such a snail's pace that the Maori dubbed him 'The Lame Seagull'.

Von Tempsky and his friend McDonnell heard that the Hauhau holding Weraroa were not united in their resistance, and the latter's kupapa (Maori troops fighting on the colonists' side) learned that the defenders were willing to negotiate a surrender. The two believed that if they asked Cameron's permission to follow up this lead, he might very well refuse, so they bypassed him with a direct approach to the Premier. The idea fitted into his new policy, and Weld gave his approval.

When it came to carrying out the scheme, they soon ran into trouble. Lieutenant-Colonel Logan grudgingly allowed the white men to go, but refused permission for the Wanganui native contingent and stopped their food supply.

Despite these handicaps, McDonnell persevered, and one night came to an arrangement that a surrender would be made to him the following morning. Logan then turned up, and on his appearance the Hauhau became suspicious and called the whole thing off. The native contingent wanted to attack, but the colonel again refused to allow them to act. Von Tempsky was so disgusted that he wrote to Weld resigning his command.

James Herwood Rocke, 18th
Royal Irish Regiment, who
was promoted brevet
Lieutenant Colonel for his
part in the action at
Nukumaru in 1865. Later
Rocke commanded the
Regular and Colonial
Troops in New Plymouth. In
the first edition of this book
this photograph was
incorrectly identified as
Captain Hugh Shaw VC.
Alexander Turnbull Library

Maori prisoners held in the
Rutland Stockade,
Wanganui. The men
wearing grey fatigue
uniforms and caps are the
regimental cooks.
Wanganui Museum

Cameron did not lose the chance to protest to Grey:

Lieutenant-Colonel Logan . . . was perfectly right . . . in ordering back from the pa
the officers and men of the Native Contingent, who, having disregard of the
authority of the Brigadier-General, opened negotiations with the enemy, were next
in defiance of all discipline and order, proposing to undertake a military service
without his knowledge or sanction . . .

I deplore that your Excellency should support with your authority the proceedings of the Colonial Minister in directly authorising subordinate officers of the
Colonial Forces to deal with the enemy, in utter disregard of their duty to the service, and the common respect due to the Brigadier-General in command.[2]

This was a far call from two years before when, after Paparata, the general
had praised the two for possessing 'that cool, deliberate kind of courage
which is so much more rare than the bravery displayed in the heat and excite-
ment of an action'.[3] They had acted with the same elan, but this time their
conduct won them nothing but censure.

In a technical, if narrow, military sense, Cameron was in the right. The two
officers had embarked on a venture sanctioned by a Minister who, however
eminent he might be, had no authority to interfere with the conduct of actual
operations. While Logan most probably sent word to Brigadier-General
Waddy, the latter had certainly not given his consent. If insubordination of
this kind became widespread, chaos must result.

But it could not be denied that McDonnell had been on the verge of
securing the surrender of a position which the general had claimed to be
beyond his powers. There was a furious reaction in Government circles. The
attorney-general wanted Cameron to be court-martialled for 'incapacity and
deliberate neglect of his instructions'. Weld went further, holding that the

colony's Parliament was powerless in the grip of a military dictatorship, and he resigned.

In their correspondence, Cameron and Grey had gone from the cordiality of 'My dear Sir George', and 'My dear General', to the stiffly formal 'Sir', as they traded accusations. Cameron decided that he had had enough, and wrote to London tendering his resignation on grounds of ill-health. The Premier then agreed to resume office.

During the months of waiting before Cameron could receive instructions from Whitehall, the campaign limped on its way. For the time being Nukumaru was left in the charge of Lieutenant-Colonel Weare and a detachment of the 70th Regiment, the threat of Weraroa being ignored — if, indeed, it existed. Waddy established a redoubt at the Waitotara, and then advanced to the Patea River, where he paused to bring up all his available forces.

On 13 March the 50th, 57th and 68th Regiments, together with a few Volunteers, marched upriver, but after a short time came under fire from Hauhau holding a position on the right flank. The Hauhau, numbering only about 200, stood no chance at all against impossible odds. To compound this their retreat, at a walking pace to show their contempt for the soldiers, resulted in very heavy casualties.

The column passed through Kakaramea and Manutahi, looting for food en route, and paused at Manawapou and the mouth of the Waingongoro River in the hope that these places might be used to land stores from the sea. With no port, or even a jetty, supplies had to be brought in by surf boats, never an easy task on this exposed coast.

Cameron made Patea his winter base, and the only activity took the form of a march by Weare from the south to link up with Lieutenant-Colonel Warre coming from the north for a formal meeting. The whole exercise over the past months had really only been symbolic, for there was no question of Maori resistance having been crushed, as Grey professed to think.

Officers and N.C.O.s of the 50th Regiment at Wanganui, 1865. Their Maori guide is at the right of the photograph.
Wanganui Museum

On 26 May Cameron wrote to Grey:

> I can see no reason to expect that the natives will ever make a formal submission, and I think that all we can hope for is that the punishment we have inflicted on some of the rebel tribes will induce the others to remain quiet for the future.

Given that another five years would pass before the last shots were fired, this view, although nearer the mark than Grey's, was still too optimistic.

The general had retired to Auckland while waiting to leave the country, and the governor set out on a bold move by tackling the Weraroa problem in person. Grey took command of an entirely colonial force consisting of Forest Rangers, the Wanganui Yeomanry Cavalry and McDonnell's native contingent. The only assistance he sought from Waddy, then at Nukumaru, was for the deployment of two companies from the 14th and 18th before the pa.

A trooper of the Wanganui
Yeomanry Cavalry, 1865.
Alexander Turnbull Library

Maori prisoners taken at Weraroa were confined aboard a prison hulk in Wellington Harbour. With their old chief Tataraimaka, most of them escaped by swimming ashore one stormy night, but a number were drowned in the attempt. *Alexander Turnbull Library*

Grey did not accept Gamble's opinion that the country, admittedly difficult, ruled out encirclement; nor did he think that there would necessarily be heavy loss of life. After a further parley with the Hauhau failed, Major Rookes led a force through the bush. On 21 July he took the Maori by surprise in an early-morning raid on Areiahi, collecting a number of prisoners. The way was now open to take up a position commanding Weraroa Pa, and the colonists started firing at long range. The defenders showed no fight at all, but made off as fast as they could scramble down the precipice. The Government force suffered not a single casualty.

Not surprisingly, Grey was triumphant, and told Parliament that the British had stood idly by and refused to help him. Waddy replied that his troops had been given orders to attack at the same time as the local units, but there had been no need to do so in the absence of resistance. Cameron, of course, had been made to look foolish, and complained of the governor's conduct to the War Office. In the fullness of time Sir George was reprimanded — one step in a new confrontation which resulted in his exchanging the role of governor eventually for that of Premier.

The homegrown forces were steadily bringing reality to Weld's dream of self-reliance. Both he and the British Government wanted the regiments to be withdrawn from New Zealand as soon as this could safely be done. The Taranaki Military Settlers and Patea Rangers, with Maori from the Lower Wanganui, carried the fight to the higher reaches of the river in the wake of the Hauhau who had so signally failed at Moutoa, and fortified a strategic site at Pipiriki. Harry Atkinson, now Minister of Defence, went on the expedition.

Major Willoughby Brassey commanded the new post, and after three redoubts had been built close to the river, the Maori returned home to help Grey take Weraroa. Their leader, Kepa te Rangihiwinui, later often known as Major Kemp, would emerge as an outstanding leader in the days to come.

Below: Topia Turoa, war chief of the Upper Wanganui. He fought against the troops at Pipiriki, but after opposing the Government until 1869 he changed sides and led a party of his tribe against Te Kooti in 1870. *Alexander Turnbull Library*

Below Right: Kepa te Rangihiwinui. *Alexander Turnbull Library*

General Sir Duncan Alexander Cameron, 1808–88. From *Picturesque Atlas of Australasia*

The Hauhau of the Upper Wanganui and their northern allies reacted to the new thrust on 19 July, when Captain Newland described the attack as the finest sight he ever saw. About 1,000 men marched with wooden trumpets four or five feet long, on which they played bugle calls learned from the British. The tattooed warriors wore their hair frizzed out, quite unlike the normal Maori style. Although inspired by Pai Marire teaching, they failed to shake the Taranaki men and settled down on the surrounding heights to lay a siege, so turning the tables on what was usually a pakeha preserve.

Brassey was in an awkward situation, many miles from help and without the supplies of food or ammunition needed to resist such an investment for very long. The prospect of leaving the redoubts to try to fight a superior force in hilltop positions was not inviting, and he resorted to the desperate expedient of writing urgent appeals in Latin, which were sent on their way down the river in empty bottles.

As the days passed, the major could not know whether his messages had been found and understood, as in fact they had. The position was too uncertain for Brassey's peace of mind, and two volunteers, Sergeant Constable and Private Edgecombe, managed to get away by canoe to summon help. Their relief may be imagined when at Hiruharama they met many of the victors from Weraroa under Major Rookes coming upstream on a rescue mission. The appearance of these reinforcements lifted the siege, the Hauhau dispersing in the impenetrable country to the north.

Taranaki too was having its share of fighting. On 12 June Warre led a punitive force of the 43rd and 70th, with Bush Rangers, from Opunake to burn the villages of troublemakers in the Warea district. The Hauhau had their revenge the following month, ambushing a patrol from the Warea Redoubt.

This called for a further riposte from Colville, late of Maketu, who led over 200 men south from New Plymouth on 2 August. He posted Major Russell with men of the 70th to make a frontal approach to Okea while he went on a flanking attack. The move was poorly co-ordinated, so that Russell's weak force was heavily engaged before Colville could come to his assistance, and more casualties were suffered than might otherwise have occurred. Colville himself was ambushed and badly wounded a few months later.

On 25 August Sir Duncan Cameron sailed from Auckland for Australia and England. Local opinion of his merits varied from his being described by one clergyman as 'an old woman in uniform', to his being presented with a jewelled sword by admirers. The War Office showed its confidence in his abilities by placing him in charge of the Royal Military College, Sandhurst, where it is to be hoped Cameron could steer future officers clear of at least some of the mistakes he had experienced in the Crimea and New Zealand.

Professor Belich has said that "General Cameron was a good tactician, a very good strategist and a superb organiser, he was the best European Commander to serve in New Zealand and amongst the best Victorian Generals".[4] In fact, the General was gifted with none of these qualities. Professor Belich tries hard to justify Cameron's professionalism in order to enhance his theories regarding Maori resistance. In fact, during the Waikato, Tauranga and South Taranaki campaigns the General fell far short of the qualities needed for a capable commander, and he was clearly out of his depth in a series of military blunders which would have led to his dismissal had he faced a European army. His catalogue of errors began when the War Office censured him for putting his life in jeopardy at Koheroa. His superiors contended that a commanding general had no business in risking his life by personally leading troops into battle. At the assault on Rangiriri Pa he threw away the lives of his only specialist artillery troops, including their commander, in an unprecedented suicidal, frontal attack. The prudent commander would have drawn back his forces and used the very men he sacrificed to shell (using mortars) the Maori out of the central redoubt, a position with no overhead cover and one which was commanded by the Royal Artillery position on the hill above.

Cameron's "greatest military achievement", the outflanking of Paterangi Pa, was not some brilliant strategy, but a course forced upon him by the breakdown of his own "much vaunted" supply system. At depots all along the line of advance, 50 per cent of the supplies were being spoiled by lack of protection from the rain.[5] A corporal of the 40th Regiment besieging Paterangi Pa stated that the men of his regiment were starving because of the lack of supplies. They subsisted for days on a handful of mouldy biscuits.[6] Cameron's need to replenish his supplies in the breadbasket of the Waikato forced him to strike at the Kingites' supply centre of Rangiaowhia.

Backed by an overwhelming force, the General failed to contain and destroy the garrison of Orakau, allowing a considerable number of the enemy to escape. Again at Gate Pa, General Cameron suffered a serious reverse in a badly handled frontal attack. The South Taranaki Campaign of 1865 saw Cameron establishing a camp at Nukumaru in a position that allowed the enemy to overwhelm his picquets and directly threaten his encampment. One must feel sorry for the General, as he became increasingly disenchanted with a war that he came to believe was being driven by settler greed for land. General Cameron had a reputation for having a cold and curt manner together with a stoic nature. This facade was seen to crumble after the disastrous rout at Gate Pa, when he was seen to dash his field-glasses, turn his back on the British fugitives and retire to his tent to conceal his emotion. Cameron's relationship with Governor Grey continued to deteriorate. Long before the General's refusal of the Governor's request to attack Weraroa Pa, Cameron had tendered his resignation. The Pa was taken by colonial troops, and soon after the Governor saw to it that this time Cameron's resignation was accepted.

Right: Kereopa te Rau (also called Tu-hawhe), of the Arawa tribe, had fought in the latter part of the Waikato War. He became one of the five special disciples of Te Ua's priesthood, and his mission was to carry the faith to the eastern coastal tribes. He was captured by Major Ropata, and excuted on 5 January 1872. *Alexander Turnbull Library*

Left: The Rev. Carl Sylvius Volkner, 1819-65, of the Church Missionary Society, was appointed to St Stephen's Church, Opotiki, in 1861. Accused of being a spy, he was killed by Kereopa. *Alexander Turnbull Library*

FIGHTING IN THE EAST

The seed of Pai Marire was sown in the west, but the first shoots of the new plant had been sharply clipped at Sentry Hill and Moutoa. While its prophet, Te Ua, stayed at home, two of his disciples set out on a mission to the east in 1865. Their activities would soon set the Government a pretty problem in trying to cope with concerted risings on opposite coasts of the North Island.

The travellers were Kereopa te Rau and Patara Ruakatauri, the former being by far the more aggressive of the two. They were accompanied by a deserter from the 57th Regiment, John Brown, who served as custodian of the dried head of the unfortunate Captain Lloyd.

They could be sure of a welcome among the Tuhoe people in their mountains and forests, and went there to spread the new gospel. This area, the Urewera, was sea-girt on three sides, giving the priceless advantage of interior lines to meet any force brought against its inhabitants — a fact which would plague both pakeha and Maori formations in the years to come.

For the present, Kereopa sought another pakeha head, first unsuccessfully at Whakatane before moving on to Opotiki. The incumbent missionary at this centre of the Whakatohea tribe was the Rev. Carl Sylvius Volkner, a German, who had recently had a church built. He happened to be away when the Hauhau arrived, but on 1 March returned in Captain Levy's ship *Eclipse*. Volkner was accompanied by the Rev. Thomas Grace, who had been driven from his mission among the Tuwharetoa people of Taupo.

The involvement of the church in political matters from the earliest days was about to incur its most serious retribution to date. The clergy had conceived it to be part of their duty to pass intelligence to the authorities of any disaffection in the places where they preached their spiritual message. Volkner, as one of these, was considered a spy. When he took his wife Emma to stay in safety at Auckland, he was warned not to return. Disregarding this advice, he had come back. In the meantime Kereopa had carried the day with the Whakatohea, no difficult matter after the worsting of the East Coast tribes at Orakau, Maketu and Kaokaoroa.

The two clerics spent the night as prisoners at Volkner's home, Peria, and next morning the German was not kept long in suspense as to his fate. He was led into his own church where Kereopa condemned him to death. The victim was taken at once to a nearby willow tree, where an inexpert attempt was made to hang him, his sufferings being ended with a shot.

In a final act of barbarism, the dead man's head was cut off, dried in the smoke of a fire, and carried into the church. Kereopa removed the eyes, placing these in the chalice, and then swallowed both, so that he was afterwards known as 'The Eye-eater'. Others were encouraged to drink Volkner's blood, and to pillage, so that they would be involved in the affair. Recently efforts have been made to deny Kereopa's deeds, but these attempts ignore the sworn evidence of Maori eye-witnesses belonging to the tribes who took part.

The death of the Rev. C. S.
Volkner at the hands of
Kereopa and his followers,
2 March 1865. *Illustrated
London News*

Grace too might have suffered but for the return of Patara from the East
Coast. Captain Levy claimed to have helped, but Grace complained bitterly
about the treatment he received from this man. Government forces had captured an important Ngaiterangi chief, Hori Tupaea, on his way from Tauranga
to Opotiki. He and Grace were held by the respective sides with a view to
effecting an exchange, as Tupaea had decided to embrace Pai Marire.

The Governor was outraged by these events, though he must obviously have
realised the risks the clergy ran when acting as his intelligence service. Grey
asked Captain Luce, R.N., to send a warship to Opotiki to arrest Kereopa and
anyone else implicated in the crime, as he saw it. On 14 May H.M.S. *Eclipse*
(Captain E. R. Fremantle) left Auckland for the Bay of Plenty. James Francis
Fulloon, a young half-caste interpreter, and a Maori in the Government service
named Tiwai were on board, the latter having been at Opotiki when Volkner
died.

Fulloon, the son of a well-born Maori woman who had married a European
trader, was a favourite nephew of Hopa Apanui, the senior chief at Whakatane. *Eclipse* made Whakatane its first port of call so that Fulloon could find
out as much as possible about the state of affairs from his relatives, one of
whom — his cousin Te Wepiha — had been an eye-witness of Volkner's
murder. He was taken aboard and the vessel carried on to Opotiki.

So far so good, but then things began to go wrong. On arrival Fremantle led
a landing party, but the boats met a hostile reception and the captain had to
retire to his ship empty-handed. He went on to Omaia, where Tiwai asked for
two of the best men to help him capture one of the murderers named Ephraim.
Instead he was given two boys. They assumed Maori disguise, but once again
the attempt ended in a fiasco. McDonnell later commented that this ill-starred
expedition caused only amusement among those it was supposed to bring to
book.

Patara Raukatauri, chief of the Taranaki people, who had been the principal leader in the fighting against the British at Kaitake. He was also one of Te Ua's five special disciples, and accompanied Kereopa to the East Coast. *Alexander Turnbull Library*

The seizure of the schooner *Eclipse* at Opotiki, 1 March 1865. *Illustrated London News*

Te Wepiha was a strong Kingite and playing a double game. After being outwardly friendly to Fulloon, he now looted the Whakatane home and store of a trader, Abraham Bennett White. News of his action reminded the public in Auckland that he had visited the *Eclipse* at Whakatane, and later events suggested that he had alerted the defence at Opotiki to be ready for Fremantle.

Fulloon was much annoyed by these insinuations. Confident of his influence with the Ngati Awa tribe, he determined to return to Whakatane to rally the people to the Government cause. He left Auckland on 13 July in the S.S. *Rangitira* for Tauranga, where Bennett White was weather-bound on his way to Whakatane in the cutter *Kate*. The latter agreed to take Fulloon with him, though both were warned by Thomas H. Smith, the Civil Commissioner at Maketu, that they were embarking on a dangerous mission.

In fact Fulloon was already too late to do any good. Another Pai Marire advocate, Horomita Horomona, had come from Taranaki and already won over the people of Whakatane by the time the *Kate* drifted in light airs off the river port on 20 July. The travellers were encouraged to think themselves welcome, but soon Fulloon and all but three of those on board were shot dead. White survived only because of the repeated misfire of a gun intended to kill him, and he later escaped back to Auckland.

Kereopa and Patara had gone further east to the area lying north of what is now Gisborne. Here the dominant tribe was the Ngati Porou, and initially the new doctrine made headway. It was, however, resolutely opposed by Ropata Wahawaha, then unknown but, like Kepa te Rangihiwinui at Wanganui, a natural leader of great courage, soon destined to win fame. He checked the Hauhau at Pukemaire, and they turned inland.

Joined by Horomona and some Tuhoe, Kereopa made for the Waikato. Rewi Maniapoto and Tawhiao, nursing bitter memories of defeat and land confiscation, were likely to lend a ready ear to his harangues. The Hauhau followed an inland route to keep clear of stronger tribes along the Bay of Plenty coast, but they ran foul of Ngati Manawa. These people had been driven by powerful foes off richer lands to the edge of the Taupo desert, but they now proved that although numbers might be lacking courage was not. The right to allow or deny passage across tribal territory was jealously guarded, as Matene had found at the cost of his life in the Moutoa incident. The Ngati Manawa effectively barred the way to the travellers until pushed back by sheer superior force, fortunately into the arms of friendly Arawa led by William Mair (by now a major) of Orakau fame.

Kereopa had failed to reach the Waikato, but the subversion he had spread among the Ngati Porou continued to give trouble. H.M.S. *Eclipse* was once again called upon, and this time to better effect. The warship landed about 100 colonial troops under Major James Fraser at the Waiapu River near East Cape. He and Major Biggs were to help the loyalists and joined hands with Ropata. In a clash on 2 August some 25 Hauhau were killed in hand-to-hand fighting. Shortly afterwards the implacable Ropata captured some of his own tribe who had gone over to the enemy and killed 11 of them with his own hand.

Captain Westrupp brought some Forest Rangers from Wanganui in time to support Fraser in another attack on Pukemaire early in October. The operation dragged on until the defenders slipped away to a new position at Hungahungatoroa. This suffered from being overlooked by another hill, and it did not take Biggs and Ropata very long to make full use of this eyrie to pour fire into the pa. When the rebels surrendered, Ngati Porou did not suffer the supreme penalty this time, and for the remainder of the wars the Government

Major James Fraser. From *Defenders of New Zealand*

Major Wahawaha Ropata, 1807–97, Ngati Porou war chief and leader of the Government faction of his tribe. He did not achieve prominence until middle age, but proved himself an oustanding leader of great courage and ruthlessness. He wears the Highland claymore presented to him by Queen Victoria for his loyalty to the Crown. *Hawke's Bay Art Gallery and Museum*

found the tribe as dependable as the Arawa.

The latter were actively working with Major Mair, who operated from Matata. As traditional enemies of Ngati Awa and Whakatohea, they needed no urging to pursue relentlessly the murderers of Volkner and Fulloon. The climax came when Horomona and his followers were rash enough to shut themselves up in a pa at Te Teko, beside the Rangitaiki River. Mair was by now an old hand in dealing with this type of defence. Rather than waste lives, he encouraged the sub-tribes among his men to dig saps in friendly rivalry, and as a result was soon accepting the surrender of the Hauhau. William

Major Brassey. From
Defenders of New Zealand

Major Charles Stapp. From
Defenders of New Zealand

Mair was one of the unsung heroes of the wars, and should certainly have joined his brother Gilbert in receiving the honour of the New Zealand Cross.

The Government could not afford another loss of face at Opotoki on the lines of the *Eclipse* venture, and now set in train a much more determined thrust. British participation was once again limited to a single warship, the corvette H.M.S. *Brisk,* under Captain C. W. Hope, which sailed from Auckland on 1 September. The landing was to be made by colonial troops and a native contingent from Wanganui under McDonnell. The men were brought in the transports *Ahuriri, Ladybird* and *Stormbird;* during the voyage a shallow-draught steamer, *Huntress,* which had been used as a dredger at Napier, joined the flotilla.

By the time the ships reached the rendezvous at Hicks Bay, near East Cape, *Brisk* had already been waiting for five days. On board was Von Tempsky, who had expected his Forest Rangers to be with the force and had come from leave in Auckland to join them. They had, however, refused to sail, and their leader elected to serve as a volunteer under the military commander, Major Brassey.

Captain Hope brought his little fleet to Opotoki, but was destined to have his problems in the days ahead. Because the entrance to the river port was obstructed by a harbour bar, only *Huntress* could be used as a landing craft. Brassey, Von Tempsky and Major Charles Stapp, with 200 volunteers, crammed into the ship and headed for the shore.

For pilot they had Captain Levy, who had brought Volkner to his doom. This man was in a difficult position. He earned his living in the coastal trade, and as a Jew was looked upon with favour by the Hauhau as a fellow victim of Christian persecution. Yet he could hardly refuse to obey Government orders. To avoid any risk of confusion, Hope took Levy up to the masthead, from where the marked channel leading into the river could be clearly seen. The captain's well-meant effort did him little good, for as he commented bitterly of *Huntress* in his subsequent despatch:

> She proceeded into the River, and ran aground either through imbecility or gross treachery on Mr Levy's part.[1]

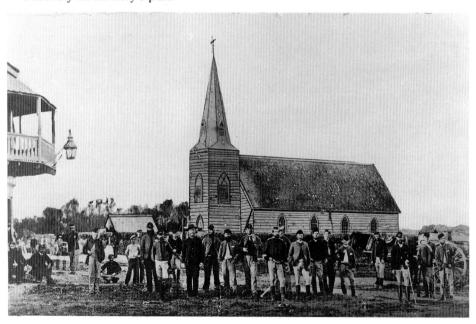

Men of the Opotiki Expedition, Patea Rangers and Wanganui Yeomanry Cavalry, photographed in front of Volkner's church, Opotiki. *Alexander Turnbull Library*

The ship lay stranded on a sandspit, her decks closely packed with men in easy range of enemy fire. In this desperate situation, it was vital to get the troops ashore before the Maori seized the opportunity to attack. Brassey and Von Tempsky, with the first 50 men to clamber over the side, ran to take possession of a nearby commanding hill from which they could cover the rest of the disembarkation.

Instead of landing McDonnell and the native contingent, Hope left them where they were and sent every boat he had to put men ashore from *Huntress*. To make matters worse, the hitherto perfect weather suddenly broke and a strong north-west wind whipped up a dangerous surf on the exxposed coast. The soldiers were scarcely on the beach when *Brisk* fired a gun to recall the boats. Hope took his ships to sea and hove to for the night.

The party ashore was in an unenviable position. Without the ships, they had only a 6-pounder gun in *Huntress* for artillery support, and even that might be of limited use while the steamer was aground. There were no tents, very little food and no more than limited ammunition:

> The men burrowed into the sand, making rifle-pits without spades, and forming some shelter against the biting wind and beating rain; many of the men and most of the officers had not even greatcoats with them; but there was wood, consequently fire, consequently some comfort. Half the force was kept under arms during the night.[2]

The rain had some beneficial effects. It damped down the sand which the gale had been blowing into everyone's eyes, and after some desultory shooting the Maori decided that fighting could wait until the morning.

Captain Stoker, of *Huntress*, was not idle. His ship was in a most vulnerable position, with the surf dashing right over her, and he was able to refloat her as the tide rose. A berth inside the bar provided a far more comfortable night for the crew.

The morning brought no abatement of the gale, and there was no telling how long the soldiers might have to wait for supplies to be landed. Rather than cool their heels, it seemed a better plan to attack without delay. The Patea Rangers were sent to a ridge to hold off any attack, and all the rest of the men returned to *Huntress*.

It seemed that this unlucky vessel was more suited to the peaceful work of dredging than to the demanding role of war. The overnight rain now poured down the river from the Urewera ranges. Despite all Stoker could do with steam and sail, his heavily loaded ship could make no headway against the strong current. He dropped anchor and allowed her to drift slowly back to the river mouth.

While time was being lost in these futile manoeuvres, the Hauhau had come down to the beach and occupied the trenches abandoned by the soldiers. Brassey therefore put his men ashore on the opposite side of the river entrance. After spending a rough night at sea, Hope had taken his squadron to shelter in the lee of Whale Island. He was most uneasy about the plight of the party ashore, and that afternoon went to Opotiki. Although he was able to see that the *Huntress* was afloat, and the troops safe for the moment, he could not anchor in the heavy seas and had to return to shelter. Once again the volunteers were in for an uncomfortable night with a violent thunderstorm and more heavy rain. Stoker took advantage of the darkness to move *Huntress* into a creek where her gun could be of some use.

Once again the right of passage across tribal territory was giving trouble,

Weapons of the Forest Rangers: the breech-loading .537 calibre Calisher and Terry carbine; a short Victorian fighting knife (this is not the Bowie knife carried by Von Tempsky's men, which had a blade nine inches long); the .36 calibre Navy Colt revolver, popular with the Rangers. *T. Ryan and N. Ogle*

this time to the Government. When the punitive expedition was in the planning stage, the Ngati Awa people had let it be known that they and their neighbours in the Whakatane district would feel called upon to fight any land force which might come to Opotiki from the west. If, however, the attack was made from the sea, they would remain neutral. Brassey and Hope probably wondered whether this was such a wise option after all.

Brassey now decided to postpone another assault until McDonnell could land the native contingent. He divided the small force ashore to defend the bridgehead, setting the Patea Rangers to hold the landward approach while Von Tempsky and the rest would meet any attack across the mouth of the river.

Dawn brought the long-expected attack against the front held by the Rangers, who soon beat it off. Von Tempsky expected a movement against the river bank he held, but he and his men were quite unprepared for the form it took. A tall Maori came walking along the opposite beach. He did not carry a flag of truce, but from his unconcerned manner it was at first thought that he must be friendly.

At last someone fired at him, at which the man made the Pai Marire gesture which was supposed to ward off bullets. A volley followed, and Lieutenant Bell crossed the river by boat to recover the body. Levy recognised him as one of the Maori who had taken part in the Hauhau rituals following the death of Volkner.

The troops, however, were more concerned with the desperate food situation than with the enemy. That afternoon H.M.S. *Brisk* led the squadron back from Whale Island. At first Hope tried dropping kegs of biscuit overboard in the expectation of their floating ashore. Despite the high surf which was still running, Lieutenant Fitton and a boat's crew volunteered to try to take extra supplies. They were overturned as they approached the beach, luckily without loss of life, and there were plenty of eager hands ready to retrieve their cargo from the sea.

Next day the sea had at last subsided sufficiently for McDonnell and his impatient native contingent to be landed. The major urged on the sailors manning his boat with the offer of a couple of sovereigns if he landed first, and soon his entire force was safely ashore.

Far left: Trooper William Wallace, Wanganui Yeomanry Cavalry, who took part in the charge at Te Tarata, Bay of Plenty, on 4 October 1865. *Alexander Turnbull Library*

Captain St Aubyn, of the Wanganui Yeomanry Cavalry, who took part in the Opotiki Expedition. *Alexander Turnbull Library*

Brassey tried to apply his formal training and ordered McDonnell to capture and hold a position. After their long confinement in cramped conditions aboard *Ladybird,* the kupapa could not contain their pent-up energies. They drove the enemy before them in a headlong rush to the village itself. With water up to their armpits, the Patea Rangers waded across Huntress Creek at half tide and advanced up the other bank of the river while *Brisk* laid down covering fire.

The pressure was too much for the Hauhau, who gave up the settlement. But so ragged were the appearance and movements of the invaders that Von Tempsky feared the troops might be mistaken for the enemy, so he climbed the niu pole to fly a borrowed red scarf as a signal for the naval gunners to cease fire.

Opotiki was well provided with ducks, fowls and pigs, which did not take long to find their way into the soldiers' cooking pots. Brassey took over Volkner's church as his headquarters. The building was also pressed into service as a barracks and was loopholed for defence. The martyr could hardly have expected his church to be put to such uses when it was completed only the year before.

St Stephens Church, Opotiki, loopholed and with an earthwork redoubt to protect it, served as Major Brassey's headquarters. *Alexander Turnbull Library*

The Hauhau had fallen back but a few miles, and built some pa to resist any further penetration by the Government force. Soon after an indecisive skirmish near one of these pa, Te Puia, McDonnell chased a handful of Maori who engaged one of his patrols to Te Tarata, about four miles from Opotiki on the east bank of the Waioeka River. The major called up reinforcements, and soon had the position invested on three sides, the fourth forming the crest of a precipice falling to the river 20 feet below.

The sound of firing stirred the garrison at Te Puia to try to relieve their comrades, and this move led to one of the few cavalry charges of the New Zealand

Wars. The Wanganui Cavalry seized the opportunity when the enemy was in open ground. The Maori on foot could not stand up to the horsemen, and had it not been for the latters' blunt sabres would have suffered heavy casualties.

This rough handling of their friends did nothing to cheer the men in Te Tarata. At eight o'clock that evening they called a truce to inquire the terms of a possible surrender. McDonnell told them that those who took part in Volkner's murder would have to stand trial, while the rest became prisoners of war. They were given an hour to think things over.

Before the truce expired, the defenders were seen to be chopping away the vines which bound together the posts of the palisade, evidently intending to throw down the stockade and break out of the trap. They started firing again, and McDonnell replied with the gun brought from *Huntress*. This made a wild screeching noise as its charge of chain-shot and bits of old iron flew over the heads of the troops.

The following morning Brassey planned to march on Te Puia, but McDonnell's scouts found it abandoned. The Whakatohea had at last accepted that they were no match for disciplined and well-armed troops in pitched battles; many soon came forward to surrender, while the more defiant took to the rugged country of the Waioeka Gorge.

Kereopa retreated even further into the recesses of the Urewera attended by a mere handful of those who had joined enthusiastically in the mass hysteria earlier in the year. McDonnell pursued him with vigour and very nearly captured the Eye-eater at Koingo in the valley of the Waimana. He again escaped, though five of his followers were shot. It would be some time before he was finally captured. Both Horomona and Kereopa eventually suffered the death penalty.

While the latter actions were taking place, Von Tempsky had returned to Wellington to try to settle the dispute involving his company. He found that they had refused to go on the Opotiki expedition because the pay offered was only three shillings and sixpence a day in place of the five shillings they were receiving. The major sent Westrupp to Wanganui with a letter, explaining that with allowances the new rate would be a little over four shillings.

Major G. F. Von Tempsky, about the time of his court martial, 1865. *Hawke's Bay Art Gallery and Museum*

Major (later Sir) Harry Atkinson. From *Defenders of New Zealand*

Von Tempsky himself now fell foul of authority. He was ordered to go to Waiapu to serve under Fraser, but promptly refused on the grounds that he could not be expected to serve under a man who was junior to him. Von Tempsky's pride was always rather touchy, and to emphasise his feelings he sent a resignation with the reply.

The Defence Minister, Harry Atkinson, did not like Von Tempsky. He rejected the resignation, and got over the seniority complaint by changing the destination from Waiapu to Napier. Von Tempsky, however, now raised a fresh objection. He claimed that, by the terms of their engagement, the Forest Rangers were enlisted to serve only in the Auckland Province. If they were required outside this area, as at Napier, then it was necessary to seek their agreement first. He did have some grounds for this complaint, since he had raised it long before in a memorandum to the Defence Minister, suggesting a change to cover the whole North Island.

Westrupp brought the Forest Rangers to Wellington, but only some of them were prepared to go to Napier under the new terms. Those who refused were placed in detention. Since discussion failed to budge Von Tempsky, he was put under close arrest. All were court-martialled, but a change of Government saw the replacement of Atkinson at the Defence Office by Colonel T. M. Haultain who, like Von Tempsky, was a veteran of the Waikato campaign. The findings of the court were passed to Grey, who soothed the defendant's feelings so that both he and his men were returned to duty shortly afterwards at Wanganui.

While these events were in progress, the Hauhau farther east were again on the warpath at Poverty Bay. Donald McLean, the Hawke's Bay Provincial Superintendent, invited the dissidents to meet him. While later initiatives along these lines were to prove fruitful, on this occasion he had no success; force had to take over from diplomacy.

Resistance crystallised at two pa at Waerenga-a-Hika and nearby Pukeamionga. Fraser selected the latter, but when Maori at Waerenga were

Bishop William Williams's house at Waerenga-a-Hika, showing the weatherboards removed for rifle fire by Major Fraser's men. *Alexander Turnbull Library*

seen leaving he turned his attention there instead. Siege had always proved the least costly way of reducing pa, so Fraser settled down to wait, keeping up a steady fire and later starting a sap.

The unlucky sappers were surprised by a strong rebel reinforcement coming from Pukeamionga, and six were killed. On the following day, a Sunday, the Hauhau tried following the doubtful precedent set by the British at Ruapekapeka and Rangiaowhia. Two formations advanced across open ground against Fraser's men, who were well dug in, and they suffered as severely as Despard's unfortunate troops had done 20 years before.

The Hauhau broke, retreating on their pa, and the action dragged on for days until a 6-pounder gun was brought up from the paddle steamer *Sturt*. When this began to smash a way through the palisade of Waerenga the defenders gave up and 400 were taken prisoner. Most were deported to the Chatham Islands — a measure which, like confiscation, did not turn out as brilliantly as its originators had hoped.

Below: The remains of Waerenga-a-Hika Pa, Poverty Bay, after its surrender and destruction on 22 November 1865. The mission house of Bishop William Williams, used as Fraser's headquarters, stands in the middle background. *Alexander Turnbull Library*

Lower plate: Captain Charles Westrupp's Forest Rangers camp, Poverty Bay, 1865. *Alexander Turnbull Library*

Wiremu Tamehana
negotiates with
Brigadier-General Carey
and then surrenders, in
1865. *Illustrated London
News*

Wiremu Tamehana, the man who at the time of the Waikato war first called upon these eastern tribes to rise, had already made a formal submission to Brigadier-General Carey in May. As he was by far the most statesman-like leader of the Maori cause, his action held symbolic importance. On the other hand, it did nothing to lessen the will to resist in such chiefs as Rewi Mania-poto, Tawhiao and Titokowaru.

Wiremu Tamehana negotiates with Brigadier-General Carey and then surrenders, in 1865. *Illustrated London News*

A RAGGED LITTLE ARMY – campaigning in the 1840s
Five illustrations by Tim Ryan.

Left: The 99th (Lanarkshire Volunteers) was the only Scottish Regiment, albeit a Lowland one, to serve in New Zealand. This field officer has removed from his shell jacket the bullion shoulder straps, to preserve them from the harsh campaign conditions; the waist sash has been omitted for the same reason. He carries a non-regulation, single-shot, percussion pistol and the standard field officer's sword carried in a brass scabbard. Many of the memoirs of the 1845-46 campaigns report the dire state of the clothing of the troops during a harsh winter campaign.

Above: An officer of the 58th (Rutlandshire) Regiment of foot who wears the 1834 pattern, single-breasted, blue frock coat, with eight regimental buttons down the front. He has removed the bullion shoulder straps for practical reasons. He wears the crimson silk sash wrapped twice around the waist over a black patent leather sword belt with snake clasp. His blue forage cap has a black leather peak and chin strap, with a band of black silk oak-leaf lace surmounted by the regimental number.

Above: The corporal of the 58th (Rutlandshire) Regiment is dressed in the red undress shell jacket with black facings of his regiment. Because the 58th had recently arrived from Britain, they were the only regiment to be armed for the war in the north with the new 1839 pattern, smoothbore, percussion musket. This was a huge advantage because a percussion musket could be fired in all weather conditions without misfiring. This soldier has a small percussion cap pocket sewn into his shell jacket.

Above: This soldier of the 96th Regiment on piquet duty is lucky to wear a tattered greatcoat with yellow regimental facings. Such 'watch' coats were in short supply so were restricted to sentries patrolling at night or in wet weather. He wears buff leather equipment and the standard pattern waterbottle. The soldier is armed with the obsolete 'New Land Service' flintlock smoothbore musket.

Left: The uniform of this Sergeant of 99th (Lanarkshire Volunteers) Regiment shows the wear and tear of a hard campaign. He wears the undress shell jacket with sergeant's stripes on his right upper arm, and his waist sash has stripes of the regimental facing colour. He is equipped with a sergeant's sword as well as his bayonet. His trousers are of the grey tweed summer type which contemporary paintings show being worn by troops involved in the Northern War.

UNDRESS UNIFORMS AND BLUE JUMPERS – British officers' dress of the 1860s
Three illustrations by Brian Conroy.

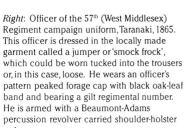

Right: Officer of the 57th (West Middlesex) Regiment campaign uniform, Taranaki, 1865. This officer is dressed in the locally made garment called a jumper or 'smock frock', which could be worn tucked into the trousers or, in this case, loose. He wears an officer's pattern peaked forage cap with black oak-leaf band and bearing a gilt regimental number. He is armed with a Beaumont-Adams percussion revolver carried shoulder-holster style.

Left: Lieutenant 18th (Royal Irish) Regiment, Auckland, 1864. This officer wears the navy blue undress forage cap, with a peak of patent leather and a red band, denoting a Royal Regiment, bearing the gilt regimental number and bullion harp badge. He is dressed in the 1852 pattern, double-breasted frock coat with gilt regimental buttons and a twisted crimson cord on the left shoulder. A crimson sash is worn over the left shoulder. His sword is of the 1822 company officer's pattern in a black leather scabbard with gilt mounts.

Right: This senior field officer, 1866, wears a navy blue officer's pattern 'pillbox' undress cap with a bullion oak-leaf band. He wears a dark blue, black-braided patrol jacket that was worn in New Zealand from 1863 onward. His waistcoat is the scarlet officer's pattern closed with hooks, with gilt false buttons and edged with gold lace. This officer carries the 1822 pattern officer's sword. His black knee boots are fitted with silver spurs.

RED COAT TO BLUE JUMPER
The uniforms of other British ranks in New Zealand during the 1860s
Three illustrations by Brian Conroy.

Right: Campaign uniform of a Private in the 65th (Yorkshire North Riding) Regiment, Waikato, 1864. This soldier wears the blue 'pork-pie'-type forage cap bearing a bugle horn over brass regimental numbers and surmounted by a green tourie or tuft denoting the light company of the regiment. He is dressed in a locally made 'smock frock' over which he wears buff leather equipment. His blanket and/or greatcoat wrapped in an oilskin sheet is worn over the left shoulder with his haversack over his right.

Left: Colour Sergeant 65th (Yorkshire North Riding) Regiment walking-out dress, New Plymouth, 1861. This NCO wears the usual 'pork pie' Light Company forage cap. His tunic is of the 1856 single-breasted pattern, bearing the Colour Sergeant's insignia of three white chevrons surmounted by crossed swords, the Union Flag and a crown. A crimson worsted sash is worn over the right shoulder. He carries a swagger stick.

Right: Sergeant 18th (Royal Irish) Regiment wearing full dress on parade at Wanganui in 1865. This NCO wears the 1855 shako (which seems to have been worn in New Zealand as late as 1866), bearing the regimental pattern shako plate and a white-over-red tuft denoting the battalion company. His tunic is of the 1856 pattern, with blue regimental facings and three white worsted chevrons denoting a sergeant, on a backing of the regimental colour, which was worn on the upper right arm. A crimson worsted sash is worn over the right shoulder. He is armed with the pattern 1856, two-band Sergeant's Enfield rifle with sword bayonet.

1860s DRESS UNIFORM RECONSTRUCTIONS OF THE 65th (YORKSHIRE NORTH RIDING) REGIMENT OF FOOT

Re-enactors: The 65th Regiment; photographs by Tim Ryan.

A sergeant and two privates of the 65th Regiment dressed in the single breasted, 1856 pattern tunic.

Left: The dress uniform of an Ensign in the 65th Regiment about 1860. The green ball tuft on this officer's 1855 pattern shako denotes the Light Company of the Regiment.

Ensign Bonnett of the 65th Regiment, wearing his undress peaked cap and carrying a typical walking cane, together with his sergeant and two men of the Light Company pause beside an Auckland road.

Men of the 65th Regiment inspect a photographic image that has just been obtained by their officer on his wet-plate camera. We are indebted to a small number of 19th century British officers for the photographs they took whilst on campaign in New Zealand.

Ensign Bonnett, wearing the 1856 pattern dress tunic with white facings denoting his regiment, poses beside a six-pound Armstrong gun.

Below: Picquets (sentries) of the 65th Regiment guard an Auckland watermill.

Private Webb is equipped with a main ammunition pouch suspended from his cross belt; from 1859 it held 50 rounds. The smaller expense pouch on his waist belt contained 10 rounds, oil bottle and cleaning materials.

1860s CAMPAIGN UNIFORM RECONSTRUCTIONS OF THE 65th (YORKSHIRE NORTH RIDING) REGIMENT OF FOOT

Re-enactors: The 65th Regiment; photographs by Tim Ryan except for b and c which are by Matthew Bonnett.

(a) Prolonged campaigns in all weather conditions meant a great deal of wear and tear and modification to uniforms worn by the British Army in New Zealand. This photograph illustrates the appearance of a soldier in a ragged grey greatcoat and an officer who has modified his sword belt into a shoulder strap for suspending his percussion pistol.

(b) Contrary to present-day thinking, the British Army did modify its tactics to cope with bush fighting. Under energetic officers several regiments took the struggle to the Maori on his own ground, even ambushing tribal war parties.

(c) The Enfield percussion rifle and its socket bayonet were considered at the time as being the zenith of the muzzle-loading rifle. It was this weapon that was used so effectively during the Indian Mutiny.

(d) The threat of ambush was always present in the rough fern and bush country of New Zealand. Supply columns had to be adequately protected by an escort of troops which in some cases were accompanied for greater protection by artillery.

(e) The Imperial Forces' direct involvement in fighting the New Zealand Wars ended in 1867, by which time they had become a toughened fighting force used to the conditions of the country. The Maori had learned the superiority of the combination of British Army discipline and the bayonet in hand-to-hand conflict.

(h) *Left*: A wet-plate image of the 65th Regiment re-enactors, showing the realism of their uniforms when photographed with a 19th century camera. Collodion by Brian Scadden

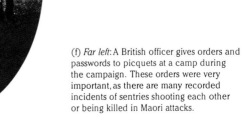

(f) *Far left*: A British officer gives orders and passwords to picquets at a camp during the campaign. These orders were very important, as there are many recorded incidents of sentries shooting each other or being killed in Maori attacks.

TENTING TONIGHT, CAMP LIFE IN THE 1860s
Re-enactors: The 65th Regiment; photographs by Tim Ryan.

Regimental standards and discipline were difficult to maintain in the boredom of life in military camps.

The experience of Imperial and colonial soldiers living in bell tents or marquees, winter and summer for months or even years, was a common occurrence. This life toughened the troops stationed in New Zealand, which was considered one of the healthiest of all the British colonies. A priority was winter hutment of all soldiers stationed in the camps and frontier fortifications. However, these cold, unlined barracks, with dirt floors and hard wooden sleeping platforms, were only one step up from living under canvas.

Drunkenness was endemic in both the Imperial and Colonial Forces where the wet canteen was often the only place of recreation in military camps.

The company fireplace was kept constantly burning, providing as it did, a hot billy of tea or coffee for the sentries coming off duty.

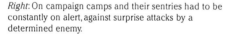

Right: On campaign camps and their sentries had to be constantly on alert, against surprise attacks by a determined enemy.

Military food was unrelentingly uninteresting and often sub-standard. Staples consisted of biscuits (baked flour, lard and salt), boiled salted beef and pork, camp bread, potatoes and, when they could be obtained, vegetables such as cabbage.

Right: Cleaning equipment, maintaining weapons and ammunition were part of the daily routine of camp life.

THE ROYAL ARTILLERY IN NEW ZEALAND

Photographs by Tim Ryan except (e) which is by Matthew Bonnet and (d) by Ernie Thompson. Reconstructed 6-pounder Armstrong gun by Darryl Hicks.

(a) The 6-pound Armstrong gun and a 4-and-2/5ths-inch brass Coehorn mortar, together with a genuine Armstrong ammunition box and six-inch shells, plus shells and equipment for the mortar.

(b) A soldier of the 65th Regiment stands guard over a 4-and-2/5ths-inch Coehorn mortar and its equipment plus the 6-inch Armstrong ammunition box and shell.

(c) Detail of the George III cypher on the 5½-inch Royal mortar, marked below the breech ring with the founder's name (H.C. King) and the date of manufacture, 1806.

(d) Detail of Queen Victoria's Royal cypher cast onto the barrel of an Armstrong gun.

(e) Soldiers of the Light Company of the 65th Regiment examine the 6-pound, breech-loading Armstrong gun.

(f) A rare original example of the 6-pound Armstrong gun, with carriage reconstructed according to contemporary plans. The Royal Artillery brought the barrel of this gun to New Zealand in 1861.

(g) Possibly the only example of the 5½-inch Royal mortar that has survived in New Zealand, together with one of its shells and a rare cutaway Woolwich 4-and-2/5ths-inch demonstration shell.

(h) A glass-plate image of an officer of the 65th Regiment posing beside a 6-pound Armstrong gun. Wet plate collodion by Brian Scadden

MAORI WARRIORS AND THEIR WEAPONS

Maori arms given up at Te Papa on the 25th July 1864. Engraving after a sketch by Lieut H.G. Robley, which appeared in *The Illustrated London News* of 24th September 1864.

1. Small tomahawk (patiti).
2. Cartouche box (hamanu), to carry eighteen rounds; the smaller boxes nine rounds. Their cartridges (karriri) are very neatly made up.
3. Patu pounamu or greenstone club.
4. Whalebone club or kotiate and wooden patu.
5. Spear (tao) either of hard wood sharpened or with a bayonet fixed.
6. Long-handled tomahawk or kakauroa.
7. Guns (pu) mostly flintlock (ngutu-parera), single-barrelled (hakimana), double-barrelled (tupara) shot guns or percussion muskets.
8. Taiaha or long club ornamented with dog skin and parrot (kaka) feathers.
9. Bayonet (peniti) and two paper cartridges.
10. Wooden battleaxe or tewhatewha.
11. Wooden cartridge roller.

Maori warrior after an illustration in *L' Univers Illustré*, 1868. The illustration is based on a sketch by Lieut H.G. Robley, 68th Durham Light Infantry, coloured by Tim Ryan.

Below: Flintlock, dated 1789, of the type that the Maori called ngutu-parera or duck's bill.

It was customary for Maori warriors to shed their clothing for war. This Toa is equipped with wooden cartouche boxes (hamanu). His flax bag would contain cartridge paper and musket balls. European turkey feathers decorate his hair. From his wrist is suspended a carved wooden cartridge roller.

All ammunition, musket balls, flints and other equipment had to be carried for long distances whilst on campaign. This warrior has manufactured flax bags (kete) in imitation of European ammunition boxes. His face is tattooed (moko) together with his thighs (puhoro) and buttocks (rape). In his hand he carries a powder horn.

This Toa has readied himself for combat by wearing only a flax war belt in which he has tucked his tomahawk (patiti). He is also armed with a taiaha long club.

Detail of scrimshaw work on a European powder horn dating from the 1860s, portraying a Maori haka.

MAORI WARRIORS AND THEIR WEAPONS

Three rifles that have been in Maori hands. From the top: (1) A .451 Whitworth target rifle dated 1860, which fired a hexagonal bullet. The wood of this rifle is covered with fine European-influenced Maori carving. (2) A .577 Snider artillery carbine which is also profusely carved in a more traditional Maori style. (3) A .577 two-band, Enfield-type, government-issue rifle, which has been inscribed with the owner's name in missionary script.

Maori weapons. From the top: (1) A trade-type flintlock musket and cartouche box; (2,3 and 4) long and short-handled tomahawks (kakauroa and patiti); (5) tower-type flintlock military pistol.

Maori weapons. Left to right: (1) Carved .577 Snider carbine; (2) Long-handled tomahawk; (3) Carved .451 Whitworth rifle: (4) Short-handled tomahawk (patiti) and cartouche pouch.

Two of Te Kooti's warriors prepare to carry a pig, which they have killed, to their camp. By 1872 Te Kooti and a handful of his followers were being hunted deep in the bush-clad ranges of the Urewera by several columns of Government Kupapa troops. The Ringatu warrior on the left carries a captured Calisher & Terry carbine. *Painting by Sid Marsh*

Flintlock trade musket, bullet mould, long-handled tomahawk (kakauroa), short whale-bone-handled tomahawk (patiti) and tower-type flintlock pistol.

Right: Maori warriors of the late 1860s. The Toa on the right is of the chiefly class and wears a fine kaitaka cloak with taniko borders. His hair is decorated with non-native turkey feathers, a fashion shown in photographs of the period. He is armed with a long-handled tomahawk or kakauroa and a whalebone club or koitate. The warrior on the left is armed with the latest breech-loading weapon, the Snider, which would probably mark him as Kupapa or Government Partisan.

COLONIAL FORCES

All photographs by Tim Ryan.

Weapons of the Forest Rangers: Bowie knife, .539 Calisher & Terry carbine, 54-gauge Dean-Adams percussion revolver and .36-calibre Colt percussion revolver.

Corps of Forest Rangers. Left: Officer in the blue campaign uniform. He is equipped with a sword, Beaumont-Adams percussion revolver, and suspended from shoulder straps are a telescope and waterbottle. Right: This private is armed with a Beaumont-Adams revolver, .539 Calisher & Terry carbine and 'Bowie' knife. He carries his blanket wrapped in a waterproof sheet over his shoulder, and his haversack contains three days' rations. Under the blanket would be a 20-round cartridge box suspended from a shoulder strap. *Painting by John Belcher*

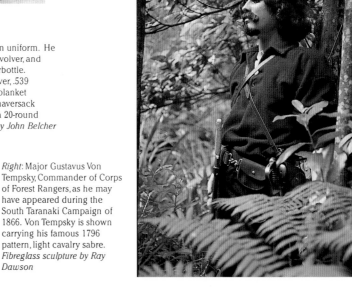

Right: Major Gustavus Von Tempsky, Commander of Corps of Forest Rangers, as he may have appeared during the South Taranaki Campaign of 1866. Von Tempsky is shown carrying his famous 1796 pattern, light cavalry sabre. *Fibreglass sculpture by Ray Dawson*

A Forest Ranger, armed with the first British bolt-action, breech-loading Calisher & Terry carbine, Bowie knife and percussion pistol, talks to a soldier of the 65th Regiment.

Right: A Forest Ranger leads a detachment of the 65th Regiment along a bush track in Taranaki.

COLONIAL FORCES

This officer of the Taranaki Rifle Volunteers wears the navy blue uniform and red waistcoat of this Militia unit. His peaked cap is based on the British officers' undress forage cap. This uniform belongs to a small collection of garments of the period held by the Taranaki Museum, which are very probably the only campaign uniforms to have survived from the New Zealand Wars. *Tim Ryan*

Armed Constabulary, Panekiri Range, Urewera, 1872. During the last months of the New Zealand Wars small units of Armed Constabulary attempted to run Te Kooti to ground before he reached the sanctuary of the King Country. These soldiers travelled light but were well armed with Snider breech-loading carbines. Pictured is the standard-issue Snider artillery carbine, whilst the officer carries the lighter, non-standard cavalry carbine. *Painting by Sid Marsh*

Upper: A Government pattern, .57 Enfield, two-band rifle. Lower: New Zealand Militia equipment dated 1862. The belt bears the Militia locket and supports the ball ammunition pouch and a frog suspending a sword bayonet of the Yataghan type. *Tim Ryan*

English and American percussion revolvers were popular throughout the New Zealand Wars. In the Imperial Forces most British officers carried revolvers, which were not supplied by the English Government, but were privately purchased by individual officers. In the New Zealand Local Forces the Colonial Government supplied large numbers of revolvers to officers, but also to other ranks of specialist units such as the Forest Rangers and the Armed Constabulary.
Left to right: (1) Militia Officer's 'pillbox' cap; (2) .439-calibre Tranter third model, double-trigger percussion revolver; (3) .50-calibre 1851 Adams percussion revolver and holster; (4) .31-calibre Colt pocket percussion pistol and holster; (5) .36-calibre Colt navy percussion revolver. Surrounding the hand guns are pistol tools and artefacts of the period. *Tim Ryan*

NEW ZEALAND ARMED CONSTABULARY IN THE FIELD
Re-enactors: Bruce Stewart and Bruce Cairns.
Painting by Malcolm Thomas; photographs by Tim Ryan.

Reconstruction of an Officer and a Constable (Private) of the Armed Constabulary during the Urewera Campaign. The officer checks his watch prior to an attack.

Model photograph by John Belcher of an officer of the Armed Constabulary who carries the Calisher & Terry breech-loading carbine. He is dressed for the difficult pursuit of Te Kooti 1869-72.
John Belcher

Scouts & Guides 1870

Above: The Corps of Guides were the lesser-known Armed Constabulary successors to the Forest Rangers. Colonel George Whitmore formed the Corps in 1869 during the South Taranaki Campaign against Titokowaru, with the intention to create a small body of picked scouts who could reconnoitre the bush-clad terrain in front of advancing columns. The Corps went on to take part in Whitmore's invasion of the Urewera. In 1870 they were disbanded when Maori Loyalists (Kupapa) took over the pursuit of Te Kooti. Left: Sergeant Arthur Carkeek of the NZ Armed Constabulary who won the New Zealand Cross in 1870 for carrying a vital message through hostile country, when no one else would take the risk. Right: Captain F. Swindley, who commanded the Corps of Guides during Whitmore's Urewera Campaign. Both men are armed with the breech-loading, .539-calibre Calisher & Terry carbine

The rank of this officer of the NZ Armed Constabulary is distinguished by his 'pillbox' forage cap with a band of silver lace. He is equipped with a blanket roll and waterproof haversack and carries a sporting version of the Snider rifle, a weapon often carried by officers.

Right: The Constable in the foreground wears the Armed Constabulary peaked forage cap bearing the first pattern AC badge. He is armed with the breech loading Snider artillery carbine which was issued to this unit.

Above: This Private of the NZ Armed Constabulary is equipped for campaign in 'shawl dress', a practical mode of clothing copied from the Maori and very suitable for crossing the many rivers and streams encountered in the mountains. His blanket is wrapped in a waterproof sheet.

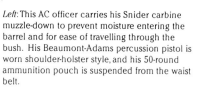

Left: From left, the .539-inch (30-bore) breech-loading, bolt-action Calisher & Terry carbine widely used by the New Zealand Armed Constabulary from 1868 until the early 1870s. Its main drawback was its combustible cartridge that was difficult to keep dry in bush conditions.
Right: the .451-inch Westley Richards carbine, nicknamed the 'Monkey Tail' because of its distinctive hinged breech cover. Captain Gilbert Mair, NZ Cross, carried a carbine of this make.

Left: This AC officer carries his Snider carbine muzzle-down to prevent moisture entering the barrel and for ease of travelling through the bush. His Beaumont-Adams percussion pistol is worn shoulder-holster style, and his 50-round ammunition pouch is suspended from the waist belt.

THE COLONISTS LEND A HAND

Although the active role of the regiments was virtually at an end, the country would have cause to be grateful for a legacy they left behind. Many a time-expired soldier, attracted by the mild climate and the chance to acquire property which would have been beyond his reach at home, elected to take his discharge locally, which generally meant that he would never see the British Isles again.

The most illustrious of these new citizens was Lieutenant-Colonel George S. Whitmore who, like most of his comrades, had learned his trade long before coming to New Zealand with service both in South Africa and the Crimea. He held the appointment of Military Secretary to Cameron, and was naturally fully aware of the general's sentiments. Whitmore shared these to the extent of resigning at the same time as his chief, but for all his stand on principle was to prove no sluggard in following the colonial passion for collecting whatever land came his way.

The British Army had used Whitmore's talents mainly in the administrative field, but its departure would soon give him the chance to prove himself as a fighting soldier. He chose to settle at Hawke's Bay, also the home of such powerful figures as Donald McLean and Mr J. D. Ormond. Although Whitmore would make his mark by the exercise of his military skill, he also had political ambitions, and cultivated those who could be useful to him.

While a new advance was going well in the west, trouble flared up again in the east. Ngati Kahungungu, a tribe divided against itself, had warriors on both sides in a skirmish at Omaruhakeke on Christmas Day 1865, and later near Lake Waikaremoana. Ropata and his Ngati Porou once again proved effective. Prisoners were killed after the second engagement, a barbaric discouragement to further insurrection.

Tareha, chief of the Ngati Kahungunu tribe of Hawke's Bay, who was prominent in the fighting of 1866. *Hawke's Bay Art Gallery and Museum*

In October 1866 the settlement of Napier was fortunate to have a trained and experienced officer of Whitmore's calibre to call upon. The Ngati Hineuru, living in the ranges behind the town, harboured a Pai Marire disciple named Panapa. The withdrawal of the British garrison from the town seemed to invite a Hauhau attack, for which outside support was not lacking.

Led by Te Rangihiroa, about 130 Maori advanced to be met by an equally scratch force under Whitmore. The latter left Major Fraser with the best troops to protect the town, while he took volunteers and kupapa to engage the Maori at Omarunui. Although the Hauhau had the advantage of a river line for their defence, they inexplicably allowed their enemies under Major Lambert to cross before firing.

The action soon became spirited, and Whitmore ordered Lambert's men to take cover along the river bank while the whole force concentrated its fire upon the village. When the Maori surrendered they had lost 21 dead to one on the Government side. At the same time as this action was being fought, a mounted detachment of Maori under Te Rangihiroa was ambushed by Fraser's command, losing a further 21.

Lieutenant-Colonel (later Major-General) George Stoddart Whitmore, 1830–1903, was a man of enormous energy and much experience of irregular warfare before coming to New Zealand. His quick temper was not always appreciated by the men who served under him, but he remained one of the few outstanding leaders of the wars. *Alexander Turnbull Library*

Trooper Chill, of the 3rd Napier Mounted Division of Volunteers, who took part in the Battle of Omarunui near Napier in 1866. *Alexander Turnbull Library*

Military barracks and redoubt on Bluff Hill, Napier. Built by men of the 65th (Yorkshire) Regiment in 1858, it was occupied by various regiments until 1867. *Alexander Turnbull Library*

On the other side of the North Island another leader, fated to become Whitmore's bitter rival, was also in action. Tom McDonnell, hero of Paparata and a score of fights, would add little to his laurels over the next two years. After Chute's return to Wanganui, surveyors were hopefully sent out to parcel up confiscated land for military settlers. The affected tribes at once began to do their best to stop the work, as they would for many years to come. McDonnell was given a mixed force of volunteers and the Wanganui Native Contingent to provide security for the work.

After an ambush of surveyors on 16 June, he made a provisional truce with the Ngati Tupaea, the tribe concerned, and then raided their village of Pokaikai at daybreak on 1 August. It was a deed reminiscent of some of his father's doubtful practices at Hokianga, and was condemned at an official inquiry.

Such actions on both sides were bound to cause the situation to grow steadily worse. On 23 September the Hauhau surprised a ration party en route to the base at Waihi Redoubt. One man, Trooper Haggerty, was tomahawked, though his three companions managed to escape. This in turn led to a patrol under Ensign Northcroft posing as surveyors to invite an ambush and then pouncing on their unsuspecting foes.

The skirmishes escalated. On 1 October McDonnell attacked the Ngati Ruahine at Pungarehu, and a spirited engagement saw the retreat of the defenders and the destruction of their village. Northcroft gallantly risked his own life to rescue a wounded man, and the Government force inflicted heavy casualties for the loss of three men. Grey himself came to Patea, and after McDonnell's brother was wounded at Te Popoia asked for troops from the 18th Regiment to reinforce the volunteers in destroying the position.

In the Bay of Plenty the Pirirakau, a small tribe in the country behind Tauranga, had not surrendered to the Government at the same time as their larger allies, the Ngaiterangi. They did not lack support from other dissidents, and took to harassing surveyors on confiscated land. When their depredations reached the point of murder, Lieutenant-Colonel Philip Harington led the 1st Waikato Militia, who had settled in the district, against the Hauhau, supported by a detachment from the 12th Regiment. This was the last time Imperial troops were in action in New Zealand.

They achieved little, and Gilbert Mair was lucky to escape after being trapped when his horse was shot from under him. He and his brother, like the McDonnells, were sons of very early settlers in the north. Despite the bitterness of the wars, both held the respect of the Maori to a remarkable extent, Gilbert being affectionately known as 'Tawa'.

William Mair enrolled 200 Arawa, and with some help from the soldier-settlers steadily drove back the Pirirakau. While his friendly Maori were so engaged, a raiding force from the Waikato struck at their homes in the Rotorua lake country. On 17 March 1867 Gilbert, as the only white man there, rose to the challenge with all his accustomed energy.

Having only 39 men to oppose a force put at some hundreds, he managed to reach some trenches of an old pa at Te Koutu. The enemy, led by Pare Turanga, a chieftainess, fought to dislodge the small party, but Mair disposed his men with such skill that the raiders began to give ground. The Arawa pushed home their advantage, killing 11 of the enemy for the loss of one of their chiefs.

Those defeated by the two brothers combined to build a pa at Puraku to command the Rotorua basin. At considerable risk, Gilbert kept them under

Sergeant-Major Jackson, of the 1st Waikato Regiment, who fought the Pirirakau tribe during the Tauranga bush campaign of 1867. A painting by J. McDonald. *Alexander Turnbull Library*

The Arawa mail carrier, Wi Popata, is ambushed and killed by a war party under Eru Tamaikowha in 1867. A painting by J. McDonald. *Taranaki Museum*

Eru Tamaikowha. From *Pictures of Old New Zealand*

Major St John. From *Defenders of New Zealand*

observation from the dominating peak Ngongotaha. Later he joined McDonnell and Major St John with a force of 500 to storm Puraku, but the resolve of the Hauhau soon melted before the advance.

The Urewera posed a new threat to Opotiki, for Eru Tamaikowha started on the warpath. On 27 June Abraham Bennett White, a survivor of the *Kate* incident, was riding with Wi Popata, an Arawa mail man, along the beach from Whakatane. The following morning a chief named Waiteria came upon their headless bodies at the Waiotahi stream, and then found White's head set upon a rock. Later two other men were murdered.

Major St John was now officer commanding at Opotiki, and Henry Mair enrolled the Opotiki Volunteer Rangers with J. R. Rushton and his friend David White, late of the Patea Rangers. St John, while likeable and brave, lacked drive. His forays against Tamaikowha achieved little, and in one instance his treacherous conduct was little better than McDonnell's at Pokaikai.

A and C Companies of the 18th Royal Irish Regiment on parade at the Rutland Stockade, Wanganui. The soldiers wear blue campaign dress. A goat, the regimental mascot, is at the right of the photograph. *Wanganui Museum*

The 57th (West Middlesex) Regiment on parade at Wanganui. Other ranks wear the full dress uniform under the regulations of 1861; this would not have been worn on campaign. *Wanganui Museum*

CHAPTER 18

A MARCH ROUND MOUNT EGMONT

While the authorities could reasonably feel that they had gone some way to restoring the situation in the east, on the other side of the North Island it was only too apparent how little had been achieved by the Lame Seagull's slow and costly expedition:

> An army of 6,000 British soldiers, commanded by a British general, and amply provided with all the munitions of war, had been concentrated upon a small portion of the western coast of New Zealand for the purpose of establishing British supremacy over that portion of the Northern Island which lies between Wanganui in the province of Wellington, and New Plymouth, the capital of Taranaki. The result of that campaign . . . was a complete failure, a heavy expense to Great Britain and this Colony, and an irreparable breach between General Cameron upon the one hand and Sir George Grey and the Colonial Government upon the other. Emboldened by the complete failure of that campaign the rebel natives not only retained possession of the entire country between Wanganui and New Plymouth, but were also emboldened to look upon the British soldier with the utmost contempt. Their pas, or natural fortresses, considered by General Cameron to be impregnable, were strengthened, and with the utmost confidence they considered themselves masters of the position. The various outposts planted by General Cameron were merely isolated and closely beseiged military redoubts, as the officers commanding had positive orders not to allow their men to go further than some two or three hundred yards beyond the breastwork, and by no means to fire upon a native until fired upon. Thus the whole country, with the exception of these isolated positions, was in the hands of the enemy, who laid ambuscades and shot down soldiers in charge of military convoys as well as Government messengers and unoffending settlers.[1]

Walter Buller. From *Defenders of New Zealand*

Such a state of affairs could not be allowed to continue. The native contingent returned to Wanganui in the *Stormbird* on 28 November 1865, leaving the Patea Rangers at Opotiki, where a military settlement was formed. When McDonnell landed with his men, he was met by Dr Isaac Featherston, Superintendent of Wellington, Walter Buller, the Resident Magistrate, and his old comrade Von Tempsky.

On Boxing Day the superintendent unveiled the Moutoa monument in the presence of a large crowd, including about 500 Maori. He spoke highly of those who had fought so valiantly in the island battle, no doubt having in mind the problem with which he would have to come to grips the next day.

There was discontent bordering on mutiny in part of the native contingent, this largely the work of one of the chiefs, Mete Kingi. He had always been a difficult man to deal with, his high opinion of his own value not being generally shared, and he spoke out against any further participation at the meeting called to enlist support for a new expedition.

Far from being disconcerted, Featherston spoke up confidently, praising the warriors and appealing to their patriotism, though one might have doubted the wisdom of the latter approach. Probably the prospect of being

Mete Kingi. From *Defenders of New Zealand*

paid for fighting won over his audience, which was soon roused to such enthusiasm that he was able to disarm and reject the malcontents. The upshot was:

> The Native Contingent was reinforced, and mustered 286 fighting men, with several of their women who invariably accompany such expeditions; carry heavy loads, act as hewers of wood and drawers of water, cook, and frequently fight with the most determined bravery. Upon the field of battle these ladies are perfect amazons and thoroughly despise the man who in the hour of danger would exhibit either fear or cowardice. The Contingent, unaccustomed and unwilling to observe the rules of civilised warfare, or to submit to what we call discipline, expected to carry on war after their own fashion, and it required considerable tact to bring them under control.[2]

Dr Isaac Earl Featherston. From *Defenders of New Zealand*

The new leader was Major-General Trevor Chute, Officer Commanding in Australia and New Zealand. He was bolder and had more drive than Cameron, and was determined to show the Taranaki dissidents that there would be no snail's-pace advance this time. Some of the British regiments had already left the country, and while most of those remaining took part in the new venture at some stage Chute had only part of the 14th, with artillery and transport units, and the native contingent, when he marched out of Wanganui on 30 December for Waitotara.

The general found that his Maori auxiliaries could bring problems with discipline and rations, and was thankful to have Dr Featherston to deal with them. On arrival at Weraroa Chute was held up for two days while the native contingent collected horses, which they claimed belonged to the dissidents, and prepared food they would need on the journey.

Von Tempsky and his handful of Forest Rangers joined the column, which crossed the Waitotara on 3 January 1866. After going about eight miles, it camped near a supposedly impregnable pa at Okotuku. McDonnell led a reconnaissance party, and taking the defence by surprise entered without opposition. They set the whare on fire before returning to camp.

Next day Chute learned that the place had been reoccupied. He set out through dense bush, along a track made difficult by ravines, rocks and supplejacks, emerging on a tableland under cultivation. On leaving the forest cover the force came under heavy fire from the pa. The Forest Rangers were sent to the left with some of McDonnell's men, while others took the right flank.

Captain Vivian led the 2nd Battalion of the 14th in a frontal attack against a thick palisade built of fallen logs held in place by stout upright stakes. This stretched across a narrow neck of land from one precipice to another. On this occasion a move which had often proved costly in the past paid off, for the troops burst into the pa with only five men wounded. The defenders lost six killed, and other casualties were carried off in their flight. Some of the native contingent gave chase, killing another and capturing a chief.

The new commander had won his first fight, and was perhaps lucky to get off so lightly. The native contingent demanded rest on 5 January, so the troops passed the time destroying enemy crops. Next day the column went on to the Whenuakura River, where it camped on high ground in the vicinity of the next objective, Putahi Pa. Reinforced by the arrival of detachments of the 18th and 50th Regiments brought up from Patea, the impetuous Chute would have liked to attack at once, but found this impossible without first reconnoitring the position.

Major-General Trevor Chute, 1816–86, was born in County Kerry, Ireland. A veteran of the Indian Mutiny, he first came to New Zealand in 1863 in command of the 70th Regiment. Later posted to Australia, Chute returned in 1865 to fight the successful Southern Taranaki Campaign. Although an energetic soldier, he had little understanding of the Maori, and his impetuosity left problems long in its train. From *Picturesque Atlas of Australasia*

Dr Featherston and Major-General Chute, (at left) watch the force march past. Von Tempsky, with dogs, leads his Forest Rangers at the right. A painting by Major G. F. Von Tempsky. *National Museum*

Forest Rangers' camp near Te Putahi Pa on the Whenuakura River, Taranaki, on 7 January 1866. Dr Isaac Featherston, Superintendent of Wellington Province, stands by the cartwheel. A painting by Major G. F. Von Tempsky. *Alexander Turnbull Library*

A reporter from the *Wanganui Times* described it:

> On the proper left bank of the Whenuakura, the Hauhau pa of Putahi is strongly situated on a plateau supported by precipitous spurs, and cleft everywhere by deep forest gullies. The road from Ngamutu comes opposite the pa to a fern plateau of similar elevation to that of the pa; thence the road descends precipitously to a grassy valley intersected by a wooded stream, and ascends the back of a steep fern spur, where each undulation has its arm of forest into or on to each turn of the road, forming a succession of ambuscading places, equalled in convenience to a wily foe by few places in New Zealand. This was the strength the Putahi Hauhaus had relied upon for a long time. Their flag had been planted in the face of the Patea garrison ever since the first arrival of the troops, and at no time had the natives taken the trouble of fortifying their place much; its approaches, if well watched, would prove more formidable than the strongest pa in New Zealand.[3]

One of the general's habits, which probably did not endear him to everyone, was to start the day at a very early hour. The time chosen on 7 January was 3 a.m., when the force set off on a circuitous route. After they had crossed a tributary of the Whenuakura by a bridge built the previous evening, the going was fairly easy until about two miles from the pa, when

> The march may be described as one continued struggle through a dense primeval forest and bush, over ravines and gullies which could in most cases only be ascended by the aid of supplejacks, and then only with great difficulty. The extreme distance to be traversed could not have exceeded four miles, but the obstacles and obstructions opposed to us made it a severe task of four hours.[4]

On reaching the clearing in which the pa stood, the native contingent and Forest Rangers covered the enemy while the Regulars emerged from the bush to take up battle formation. Once again the 14th Regiment was in the centre, with the 18th on the right and 50th to the left. Von Tempsky's Rangers opened fire from 300 yards, interrupting a haka, and shooting soon became general. Starting from 400 yards, the assault troops advanced with caution in the face of the enemy fusillade. When the distance had narrowed to 80 yards the order to charge was given. This was carried out with cheers, and once again a frontal attack was irresistible.

McDonnell was wounded in the foot early in the engagement, but, supported by Sergeant Samuel Austin of the Wanganui Volunteer Contingent, insisted upon remaining in charge of his men. Later in this campaign, by a coincidence, Austin also rescued the major's brother William who was lying wounded and in danger of being tomahawked. These deeds were later rewarded with the New Zealand Cross.

The native contingent pursued the fugitives, while the troops completely razed the pa. Colonel H. E. Weare led 100 men from Patea to ambush the expected line of the enemy retreat from Putahi to Kakaramea. Only five Maori, however, walked into this trap. Sixteen dead were collected, the Government loss being one man killed and seven wounded. Chute was proving that he could get quick results from frontal attack without incurring the disastrous casualties suffered at Gate Pa and Rangiriri.

During the sack of Putahi, articles were found which had formerly belonged to two murdered settlers, Arbon and Hewitt, as well as a whaleboat concealed near the river which had been stolen from the steamer *Gundagai*. To square accounts, the native contingent collected large quantities of potatoes to help the none too plentiful stores of the commissariat.

Kakaramea had been the scene of a skirmish between the Forest Rangers and Hauhau the previous May. Scouts now found the country deserted and so contented themselves with burning the empty villages as they passed through. Chute carried on via Manawapou to Tangahoe. The 18th and 50th Regiments returned to Patea, to be replaced by 240 men of the 57th from Waingongoro and Manawapou.

Forest Rangers' camp in the bush during Chute's march. Von Tempsky smokes a pipe at the left. Next to him is Assistant-Surgeon William Manley, who won the V.C. at the Gate Pa. A painting by Major G. F. Von Tempsky. *Alexander Turnbull Library*

Reconnaissance by Ensign William McDonnell in the vicinity of Ketemarae, a bush settlement where the track branched off to pass round the northern rim of Mount Egmont, disclosed a food-growing area protected by strong pa. Further scouting revealed that the Maori meant to make a stand at Otapawa, about five miles from camp.

As soon as the energetic commander had the necessary information, he wanted action. At 2.30 a.m. the next day a force of 600 followed, as silently as possible, a good bullock track for the first two and a half miles. The going then became rough, until a point was reached where the whare of the pa could be seen on the other side of a valley. Chute decided it would be easier to set up his Armstrong battery here than take the guns any farther.

Otapawa was the hardest nut he had to crack in this campaign, for it was said never to have fallen under any previous attack. It must also be remembered that the force at his disposal was only a tenth the size of Cameron's. The pa was well defended with both palisades and trenches, the left front ending in fenced cultivations and the right at a tongue of bush.

The 57th and 14th Regiments shared the attack and rushed towards the defences. The defenders were under better control this time, waiting until the troops were within 40 yards before opening 'a most severe and unusually well directed fire from the whole front of the entrenchment and the bush on its right'.[5]

The cross-fire from the bush was taking its toll, and Lieutenant-Colonel Hassard led some of the 57th to clear it. In doing so he fell mortally wounded, but the Maori were driven out. At the other end of the front, Lieutenant-Colonels Butler and Trevor fought their way into the position through the cultivations. The garrison gave way under the pressure and fled down a steep wooded gully at the rear, where a detachment of the native contingent awaited them.

Casualties were heavier than usual, seven killed and 14 wounded, while Maori losses were put at about 50. Young William McDonnell, who deputised for his injured brother in charge of the native contingent, earned Chute's

William McDonnell. From *Defenders of New Zealand*

The storming of Otapawa Pa, South Taranaki, on 14 January 1866. In the foreground Lieutenant-Colonel Jason Hassard, commanding the 57th (Middlesex) Regiment, is carried from the field mortally wounded. In the middle distance Chute issues orders. A painting by Major G. F. Von Tempsky. *Robert McDougall Art Gallery*

Officers of the 57th (Middlesex) Regiment photographed in Auckland in the late 1860s. *W. Salt*

highest commendation. After carrying out the usual total destruction of the enemy position and crops, the general turned his attention to Ketemarae.

The force started out at 4.15 a.m. on 15 January. Although this settlement and others nearby had been fortified, all were deserted after the reverse at Otapawa. The Forest Rangers and native contingent scoured the bush in the neighbourhood, finding and scattering small parties of Hauhau. Resistance had been expected at the strong pa of Puketi, but Butler's column found this too had been abandoned.

Cameron had clung to the coast when he came this way. Chute, bold as ever, meant to march through the forest clothing the foothills of the great volcanic cone of Egmont to prove once and for all to the enemy that they would find no sanctuary in these fastnesses. It was an ambitious venture, destined to have its share of anxious moments.

At 4 a.m. on 17 January 1866 a force of 400 men left Ketemarae for Mataitawa. Having been in the country only a few months and lacking adequate information about the task before him, Chute perhaps under-estimated its magnitude. The track had for some years been used only by the dissidents, and all he could find out about it was that Maori claimed to be able to do the journey easily in two days but that British soldiers would need three.

At first all went well, the troops marching along a good dray road through a village and cultivations, from which the few occupants soon disappeared. Then Chute's luck ran out. Instead of the three-day march he had been led to expect, he discovered that

> To accomplish a distance of about fifty four miles the force was eight days actually on the move, and never less than ten hours in any one day. I thus found that I had been quite misinformed as to the length and nature of the track, which had even been represented to me as practicable for pack horses, except in two or three places where slight improvement would be required. So far from this being the case, there were no less than twenty one rivers and ninety gullies, the precipitous banks of many of which presented formidable obstructions to our advance, and re-quired great labour to make them passable: and except for about two miles after entering the forest, working parties in advance were constantly employed in cutting down trees, supplejacks, &c, to admit of the passage of the pack-animals. In addition to these obstructions, the weather, which had been fine for the first three days, changed to continuous rain, which increased our difficulties in cros-sing the gullies and necessitated the construction of corduroy road over swamps, which might otherwise have been practicable.[6]

Right: British troops crossing the Tangahoe River, 1865. This painting by Lieutenant-Colonel E. A. Williams illustrates the difficulties of Chute's advance. *Alexander Turnbull Library*

Quite apart from the discomfort it caused, the high rainfall here fostered a moss-hung, entangling jungle in which the clinging lawyer vine was plentiful. These troubles soon gave way to one even more serious. Believing what he had been told, the general had brought rations for only three days, and to compound the difficulty the native contingent had left part of theirs behind.

By the evening of 19 January, Chute began to have serious doubts about his position and ordered the rations to be halved, an added hardship when the men were having to exert so much energy to push their way through the bush. Chute lost patience with Pehimana, the reputed guide. Men were sent up trees to take compass bearings on the peak of Mount Egmont, which could not be seen from the ground.

Next day Captain Leach and Ensign McDonnell were sent on ahead with a detachment from the native contingent to make sure of the route and, if possible, to bring back food. By the following evening, having heard nothing from the scouts, Chute had to call a halt after moving on only six miles all day. Both the troops and the pack animals were worn out by their exertions.

On 22 January the force rested in 'a sea of mud and water', by now eating horseflesh and the little biscuit still available. Anyone as restless as Von Tempsky could not bear to sit idle all day, so he left to explore and to his delight met William McDonnell on his way back. The latter brought the glad news that the advance party had reached Mataitawa and that Leach was following with men of the 43rd and 68th Regiments carrying the much-needed supplies.

Right: Bullock drays crossing a river below Mount Egmont. Often flooded by continuous rain, every river presented an obstacle. A painting by Lieutenant-Colonel E. A. Williams. *Alexander Turnbull Library*

After another very wet night the force marched — if their laboured progress could be so described — at 7 a.m. Conditions were every bit as bad as before, but now they at least knew that Mataitawa was no more than 20 miles distant,

and Colonel Warre had laid on food for the rest of the journey.

It was not until 10.30 a.m. on 25 January that the bedraggled troops emerged from the forest trek they would never forget into the bright sunshine of the Mataitawa Valley. Their relieved commander allowed a halt so that everyone could dry out sodden clothes and kit, which were soon spread over the ground in every direction. That afternoon the soldiers moved on to camp at Wawaikaihi, about three miles from New Plymouth.

'Queen Victoria' (Takiora) of the Nukumaru tribe. This woman warrior fought for the Government, and guided Generals Cameron and Chute during their West Coast campaigns. She was said to be the first to enter Weraroa Pa.
Alexander Turnbull Library

The 26 January was a day of rejoicing in New Plymouth. When the extent of General Chute's successes were known, it was determined that he should have a public reception. A triumphal arch twenty feet high was erected on the Hautoki bridge; an address drawn up, and a most substantial dinner sent out to the whole force.[7]

That same afternoon, while these preparations were in train, the tireless Chute embarked 100 men of the 43rd Regiment in the S.S. *Ahuriri* to reconnoitre the estuary of the Mokau, since Warre reported that hostile Maori had been seen at nearby White Cliffs. This river was the traditional highway for the Waikato tribes to come south to Taranaki whenever fighting was in prospect. By the time the detachment arrived, the weather had deteriorated again, and as the few whare along the banks appeared deserted the ship returned to port without incident.

Next day the hero of the hour marched at the head of his troops to the town, halting at the ceremonial arch. There he was received by the Superintendent of Taranaki, who read an address of welcome and thanked the force for its exploits during the past eventful month. In his reply the general looked forward to 'the establishment of a permanent peace, to be attended by the uninterrupted prosperity of this province'.[8] Once again this hope, like others before it, would prove to be too optimistic.

Chute seemed determined to provide as complete a contrast to Cameron as he could. Despite the punishing march his men had endured since leaving Wanganui, they were given no rest, marching out of New Plymouth that afternoon to reach Oakura in the evening. The day of 28 January, like the one before, took the force past sites which had seen conflict for the last 20 years, and after crossing the oft-disputed Tataraimaka block the men camped at the Stony River.

Still unopposed, the column continued to Warea, but now came news of Maori not far ahead. They were reported to be at Waikoko, and Chute moved on to Tipoka near Cape Egmont, a post held by the Taranaki Military Settlers under Captain J. G. Corbett. This time he hoped to block any Hauhau retreat into the bush, sending Corbett and Captain Livesay off on flanking movements.

Captain John Glasfurd Corbett. From *Defenders of New Zealand*

The main body of troops left at 3 a.m. on 1 February, and after following a bush track for about six miles they emerged into a large clearing to see Waikoko before them. A frontal assault was ordered, with the 14th Regiment on the right, the 43rd on the left and the Forest Rangers taking the centre. The defenders quickly gave way, but on reaching the shelter of the bush resumed the action until they were once again driven off. The attack had been made before Corbett and Livesay were in position to close the trap, the known Maori loss being four killed. The British suffered only one fatal casualty. The whare and crops were destroyed to push the Hauhau farther back from settled areas.

Dr Featherston went on ahead, and by 2 February Chute reached Opunake, where he was disturbed to find Te Ua and some of his supporters, still under arms, living near the redoubt. The prophet was put under arrest and sent to Sir George Grey at Wellington. The latter, subtle as ever, persuaded Te Ua to accompany him on a tour of the troubled areas, with the result that the nationalist leader was discredited in the eyes of his own people. His followers at Opunake were disarmed and required to take an oath of allegiance.

Apart from small-scale punitive raids on villages by detachments from his force, Chute's fighting was over, and the band of the 18th Regiment greeted

Major T. J. Edwards of the 14th (Buckinghamshire) Regiment, which took a prominent part in Chute's campaign. The major wears the dark blue patrol jacket braided with black typically adopted by British officers in the field. *National Museum*

Far right: Colonel Robert Carey, 1821–83, was an officer who had seen much service in India. He arrived in New Zealand in 1860, and served as Deputy Adjutant-General during Chute's Taranaki Campaign. *Alexander Turnbull Library*

Colonial Defence Force Cavalry on parade at Wanganui, 1866. The York Stockade stands on the hill in the background. *Wanganui Museum*

his arrival at Patea with 'See the Conquering Hero Comes'. By 7 a.m. on 9 February the general was back at Wanganui, after a lightning campaign which had vindicated the effectiveness of his troops and earned him a knighthood.

Wellington was *en fête* for his arrival, and at a banquet Grey claimed:

> I say that we should acknowledge not only that General Chute has restored peace and tranquillity to a previously most dangerous district, but that he has given us an example which must be of the greatest possible use to ourselves, and those who are to follow us. I say that he has gained us the respect of our friends and the fear of our enemies.[9]

The Government was later to find that this acclaimed champion shared Cameron's belief that Imperial troops were being put at risk for land-grabbing under the doubtful cover of protecting the settlers. He insisted upon the departure of the regiments according to plan, and refused to allow operational control of those remaining to pass into local hands while awaiting transport.

General Chute. From
Defenders of New Zealand

Officers of the 18th (Royal Irish) Regiment at Fort Britomart, Auckland, 1863. *Hawke's Bay Art Gallery and Museum*

Soldiers of the 18th (Royal Irish) Regiment at Fort Britomart, Auckland, 1863. This photograph shows men wearing full dress with red jackets and shakos, and walking-out dress with red shell jackets. *Hawke's Bay Art Gallery and Museum*

CHAPTER 19

BRITISH REGIMENTS AND CORPS IN NEW ZEALAND DURING THE WARS OF 1845–47 AND 1860–70

12th (East Suffolk) Regiment of Foot (nicknamed 'The Old Dozen'),
C.O. Lieutenant-Colonel H. M. Hamilton
The regiment arrived in Sydney, Australia in 1854, and served in New Zealand from 1860 to 1866. It was engaged in the first Taranaki war, being present at the fight at No. 2 Redoubt. The 12th was in action throughout the Waikato War. It sustained losses at Rangiriri and took part in the battle at Gate Pa. The headquarters of the 12th moved to Napier in December 1865 and then on to Tauranga in 1866 where elements of the regiment took part in the Tauranga Bush Campaign. The Regiment embarked for England in 1867.

14th (Buckinghamshire) Regiment of Foot ('The Old and Bold'),
C.O.s Lieutenant-Colonels Austen and W. C. Trevor
Arrived in New Zealand from Cork, Ireland, in 1860, and remained until 1867. The regiment was present at the siege of Te Arei, and served thereafter in Taranaki. In 1863 it was transferred to the Waikato and took part in the actions at Koheroa and Rangiriri. Detachments fought at Gate Pa. The regiment was later stationed at Napier and Wanganui, and formed part of Chute's force in his Wanganui campaign.

18th (Royal Irish) Regiment of Foot ('Paddy's Blackguards'), C.O.s
Lieutenant-Colonels A. A. Chapman and G. A. Elliot
Came to New Zealand from Portsmouth, England in 1863, and on leaving in 1870 was the last Imperial regiment to be withdrawn from the country. After serving in the Waikato campaign, it went to Wanganui, being present at the actions of Nukumaru and Weraroa. It joined in General Chute's march of 1866, and was later stationed in a number of garrisons until its final departure.

40th (Somersetshire) Regiment of Foot ('The Excellers', from the
Roman numeral XL), C.O. Lieutenant-Colonel A. Leslie
Transferred from Australia to New Zealand in 1860 and served until 1866. The Excellers suffered severe losses at Puketakauere Pa in Taranaki, and were present at Huirangi and Te Arei. During the Waikato war the regiment fought in the actions at Rangiriri and Orakau. It remained as a garrison in the Waikato after the fighting ended, and returned to England in 1866.

43rd (Monmouthshire) Light Infantry ('Wolfe's Own'), C.O.s
Lieutenant-Colonels H. J. Booth and F. H. Synge
This regiment sailed from Calcutta, India, in 1863, and served in New Zealand in the Waikato, at Gate Pa, Te Ranga and later in Taranaki. In March 1866 it embarked for England after 15 years of foreign service.

50th (Queen's Own) Regiment of Foot ('Dirty Half-Hundred'), C.O.s
Lieutenant-Colonels N. Wodehouse, H. E. Weare, R. Waddy
Arrived in New Zealand from Ceylon in 1863 and served until 1866, when it departed for Sydney. The regiment took part in the Waikato campaign, being

present at the Battle of Hairini. In 1864, on being sent to Wanganui, the 50th fought at Nukumaru and later in Chute's march.

57th (West Middlesex) Regiment of Foot ('The Die Hards'), C.O.s Lieutenant-Colonels H. J. Warre and R. A. Logan

Like many of their comrades, these troops had served in India, coming to New Zealand from Madras in 1860. The regiment served at Te Arei in the first Taranaki war, and remained as the garrison on the west coast of the North Island. The regiment fought at Katikara and Poutoko in the second Taranaki war, and during Chute's expedition sustained heavy casualties at the Battle of Otapawa. It remained in South Taranaki and the Waikato until 1866.

58th (Rutlandshire) Regiment of Foot ('The Black Cuffs'), C.O. Lieutenant-Colonels E. B. and R. H. Wynyard, also C. Bridge

This regiment was an early arrival in New Zealand, coming from Sydney in 1845 to take part in the actions at Okaihau, Ohaeawai and Ruapekapeka. It went south for the Wellington and Wanganui disturbances, being engaged at Boulcott's Farm, Horokiri and St John's Wood. During a long period of garrison duty in Wanganui, it built the Rutland Stockade before sailing from New Zealand in 1858.

65th (Yorkshire North Riding) Regiment of Foot ('The Royal Tigers'), C.O.s C. E. Gold and A. F. W. Wyatt

Arrived in Wellington from Australia in 1846, and stayed until 1865, so achieving the longest period of service in New Zealand — nearly 20 years. Active in Wellington and Wanganui in 1846–47, the regiment distinguished itself in the Taranaki and Waikato campaigns from 1860 to 1866. The Maori called the regiment the 'Hikety Pips' (65th), and greatly respected the men.

Soldiers of the Light Company, 65th (Yorkshire North Riding) Regiment. From left to right: Bugler Austin, Company Sergeant-Major William Acheson, Private Tobin, Lance-Corporal Lennox, Sergeants Feltham and Russell. *Alexander Turnbull Library*

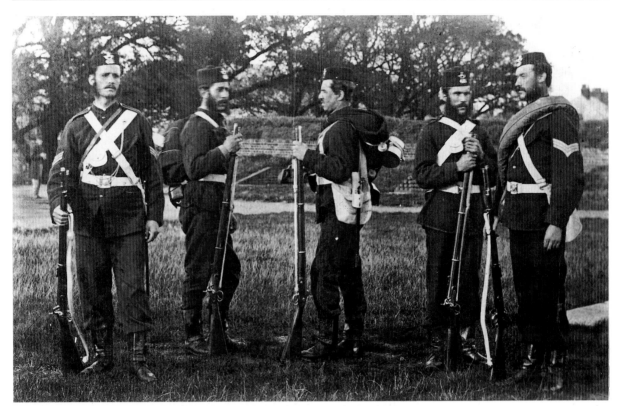

68th (Durham) Light Infantry ('The Faithful Durhams'), C.O.s Lieutenant-Colonels H. H. Greer and Morant

One of the last to be brought to New Zealand, this regiment was drawn from Burma in 1864. Its involvement in the Waikato war included the engagements at Gate Pa and Te Ranga. Later the 68th went to Taranaki for Chute's march around Mount Egmont, and was stationed in the Wanganui area until it returned to England in 1866.

70th (Surrey) Regiment of Foot ('The Glasgow Greys'), C.O.s Lieutenant-Colonels T. Chute, T. J. Galloway and T. E. Mulock

Reached New Zealand in 1863 in time to take part in the fight at Katikara, Taranaki. On moving north, the regiment saw action at Koheroa, Cameron Town and Orakau before returning to Taranaki. There the 70th was at Kaitake and in Chute's Taranaki campaign. When it returned to England in 1866, the regiment had been on foreign service for 17 years in India and New Zealand.

80th (Staffordshire Volunteers) Regiment of Foot ('The Staffordshire Knots'), C.O. Major T. Bunbury

A detachment of this regiment was stationed at the Bay of Islands from 1840 to 1845, under the command of Major Bunbury. It took no part in the campaigns of 1845–46, having returned to Australia prior to the outbreak of hostilities.

96th Regiment of Foot ('The Bendovers') C.O. Lieutenant-Colonel W. Hulme

The Grenadier Company of the 96th went to Wellington in 1841, and other detachments arrived in 1843 and 1844. By 1845 the whole regiment had been moved from Hobart, and took part in the action at Kororareka. It was present at Puketutu during the war in the north, after which a detachment was transferred to Wellington in time for the operations in the Hutt Valley. In 1847 the regiment was sent back to Tasmania.

99th (Lanarkshire Volunteers) Regiment of Foot ('The Queen's Pets'), C.O. Lieutenant-Colonel H. Despard
Detachments of the regiment reached New Zealand in 1845, and took part in the Battle of Ohaeawai and the capture of Ruapekapeka Pa. In common with the 96th, it went on to Wellington for service in the Hutt Valley and at Horokiwi. In 1847 the regiment returned to Sydney.

Royal Artillery C.O.s Captains Henderson, Watson, Mercer, Strover, Barstow and Williams
No. 2 Company, 6 Battalion served in New Zealand during 1845–47. After the early actions, the remaining detachment was absorbed into 7 Battalion in 1858. The Artillery force was stationed at Auckland, Wanganui, New Plymouth and Napier. In 1861 it was strengthened by C Battery, 4 Brigade and new equipment. The Gunners served in Taranaki, Waikato and at Tauranga, being present at all the sieges in 1860–66. The last detachments were withdrawn in 1870.

Royal Corps of Sappers and Miners
This corps consisted of non-commissioned officers and privates only. A strong detachment arrived in Australia in 1835. During the period 1845 to 1847 the men of the corps were responsible for road making and sapping in several sieges. In 1857 the NCOs and other ranks merged with the existing Corps of Royal Engineers (who before that date consisted of officers only) to become the Royal Engineers.

Royal Engineers C.O.s Lieutenant-Colonel Bolton, Captain Collinson, Lieutenant Lugard
Detachments of the ubiquitous Royal Engineers served in New Zealand during the period 1860–70. They took part in many sieges and built roads, bridges and blockhouses. Their use of the field telegraph to link posts in the Waikato and Taranaki is one of the earliest recorded on campaign.

Army Medical Department
Regimental surgeons and colonial service surgeons were attached to all army units during 1860–66. They established military hospitals throughout New Zealand.

Army Hospital Corps
Detachments of the Army Hospital Corps reached Auckland in 1861. Military hospitals were established in Auckland, New Plymouth, Napier and Wanganui. This was the first campaign in which the British Army discontinued the regimental hospital system in favour of general care. The last of the Corps left New Zealand in 1870.

Commissariat Staff Corps
Sections of the Commissariat Corps served in New Zealand between 1861 and 1870. These were responsible for the supply of food, forage and fuel to the British Army. Commissary-generals officially ranked as brigadier-generals, and commissary clerks as ensigns.

Military Train and Horse Transport Corps
The military train was established in 1856 because of lessons learnt in the chaotic Crimean campaign. Detachments served in New Zealand during the period 1861–66. The 4th Battalion of the Military Train arrived in Auckland in 1864, and remained until 1867. It served both as cavalry and in a transport

and supply capacity, as in the Indian Mutiny.

Royal Marines

The Marines have a long association with New Zealand. They first landed in 1769 with Captain Cook. In 1845 detachments took part in the war in the north, being present at the burning of Otuihu Pa and the battles at Puketutu, Ohaeawai and Ruapekapeka. Moving south, they assisted in operations at Porirua in 1846. Detachments were next in action during the first Taranaki war in 1860 at the Battle of Waireka, and in the Waikato campaign of 1864 they were in the hard-fought engagement at Rangiriri. Marines from Sir William Wiseman's squadron formed part of the attacking force at Gate Pa.

Naval Brigade

Like the Royal Marines, sailors went into action on land both in 1845–46 and 1860–64, often combining with the Marines to form a naval brigade, or serving as artillerymen ashore. Seamen were present at Kororareka, Puketutu, Ohaeawai and Ruapekapeka during the war in the north. They took part in the kidnapping of Te Rauparaha. During the 1860s sailors served in Taranaki, Waikato and Tauranga, the major engagements being at Waireka (1860), Rangiriri (1863) and Gate Pa (1864).

Far left: Captain Smith, Royal Artillery, 1864. *Hawke's Bay Art Gallery and Museum*

Corporal Goddard, of the 43rd (Monmouthshire) Light Infantry, in blue campaign uniform. He died of wounds at New Plymouth in 1866. *Alexander Turnbull Library*

A square formed by men of the 18th (Royal Irish) Regiment. The photograph, which shows the men in campaign dress, was taken at the Napier Barracks, 1866. *Hawke's Bay Art Gallery and Museum*

No. 5 Division of the New Zealand Armed Constabulary on parade at Wellington. *Alexander Turnbull Library*

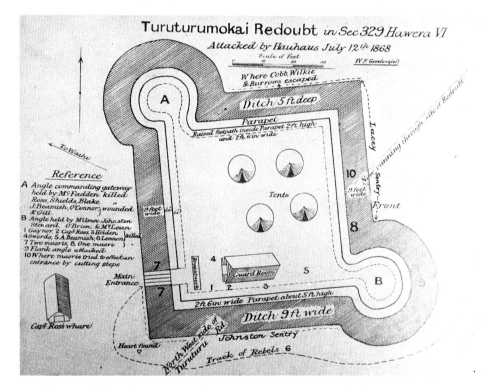

Turuturumokai Redoubt *in Sec 329 Hawera VI*

Attacked by Hauhaus July 12th 1868

Scale of Feet

W.F. Gordan (del)

Where Cobb, Wilkie & Burrows escaped

Ditch 5 ft deep

Parapet

Raised footpath inside Parapet 2ft high and 2ft 6in wide

A

To Waihi

Reference

A *Angle commanding gateway held by McFadden killed Ross, Shields, Blake, J. Beamish, O'Connor, wounded & Gill.*
B *Angle held by Milmoe, Johnston Stewart, O'Brien, & McLean*
1 *Gaynor, 2 Capt Ross 3 Holden 4 Swords, 5 A Beamish, 6 Lennon 7 Two maoris, 8, One maori 9 Flank angle attacked 10 Where maoris tried to effect an entrance by cutting steps.*

Main Entrance

Capt Ross whare

Tents

10

9 feet wide

Front

Lacey Sentry

Now running through site of Redoubt

8

Guard Room

Breastwork

5

B

2ft 6in wide Parapet about 5 ft high

Ditch 9 ft wide

Heart found

North West side of Turuturu Rd

Johnston Sentry

Track of Rebels 6

A plan of Turuturumokai Redoubt. *Taranaki Museum*

The Turuturumokai Redoubt at Hawera, Taranaki, attacked by Titokowaru's warriors on 12 July 1868. *Illustrated London News*

CHAPTER 20

NEW ZEALAND ARMED CONSTABULARY IN THE FIELD

For all Grey's calculated gamble in declaring the war at an end two years before and the sailing of the regiments for other climes, the continued unrest made it only too obvious that some permanent force was essential to replace the mish-mash of volunteer units. Not only was professional discipline badly needed, but settlers who had more than enough to do in trying to wrest a living from the wilderness also grudged the time for drills — not to mention turnouts for alarms that might take them away and leave their families unprotected.

To meet the need, Parliament passed a Bill late in 1867 creating the New Zealand Armed Constabulary. This was the country's first national Army in all but name, and was embodied in the following year. McDonnell put recruiting in hand and Von Tempsky and Roberts took charge of No. 5 Division, of about the same strength as their former Forest Ranger company, and though Jackson preferred to remain on the farm at Rangiaowhia, veterans flocked to enlist. Officers were given police ranks, a practice they disliked, and were often known by Army titles. The most senior of the new designations was inspector, the equivalent of major, so McDonnell remained a lieutenant-colonel in the New Zealand Militia.

By this time the gap left by Te Ua in Taranaki was being filled by another leader, Titokowaru, who had fought in one of the earliest Hauhau battles at Sentry Hill. Without question he was to prove one of the most able generals the Maori cause produced, but at the beginning he felt his way with care, preaching resistance in the villages and causing the murder of isolated civilians and an ambush of a small military convoy. His teaching went beyond the Pai Marire code, permitting ritualistic cannibalism.

Captain George Ross. From
Defenders of New Zealand

The Armed Constabulary occupied the Waihi Redoubt, and because it was not safe for men to stay on their farms after dark, settlers would spend the night at Turuturumokai, a strongpoint of the 18th Regiment two years before. Since then it had been neglected, so Captain George Ross was sent with 25 Armed Constabulary to put the defences in order.

The work went ahead at a slow pace, observed by Maori who came selling food and fraternising in an apparently friendly fashion. The place was poorly sited for defence, being commanded by higher ground nearby. By 11 July 1868, when the parapet was still only breast high, Titokowaru decided that the time was ripe to strike.

He sent a war party to make a surprise attack at dawn on Sunday, 12 July, and certainly took the garrison unawares. Sentries were outside the defences because the ground there was less muddy than inside. The guard had not been called for the usual stand-to at 3 a.m., and the sleeping men were aroused by the sound of firing to fight for their lives.[1]

McDonnell was away from Waihi where the dawn parade was in progress when the flashes of the shooting could be seen at a distance of four miles.

Major William Hunter.
From *Defenders of New Zealand*

Von Tempsky, in command, ordered Major William Hunter and his cavalry to hold the redoubt while the infantry set out to the rescue. When Hunter passed on the order to his men to stand down, they could hardly believe their ears. Some were abusive, and the troop sergeant accused Hunter of cowardice in not leading a relief of Turuturumokai.

The effect of Von Tempsky's order was that the ordeal of Turuturumokai's garrison was dragged out much longer than it need have been. Two men bolted while they had the chance and met the oncoming relief force. Ross and Lennon, the canteen keeper, were killed and their hearts cut out. By the time the panting Constabulary hurried over the last stages of their journey, the Maori drew off, leaving 10 of the garrison dead.

At the subsequent enquiry, Von Tempsky maintained that his small detachment of cavalry would have been useless if, as could reasonably have been expected, the Hauhau were in possession of the defences. There were those however, who said that he wanted to claim the credit himself, and so had been led into an error of judgement.

On his return from Manawapou, McDonnell was much upset by the losses at Turuturumokai, and was impatient to seek retribution. He had to wait for more than a month while additional troops were recruited in Wellington to reinforce him, and when they at last arrived they knew nothing of the bush in which they would have to fight.

McDonnell meant them to learn their bushcraft while on operations from the seasoned constabulary which included former Forest Rangers. After the destruction of Pungarehu, Titokowaru chose for his headquarters Te Ngutu-o-te-Manu (the Bird's Beak), a village in the dense forest.

At 5.30 a.m. on 21 August the force set out for Te Ngutu. The heavy morning mist gave way to a downpour, and the Waingongoro River was already running high as the men crossed to follow a narrow track along which they had to move in single file. At Pungarehu rifle pits lined the edge of the track, and at Te Manu te Whenua a stockade barred the crossing of a creek. Luckily none of these defences was occupied, and eventually McDonnell got his force in position. After sending Von Tempsky round to the left flank, he threw Hunter's division in a frontal attack.

The troops rushed the defences amid cheers, and after a sharp skirmish the Hauhau fled into the bush. A search of the whare yielded gunpowder and arms, which were seized or destroyed, and the huts were set on fire. While Von Tempsky was sent off with the wounded, McDonnell took charge of the destruction of the large meeting house in which Titokowaru had preached death to the pakeha.

The Maori rallied and were joined by others to harry the rearguard under Hunter on its way back. When they reached the river it was in flood. A rope was carried across, and the men made the best of getting over, either clinging to the line or to the swimming horses.

McDonnell had lost four killed, but felt a good start had been made in recovering the position after Turuturumokai:

> We reached Waihi about 6 p.m., and drenched and tired as the men were, they gave three cheers that were refreshing to hear. . . . All the fine qualities of the tried veteran were displayed by a body of men hurriedly brought together and unaccustomed to work together, three fourths of them had never been under fire, but the manner in which they crept along the bush track, and then with a cheer, which those who heard it can never forget, rushed on the formidable position on their front shows me that I have men under me on whom I can rely at all times and men whom I am proud to command.[2]

Far right:
Lieutenant-Colonel Thomas McDonnell, New Zealand Militia, who commanded the Patea Field Force at Te Ngutu-o-te-Manu. *Alexander Turnbull Library*

Major (Inspector) G. F. Von Tempsky, 1828–68, New Zealand Armed Constabulary, killed at Te Ngutu-o-te-Manu on 7 September 1868. A painting by J. McDonald. *National Museum*

Captain William McDonnell, brother of Thomas McDonnell. *Alexander Turnbull Library*

The Waihi Redoubt at Hawera, Taranaki, Lieutenant-Colonel McDonnell's headquarters at the time of the attack on Te Ngutu-o-te-Manu. *Alexander Turnbull Library*

The battle in the bush at Te
Ngutu-o-te-Manu. A
painting by J. McDonald.
Taranaki Museum

These lofty sentiments were to be all too short-lived. When Kepa te Rangihi-winui brought a native contingent of 110 men from Wanganui, McDonnell decided to try to trap his adversary at Ruaruru, not far from Te Ngutu, which was supposed to be his present refuge.

When the force left Waihi soon after midnight on 7 September the prospects seemed a good deal more favourable than those of the previous expedition. Kepa was always totally reliable, and his men could make up for the inexperience of the Wellington recruits in the bush. The weather was dry and clear, and by following a circuitous route surprise might be achieved.

The route was really the source of McDonnell's troubles. Progress was so slow that nothing had been seen of the enemy until well into the following afternoon, when the men were tired after their long trek. One of Kepa's kupapa climbed a tree and saw smoke about half a mile ahead. He also reported hearing a haka in progress.

It seemed clear to Kepa that more intelligence was needed, and he suggested to the colonel that the force should remain where it was. During the night the native contingent would spy out the land, and the rested men could make a properly planned attack next morning.

Kepa urged an attack next morning, but McDonnell rejected this sensible advice. Kepa was sent on ahead, and when he reached an enemy outpost the firing disposed of any chance to surprise the village. There was nothing for it but to follow the track, and Kepa found that this had brought them not to Ruaruru but to Te Ngutu-o-te-Manu once again.

Titokowaru had decided that his warriors would be more effectively used by placing most of them in ambush outside the palisade. While Kepa came to the front of the position, Von Tempsky led an encircling movement with his European troops through the forest and across the Mangotahi creek. They came under intense fire from the Maori, well hidden in the bush, and men quickly began to fall, particularly the recently enlisted Wellington Rangers and Wellington Rifles who, tending to bunch together for support, simply presented far better targets than the veterans in extended order.

Kepa and Von Tempsky both wanted to storm the village, but McDonnell hesitated. Eighty of his force, which he had praised so warmly only a few weeks before, took to their heels, and on reaching camp spread the wild story that the force had been wiped out. With these deserters, and men falling fast, the colonel decided to withdraw while he still had the troops fit to carry out the wounded.

Kepa was to supply the rearguard, and William McDonnell was sent to order Von Tempsky to fall back with the Europeans. William carried out his errand, but shortly afterwards 'Von' was shot in the forehead and died instantly. McDonnell then instructed Lieutenant Hastings, who referred him to his senior, Captain Buck. Both of these officers were also killed within a short time.

The death of Von Tempsky. A coloured lithograph by W. Watkins. *Taranaki Museum*

Gustavus Ferdinand Von Tempsky. From *Defenders of New Zealand*

Responsibility for the retreat fell upon John Roberts:

> I got together all the men I could find and disposed them as well as I could to resist the Hauhaus, who were pressing us hard, yelling 'Surround them, surround them!' in Maori. I formed the men into a rough half moon front, and instructed them to fire volleys:
> 'Blaze away as hard as you can, boys, blaze away!' We fired a number of volleys, and this had some effect on the Hauhaus, who kept a greater distance after that. By this time it was getting quite dusk in the bush, under the close, dense treetops. I came to the conclusion that I had better try to make my way out to camp with the wounded.[3]

McDonnell believed that Von Tempsky's division was following with sufficient officers; in fact, the Hauhau had got between Roberts and himself, and the main body came under heavier pressure. McDonnell sent his brother to hold a gorge leading to Te Manu te Whenua, where an ambush might be laid, and finally reached Waihi at 10 p.m. Then to his dismay a roll call revealed that a large number of men were missing, and it was useless to search for them before daylight.

Captain John Roberts. From *Defenders of New Zealand*

Below: Captain George Buck (ex-65th Regiment), officer commanding the Wellington Rifles, killed at the Battle of Te Ngutu-o-te-Manu. *National Museum*

Below right: The death of Corporal James Russell, New Zealand Armed Constabulary, at Te Ngutu. A painting by J. McDonald. *Taranaki Museum*

Roberts retired slowly, and one of his best men, Corporal Russell, was so severely wounded that it was hopeless to try to take him back to camp. The doomed man could not use his carbine and sat propped up against a tree. A big warrior rushed up with his tomahawk for the kill, whereupon Russell drew a revolver from his coat and shot him dead. The Maori later said that after this experience they held back and made certain that the corporal was killed before they approached him again.

The dead had to be left where they lay, but most of the wounded could walk, with some help. Now and again the troops would have to pause to fire at the enemy dogging their footsteps, and as night fell they were so exhausted that Roberts had to call a halt:

We were still within cooee of the pa, in fact we could hear the Hauhau yells and war songs all night.[4]

The captain knew he could find his way out of the bush by compass, but meant to hold this possibility in reserve. Among the friendly Maori under his command was a chief, Pehira Turei, who claimed to know the way. Roberts kept this man and his friends nearby during the weary hours of waiting and he posted a sentry to be sure that they did not slip away in the darkness.

About two o'clock in the morning the moon rose above the treetops, and Roberts could check his direction for Waihi. His guide led the way, followed by a guard with orders to shoot at any sign of treachery. The Hauhau had

Tutange Waionui, of the Ngati Ruanui tribe of Patea, one of several warriors said to have killed Von Tempsky. *National Museum*

given up the chase, but progress was agonisingly slow, with one-third of the men wounded and the rest covered with blood from helping them:

> When we started our retreat we were well in on the Egmont or inland side of McDonnell's route. By about daylight we got out on the track leading down to the Waingongoro River ford, the track we had come in the morning, and we reached our base camp, the Waihi Redoubt, about eight o'clock.[5]

A search party led by Kepa was on the point of leaving to find them, and both the men he led to safety and McDonnell owed much to the cool courage of this young man of 27.

McDonnell, after Pokaikai, was no favourite in Government circles, though his friend Dr Featherston hastened to console him:

> You will remember that I strongly urged you not to take the command of such a force (if force it could be called). . . . You however felt your honour was involved, and accepted the command of the veriest and most cowardly rabble that could possibly be collected at a moment's notice at the different seaports of the Colony.
>
> You are no sooner said to have some 800 men under your command than you are goaded by Ministers and people to immediate active operations. You and all your other brave and intelligent officers, knowing full well that you could not depend on your men standing the first volley of the enemy, yet led this rabble into action, and the result is just what every officer must have contemplated — the skedaddling of the men and butchering of the officers.[6]

Volunteers surprised by Maori at Te Ngutu-o-te-Manu. This engraving, from the *Illustrated New Zealand Herald,* gives the impression of a victory rather than a defeat. *Alexander Turnbull Library*

Colonel Theodore M. Haultain, 1817–1902, served in India and Afghanistan. In 1849 he came to New Zealand in command of the Fencibles. He later commanded the Auckland Militia and all four Waikato Regiments. He was Defence Minister in 1865, and personally conducted the Whakamarama Campaign of 1869. From *Defenders of New Zealand*

Allowance must be made for Featherston's personal bias against local troops, and the fact that he urged the return of British regiments, but McDonnell also changed his tune in seeking an excuse for his failure; his gallant recruits from Wellington were now 'drunken useless vagabonds'.

Whitmore offered his services to the Defence Minister, Colonel T. M. Haultain, stating his willingness to come under McDonnell's command even though the latter was junior to him. Accounts reaching Haultain of conditions at Waihi were so disturbing that he went to see things for himself.

On 13 September, when the troops fell in for the daylight parades, Major Hunter told Constable Keenan to take the pipe out of his mouth. He refused, and upon being placed under arrest flung his carbine on the ground. Later Constable Maunders led his comrades to demand the release of the prisoner, and was himself sent to the guardroom.

These men belonged to No. 5 Division, which the late Von Tempsky had trained with great care, and which had provided the backbone of Roberts's force in the retreat. Haultain did not wish to lose such valuable material if he could help it, and paraded the division to hear their complaints.

He found the men 'determined at any cost to get away from Patea and to return to Waikato. . . . I found the spirit of insubordination so strong that I ordered the Division to be immediately marched back to Patea.'[7] This did not help matters, since the constabulary claimed that being withdrawn from the front amounted to an indirect charge of cowardice.

At Patea Haultain addressed another parade, assuring the men that no reflection on their courage was intended. Sergeant McMinn thereupon produced a letter stating bluntly that he and his comrades would not in future take the field under McDonnell, whom they blamed for Von Tempsky's death. The Defence Minister would have none of this latest act of defiance, and told those who were prepared to accept orders to step forward. Only one did so, Sergeant Anderson. The division was disbanded, and none of the men received the New Zealand War Medal. Nor were they allowed to rejoin if they wished. Keenan and Maunders were sent to prison.

McDonnell went to Weraroa to enlist 400 kupapa for a new native contingent. He wrote to the Defence Minister, as usual in somewhat ambiguous terms, and though he did not intend his letter to be one of resignation, Haultain was not slow to accept it in this light.

Whitmore was promoted to full colonel and sent to take charge. His opinion of the troops he found had much in common with Dr Featherston's:

> With the exception of the Armed Constabulary, two thirds of the Europeans on pay here are utterly useless for any purpose whatsoever, and it is simply a waste of money to keep them on pay. I allude to the bulk of the temporary corps (Patea Rifle Volunteers and European Contingent), who are not only of no use to themselves, but give endless trouble to others, and require many otherwise available men to guard them in confinement, or tend them in hospital.[8]

The new commander resolved to rid himself of these amateurs and to rely in future on the Armed Constabulary and Kepa's native contingent. Captain Roberts went to Auckland to recruit No. 6 Division to replace No. 5, and at the same time had the melancholy task of handing the late Von Tempsky's effects to his widow.

NEW ZEALAND ARMED CONSTABULARY FIELD FORCE

New Zealand Armed
Constabulary Badge
1867–1881

The North-West Mounted Police of Canada is perhaps the nearest equivalent of the Field Force of 1867–86, but the New Zealand Armed Constabulary saw infinitely more fighting.

In 1886 the Hon. Edward W. Stafford, Premier of New Zealand, initiated the Self Reliant policy, and from that year the Government relied mainly on its own troops, with the exception of Chute's Taranaki Campaign. In 1867, when it became clear that the most severe fighting was over, the Colonial Defence Force was disbanded on 22 October. In its place an Act of Parliament created the Armed Constabulary.

The force was formed to replace the existing unsatisfactory method of defending settlements from hostile Maori by small volunteer and Militia units. These were being continually raised and then disbanded, and their discipline was often questionable. The new force, under a commandant (equivalent to a lieutenant-colonel in the Militia), combined military and police functions in a paramilitary manner, and replaced the Imperial formations which were being withdrawn or assigned to garrison duties. At its peak during wartime there were nine divisions of Armed Constabulary (including two Maori), each of 60 to 100 men.

Early in 1866 the new force first saw action in a punitive expedition up the Waimana River in the Bay of Plenty. In May the Constabulary engaged in the campaign against the war chief, Titokowaru, which involved the most ferocious fighting of the Taranaki wars. This chief inflicted a series of disastrous defeats on the Government forces.

In November 1868 the focus shifted to the east coast, where Te Kooti had raided Poverty Bay, inflicting heavy losses. The Field Force took up the pursuit of the new dissident. From 1868 to 1870 the Armed Constabulary saw action in the Bay of Plenty, Taupo, East Coast, Taranaki and Waikato districts of the North Island. One division was stationed on the West Coast goldfields of the South Island (1868), when Fenian rioting broke out amongst the miners.

By 1870, when the wars had lapsed into a guerrilla struggle against Te Kooti's band and its allies, a special unit of Maori friendly to the Crown was raised for action against him. This was the Arawa Flying Column, Armed Constabulary. It consisted of two companies, each of 100 picked Arawa tribesmen, with European officers and mixed Maori and European N.C.O.s For two years they harried the remnant of Te Kooti's warriors, until No. 2 Company fired the last shots of the North Island wars on 14 February 1872.

After the Arawa took over active campaigning, the European portion of the force was engaged on patrol and garrison duties on the borders of pakeha-settled country. Their work included building blockhouses, redoubts, roads and bridges, as well as erecting telegraph lines.

The year after the hostilities ceased, the Field Force numbered 714, consisting of a commissioner, two instructors, 10 inspectors, 21 sub-inspectors, five assistant-surgeons, eight sergeants-major and 601 constables, also depot staff. They were required to patrol and garrison the frontier areas adjoining the King Country, and to man posts all over the central North Island for the next 14 years. Numbers were progressively reduced until the discreditable Parihaka 'crisis' of 1881, when the force was increased to 1,100.

In 1881 all officers of the Field Force were transferred to the Militia list, and the word 'Armed' was dropped from the title. The fear of an invasion by a non-existent Russian naval squadron in 1885 led to the force being employed on the building of harbour defence works at the four main cities. As a result the formation changed its character, with the addition of Artillery, Engineer and Torpedo branches. When the Defence Act of 1886 came into effect, the military and police sections of the Constabulary were finally separated, the former becoming the Permanent Militia and the latter the New Zealand Police. The Armed Constabulary was therefore unique in being the origin of the Police, Army and to some extent the Navy of New Zealand.

An Armed Constabulary drum and fife band, probably at the Pukearuhe Redoubt. *Taranaki Museum*

Constables in campaign dress. The peaked forage cap has the silver A.C. badge, and a blanket in a waterproof cover is worn over the regulation jacket. Brown leather equipment is worn, with an ammunition pouch and Snider sword bayonet at the waist. The kilt (rapaki) is tailored and belted. The firearm is the Short 2-band Snider Rifle. *Taranaki Museum*

This constable in mounted order guards a prisoner. He wears the regulation cap, jacket, Bedford cord breeches and boots. The arms include a Snider carbine, revolver (probably a Tranter) and regulation sword. *Taranaki Museum*

Uniforms of the Armed Constabulary Field Force

The dress regulations were set out in the Manual of Rules and Regulations, so this was one of the very few units to be uniformly dressed. The following description of the clothing of all ranks is taken from the Armed Constabulary Manual of 1870.

Constables The uniform and kit of constables is to consist of a blue cap with peak and a band of black mohair braid 1 inch wide, blue tweed or serge patrol jacket with white metal A.C. buttons, blue tweed or serge trousers, water-tight lace-up boots, brown leather leggings, greatcoat, waterproof sheet, haversack, two blankets, swag straps, two woollen shirts, two pairs woollen socks, two pairs drawers and two undershirts.

Mounted Constables will wear the same uniform in every respect as the foot with the exception of a cavalry cloak instead of the greatcoat: and in addition to the above each mounted man is to have one pair of Bedford-cord breeches, one pair of Napoleon riding boots and hunting spurs.

Non-Commissioned Officers The uniform of N.C.O.s whether mounted or foot is to be precisely the same as that of the constables, with the addition of chevrons on the right arm according to the grade of the wearer; in the case of sergeants-major surmounted by a crown.

Officers Officers of all ranks are to be similarly dressed; their uniform will be as follows:- blue cloth forage cap with stiff peak, and silver oak leaf band 1¾ inches wide, with silver button and tracing lace on top; blue cloth patrol jacket with standing collar, braided with hussar braid and silver shoulder cords; blue cloth single-breasted waistcoat hooking to the throat, with silver beading and silver lace round edges and pockets; blue cloth trousers with black oak leaf mohair braid down the side 1¾ inches wide.

On campaign the Armed Constabulary usually modified their uniforms. The most common adaptation for the guerrilla struggles was called 'shawl dress'. This took the form of a blanket or shawl belted about the waist. The idea was borrowed from the Maori rapaki, or kilt, being worn in the bush for ease of movement and with the added advantage that it could be easily dried over a fire. The rigours of bush fighting, with the constant crossing of rivers and streams and the necessity of tramping through wet undergrowth in mountainous country, was found to be too hard on trousers, which rotted or fell apart in a short time.

The following lists, also taken from the A.C. regulations, detail appointments, weapons and equipment:

Mounted Constabulary Breech-loading carbine, cleaning rod, snap cap and chain, pouch and belt, breech-loading revolver, revolver sheath, revolver ball bag, sword, scabbard steel, sword belt, sword knot, saddle, numna, girths leather, stirrup irons, stirrup leathers, breastplate, wallets, headstall, reins, bits, curb chain and hooks, straps for cloak and wallet, carbine holster, handcuffs and key, regulation book.

Foot Constabulary Snider artillery carbine, cleaning rod, bayonet, scabbard, snap cap and chain, pouch, ball bag, oil bottle, waist belt, bayonet frog, sling, breech-loading revolver, revolver sheath, revolver ball bag, revolver waist belt, handcuffs and key, regulation book, baton and case, bull's-eye lantern.

New Zealand Armed
Constabulary Field Force
uniforms: 1. officer in full
dress; 2. foot constable; 3.
mounted sergeant-major; 4.
officer of the Arawa Flying
Column; 5. foot constable
in campaign dress.
Drawing by F. Turton

Commanding Officers of the Field Force
Lt.-Col. G. S. Whitmore, Commandant 1867–69
Lt.-Col. St John Branigan, Commissioner 1869–71
Lt.-Col. W. Moule, Commissioner 1871–75
Lt.-Col. W. C. Lyon, (Acting) Commissioner 1875
Col. the Hon. G. S. Whitmore, Commissioner 1878–79
Lt. Col. H. E. Reader. Commissioner 1879–85
Maj. W. E. Gudgeon, (Acting) Commissioner 1885
Col. Sir George Whitmore, Commissioner 1885–86
Sir George Whitmore was promoted to Major-General
in 1886.

Men of the New Zealand
Armed Constabulary and
Militia. From left to right:
Sergeant A.C.; Officer A.C.;
Militiaman. *Painting by F.
Turton*

Kepa Te Rangihiwinui
(Major Kemp), N.Z.C., chief
of Putiki, Wanganui. The
archtypal kupapa, he
fought at Moutoa Island in
1864 and at Weraroa,
Pipiriki and Opotiki in
1865. Kepa again took the
field against Titokowaru in
1867–68, and Te Kooti in
1869–70. A courageous
warrior, his unswerving
loyalty to the Government
was rewarded by the sword
of honour he wears,
received from Queen
Victoria. *Alexander
Turnbull Library*

WHITMORE TAKES COMMAND

T he new commander had a considerable advantage over McDonnell in that he was a professional soldier of long experience. While he had done well in the defence of Napier, Whitmore had yet to try conclusions with a Maori of real ability as a leader.

Titokowaru had won all along the line against McDonnell, for even though he had been caught with the defence works along the track at Te Manu te Whenua unmanned, the Maori took such full advantage of the bush to harry the rearguard on the return journey that the main body was forced to rejoin it from time to time to hold off the attacks. The second engagement at Te Ngutu was fought entirely on Titokowaru's terms, providing the greatest disaster to the Government cause since the Gate Pa.

Titokowaru's mana had, of course, risen enormously among the Taranaki tribes from these encounters, and in the weeks that followed he advanced in the direction of Wanganui to a point close to the present town of Waverley. At Moturoa the Maori leader prepared his position to meet the inevitable onslaught.

Whitmore moved his headquarters to Wairoa, as Waverley was then called, and delayed his attack until Roberts arrived with No. 6 Division. The latter landed at Wanganui on 5 November 1868, and reached Wairoa the following afternoon after a two-day march. Because of this, they were intended to form the reserve in the order of battle on 7 November.

Whitmore hoped to achieve surprise, starting out in the early hours. Captain Hawes and the Wairoa Rifles were detailed to hold a redoubt at the edge of the bush to cover any retreat, and at this point some of the native contingent refused to go any further, staying with Hawes while Kepa led the remainder. The approach was by a broad track through the forest, and Major Hunter had command of the storming party.

Encounter between volunteers and Maori, 1868. *Illustrated London News*

The Battle of Moturoa, South Taranaki, on 7 November 1868. These two sketches were drawn by an eye-witness shortly after the engagement. From *The Adventures of Kimble Bent*

Captain Goring. From *Defenders of New Zealand*

He led the vanguard through the damp, misty dawn in strict silence, and as they neared their objective with no sign that the Maori were alerted, hopes of achieving surprise ran high. Titokowaru, however, was well prepared behind a stockade built with whole tree trunks and heavy split timber sunk well into the ground.

He remembered the day at Sentry Hill when he had lost an eye, and like the British on that occasion, he allowed Hunter to come within about 10 yards before opening fire with every gun he had. Hunter, in the lead, was one of the first to be killed, and men went down all around him. Kepa had been sent on a flanking mission, but the difficult terrain and the failure of the frontal attack brought this to a halt.

With the assault stalled, the Maori took to the bush as they had at Te Ngutu to rout their enemies. Whitmore threw in No. 6 Division to help cover the withdrawal, Roberts and Captain Goring with No. 1 Division in turn holding off the enemy and then passing through the ranks of their comrades to hold the next position. On reaching the edge of the bush it was a case of every man for himself as they ran to the entrenchment Hawes had prepared.

With 22 men killed, Whitmore's opening battle had been as disastrous as the second engagement at Te Ngutu. He was criticised for allowing himself to be outwitted as McDonnell had been — and with less excuse, since his men were fresh and close to their headquarters. The colonel felt obliged to offer his resignation, but the Defence Minister could not afford to discard a colonel after every battle, and gave him another chance to redeem himself.

To compound the Government's problems, a new and formidable menace had once again arisen in the east. The windswept Chatham Islands had been chosen as a prison camp for Maori taken at Waerenga-a-Hika, and one of those sent there was a young dissident from Turanganui, now Gisborne. It is doubtful whether any charges could have been proved against him, but local worthies felt life would be more peaceful in his absence.

Conditions of captivity at the islands were lax to the point of scandalous, so the enterprising young man had little difficulty in winning over his fellow-captives. Te Kooti Rikirangi planned a mass escape, and achieved this by seizing a ship named the *Rifleman.* The crew were forced to take the prisoners, thirsting for revenge, back to the North Island.

Major R. Biggs, Poverty Bay Militia, who was killed with all his family in Te Kooti's attack on Poverty Bay, 10 November 1868. Biggs had fought in the Opotiki, West Coast and Urewera campaigns and had been instrumental in the deportation of Te Kooti. From *Defenders of New Zealand*

They landed near Poverty Bay on 10 July 1868, and Major R. Biggs tackled the situation with energy when he learned of Te Kooti's arrival two days later. The escapers made for the Urewera, and Biggs hoped to stop them at Paparatu. His force was small, and he was absent when Captain Westrupp was attacked on 20 July. That night, nearly out of ammunition and abandoned by some of his friendly Maori, the Captain was perhaps lucky to get back to Tapatoho.

At this stage Whitmore was still operating from Napier, and on his arrival wanted to enlist Westrupp's men to help pursue Te Kooti. Not only did they refuse to move another step until they had rested from their ordeal, but the colonel's own Napier contingent was also far from keen, so Whitmore had to wait until Major Fraser arrived with his Armed Constabulary.

Before he could move, Te Kooti had beaten off another attack at Te Koneke by a mixed force under Captain Richardson and Lieutenant Preece. On 31 July, in bad mid-winter conditions, Whitmore was able to set out on his quest with 200 men. Enthusiasm, however, was still low, and some Europeans and kupapa deserted.

On 8 August the force finally overtook Te Kooti at the Ruakituri River. The Maori were ready for their enemies, who were confined to a gorge as they

Te Kooti Rikirangi Te Turuki (1830–93), guerrilla leader and founder of the Ringatu Church. A man of the Ngati Porou tribe, he was related to Major Ropata but was not a chief by birth. His hit-and-run strikes were carefully planned and ruthlessly executed, and many times he was more than a match for the Colonial forces. A conjectural painting by H. G. Robley. *Auckland Institute and Museum*

Captain (later Major) Richardson. From *Defenders of New Zealand*

Lieutenant (later Captain) George A. Preece. From *Defenders of New Zealand*

approached. Despite their unfavourable situation, Whitmore's men brought to bear all the fire they could muster, and when the action was broken off it had proved indecisive. They were a long way from their headquarters, with casualties to evacuate under appalling conditions, but Te Kooti himself had also been wounded.

After Whitmore left for the West Coast, four men were murdered at Whataroa in October. Donald McLean took over the task of trying to lay Te Kooti by the heels, but he was to prove the most elusive man the Government had ever had to face.

Major Lambert took command of a stronger force than Whitmore had mustered, including Ropata with 200 Ngati Porou. He went to Whataroa, but being doubtful of the enemy's whereabouts returned to Wairoa. Te Kooti soon gave awful proof of his presence. In darkness on 9 November he made one of the lightning raids which were to become his trademark. In the attack on Poverty Bay Major Biggs and his family were murdered along with 70 others. Almost coinciding with the disaster at Moturoa, this further setback brought

Kai-iwi Cavalry Sergeant wearing a blue peaked forage cap with silver lace, brown leather equipment, blue jacket trimmed with black lace, fawn Bedford cord breeches and black boots. *Alexander Turnbull Library*

Kai-iwi Cavalry Sergeant wearing a blue peaked forage cap with silver lace, brown leather equipment, blue jacket trimmed with black lace, fawn Bedford cord breeches and black boots. *Alexander Turnbull Library*

Far left: Private of the New Zealand Militia in campaign dress. He wears a dark blue 'pork pie' forage cap, blue shirt, blue trousers, brown leather equipment and white canvas haversack and carries a navy-blue blanket slung over his shoulder. *Alexander Turnbull Library*

Lieutenant (later Major) Gascoyne: From *Defenders of New Zealand*

Colonel William Lyon. From *Defenders of New Zealand*

the fortunes of both the Government and Whitmore to a nadir. But although the road would be long and hard, things would slowly improve.

At first there was little sign of this happening. The colonel fell back as far as the Kai-iwi, followed by the victorious Titokowaru. The latter had promised his followers the sacking of Wanganui, but the town was held by two companies of the 18th Regiment, the last British troops in the country. For the moment the rebel leader contented himself with building a new pa at Tauranga-ika.

Haultain was forced to accept that, black though the situation looked at Wanganui, the Armed Constabulary must go to check Te Kooti. Colonel William Lyon, formerly of the Coldstream Guards, supported by McDonnell, must conduct a holding operation. Whitmore sailed for Poverty Bay on 2 August with most of the Constabulary. When he landed, his chief difficulty was to get reliable information as to Te Kooti's whereabouts. Lieutenant Gascoyne, Preece and Ropata had not been idle, but one of the guerrilla's greatest assets was a mobility which could all too often catch his foes off guard.

Some men who had ventured into the bush near the mouth of the Te Arai River were soon heavily engaged. Roberts, who had been on the point of sailing in the *Sturt* with 100 men, was providentially unable to do so because the ship sprang a leak. He was sent to help the hard-pressed Ihaka Whanga, a Ngati Kahungunu kupapa chief, while Whitmore tried to cut off Te Kooti's retreat — but with no luck.

Ihaka Whanga. From *Pictures of Old New Zealand*

Te Kooti made a serious mistake. As a guerrilla leader he could have had things more or less his own way, but now he decided to build a pa for a pitched battle. This was simply playing into Whitmore's hands, and the Government column lost no time in following him to Ngatapa.

Whitmore did not think much of this position as a Christmas present:

[It] is by a great deal the most difficult and strongest I have ever seen in this country; and of those in my camp, none, European or Native, has ever met with a stronger. Rising abruptly out of a confused and 'tormented' mass of forest-clad hills, a single cone-shaped mountain rises, conspicuous from its height and isolation. It is covered with bush, which had been to some extent cut down and burned. The apex of the hill, which is perhaps 2,000 feet high, is girt by a triple line of fortification, and of these the two inner ones rise to a height of 12 feet. Rifle-pits guard the front and the water, which is distant some few chains; and a scarped ridge, said to be impracticable for the descent of the garrison, terminates two, if not all three, of the parapets. These latter are built as we build fortifications, with fern and sticks. I learn that behind the ridge the apex is descended by a ladder to a second knoll on which the kainga of the women stands, and by this alone, I am informed, can the garrison escape to the rear.[4]

The force surrounded the pa as far as numbers allowed. Some stretches were thinly held, and one sector beneath a precipice which was thought impossible to descend remained unguarded throughout the action. Appeals made to the garrison to permit the women to leave were ignored, and at the end of the year the troops had settled down to a siege.

The nature of the position forced a frontal attack across cleared ground. Saps were pushed forward, and the Coehorn mortar was brought into play. This, throwing bombs high in the air, was a far more effective weapon against a well-dug-in enemy than the Armstrong guns used in earlier actions.

Armed Constabulary from No. 1 Division climbed up from the rear to the extreme right at a point so precipitous that a pickaxe had to be used to cut out standing room. This sortie threatened one end of the entrenchments, and the rebels made several attempts to dislodge the attackers, three of whom were thrown down the slope. Constables Ben Biddle and Solomon Black won the New Zealand Cross for their determined gallantry in holding their positions. Ropata also earned the decoration for his services during an earlier probing operation here.

Te Kooti was finding out just how mistaken he had been in opting for a pitched battle. The spring on which his people depended had been lost, and though the heavy rain helped to alleviate the lack of water they were so short of food that starvation stared them in the face. Surrender was unthinkable, and as Whitmore prepared for the final assault the garrison descended the cliff face thought to be impassable.

In the event, surrender would have been the better option, at least for the rank and file, since the Government force would have taken them prisoner. Just as Te Kooti had shown his Poverty Bay victims no mercy, Ropata would now exact an equally terrible vengeance. His Ngati Porou and the Arawa warriors hunted down the fugitives after killing the wounded left behind, and

Sub-Inspector (Captain) D. M. Brown, No. 7 Division A.C., killed during the siege of Ngatapa, January 1869. *National Museum*

nearly all the defeated were summarily executed when in flight.

Te Kooti himself escaped to take refuge near the Waioeka Gorge, in country so rugged and forested as to be virtually unknown to any but the local Tuhoe people. Whitmore wrote:

> . . . defeated, twice wounded, a fugitive, and failing in his prophecies, he is not likely again to trouble the district, or assemble a fresh band of assassins, even should he survive the hardships before him, or escape the vengeance of the Uriwera [sic] upon an imposter.[2]

This rash forecast could well be classed as famous last words.

Believing this eastern menace to be crushed, the colonel lost no time in shipping the Armed Constabulary back to Wanganui to deal with Titokowaru. They arrived on 16 January 1869. Like Chute he never believed in wasting time, and nine days later was on the march for Tauranga-ika.

Colonel Lyon had been holding a post on the Kai-Iwi, and a few days earlier a group of unarmed Maori youths came to nearby Handley's woolshed to raid pigs, where it was alleged that Lieutenant John Bryce, leading the Kai-Iwi Cavalry, cut them down.[3]

When Whitmore was confronted by the completed fortress at Tauranga-ika, he liked it no better than Ngatapa:

> No troops in the world could have hewn their way through a double row of strong palisades, backed by rifle-pits, and flanked by two-storied erections, such as are constructed in this fortification, defended by excellent shots and desperate men.[3]

Two Armstrong guns were brought up to start a barrage on 2 February, but had little effect on the defence. The infantry began digging in, and though the cavalry worked their way round the pa for some reason Whitmore did not closely invest the pa. After Te Kooti had slipped through his fingers because he had left a sector unguarded, one would not have expected him to take the same chance with Titokowaru. Most probably the latter's invincibility so far had made any idea of flight unthinkable.

The troops in the trenches passed the evening with rousing choruses, such as 'Oh, Susannah' and 'Marching through Georgia'; the Maori enjoyed the concert and called for encores. The singers may well have wondered how many of them would survive an attempt to storm the pa the next day.

When morning dawned, the inexplicable had happened — the pa was deserted. Lieutenant Bryce led his cavalry in pursuit, and had a brush with the rearguard near Weraroa, but the retreating Maori were able to break off the engagement.

Lieutenant (later Captain)
John Bryce. From
Defenders of New Zealand

An artillery detachment of
the New Zealand Armed
Constabulary, with two
6-pounder Armstrong guns
of the type used to
bombard Tauranga-Ika Pa.
Alexander Turnbull Library

The deserter Kimble Bent, who had been employed as an armourer by Titokowaru, later told James Cowan the story behind this strange turn of events. A woman had achieved what had proved too much for all the Queen's men. The rebel leader had coveted another man's wife, and when discovered had suffered a severe loss of mana. The other chiefs would not counttenance the defence of Tauranga-ika as he wished.

Whitmore had certainly had a great stroke of luck, and at once moved westwards to recover territory abandoned since Moturoa. On the way to Patea he called at the scene of his earlier humiliation and gave the remains of his fallen troops a decent burial.

Although driven back into the bush, the Maori showed that they were more than willing to revert to their earlier tactics of picking off small detachments. Kepa located Titokowaru at Otautu, in the Patea River valley. Whitmore set off up one bank while St John took the other. Their approach was shrouded in fog and Titokowaru and his men were initially able to inflict casualties, but with failing ammunition they had to take to the bush once again.

Whitmore energetically followed the fugitives on to the Te Karaka plateau. The Government had offered £1,000 for Titokowaru, dead or alive. Kepa, determined to avenge the death and mutilation of one of his kinsmen, Kori Raukawa, urged the colonel to extend the offer to all rebels. Supposing that the attraction of a bounty would spur his men to greater efforts, Whitmore agreed to pay £10 a head for chiefs, and £5 for others. He could not have foreseen that this everyday expression would be taken literally by the kupapa, and his horror may be imagined when these grisly trophies were produced for payment, especially as white men had joined in this practice.

Beset by desertions, lack of supplies and now this new terror of death and mutilation, Titokowaru retreated into the remote fastnesses of the forest. His fighting days were over, though in the 1880s he was to play a peaceful role as one of the chief lieutenants of Te Whiti and Tohu during their protracted civil disobedience at Parihaka.

The siege of Titokowaru's Tauranga-Ika Pa by Colonel Whitmore's Colonial forces on 2–3 February 1869. *Wanganui Museum*

Major William G. Mair, 1832–1912, joined the Colonial Defence Force in 1863, and took part in most of the actions of the Waikato War including Orakau, when he made the call for surrender and received the historic reply. He was noted for his calmness, courage and sound judgement, leading his forces with great success. Mair's tact and respect in dealing with the Maori led to the submission of King Tawhiao in 1881. He served as a highly respected judge of the Native Land Court until his retirement in 1909. *Alexander Turnbull Library*

Hawke's Bay Mounted Volunteers at the Waipawa Stockade, Ruataniwha, 1869. *Alexander Turnbull Library*

THE UREWERA EXPEDITION

As Titokowaru's star waned, Te Kooti began to prove that he was very far from the spent force that Whitmore had postulated after Ngatapa. His renewed depredations started in a modest way with the murder of a surveyor at Ohiwa Harbour near Opotiki.

He next moved against the hinterland of Whakatane, choosing as his first target a flour mill at Te Poronui, only a short distance from the little town. The engagement in March 1869 was a remarkable one, for the defence under a French settler, Jean Guerrin, consisted of only three men and three women, yet they were able to defy the bloodthirsty band for two days before the inevitable end.

This had done nothing to enhance Te Kooti's mana, and without delay he approached a pa at Tauporoa held by the Ngati Pukeko. After an attempt to take the post by treachery had failed, Te Kooti and his men settled down for another couple of days, determined to overwhelm the outnumbered defenders.

The Mair brothers lost no time in coming to grips with the latest outbreak. William, in command at Opotiki, sent Henry with the Opotiki Rangers and some Armed Constabulary, while Gilbert hastened across the great Rangitaiki swamp with his Arawa kupapa.

The latter arrived first, but not in time to prevent the fall of the pa, for they met survivors escaping after giving a good account of themselves. Mair was able to protect them by driving off their pursuers. Te Kooti moved down the river to sack Whakatane itself, the force from Opotiki also arriving just too late to prevent the settlement being put to the torch.

Te Kooti left the Bay of Plenty people to recover from his foray and turned his attention to Hawke's Bay. A diversion in the Wairoa Valley was driven off, but his main thrust was against Mohaka, where civilians, regardless of race, were killed in a manner every bit as indiscriminate as that seen during the massacre at Poverty Bay.

The survivors took a stand at two pa, the first of which, Te Huke, was overcome by means of a false flag of truce, whereupon those inside were murdered. The second post, Hiruharama, managed to hold off the enemy until the force under Ihaka Whanga, which had stopped the movement against Wairoa, returned.

The besiegers did their best to prevent the relief of the pa and managed to hold most of Whanga's force. A mere handful, volunteers to a man, followed Trooper George Hill of No. 1 Division in a determined bid to help the garrison. A veteran of long service, Hill took charge of the defence and inspired his comrades to resist until the approach of a relief party from Napier induced Te Kooti to retire at his leisure once again to the Urewera. More than 60 people were left dead as the result of his latest raids. But for Hill the tally would have been even higher, and no man better earned his New Zealand Cross.

Te Kooti did not have a monopoly on killing. In the west a marauding party of Ngati Maniapoto, passing down the Mokau, fell upon the Pukearuhe Redoubt at White Cliffs in mid February. The few people there, including the missionary John Whiteley, were all killed.

Since his force was no longer needed against Titokowaru, Whitmore embarked his troops from Opunake and Waitara en route to Auckland and the Urewera for a major drive against Te Kooti. The two ships *St Kilda* and *Sturt* landed Armed Constabulary at Mokau, and the latter fired a few rounds from her solitary gun. But the raiders had already gone.

Upon reaching Onehunga, some of the force were given a day's leave, perhaps rather niggardly in view of recent exertions, but their sense of urgency for the new campaign did not match their commander's:

> Some of the men who had long unspent arrears of pay in their possession, and had just come from a fatiguing march of two months in the bush, allowed themselves to fall into the temptation afforded by so many public houses; so that 50 men from this cause, or in endeavouring to bring away their comrades, were left behind. They have however made good their passages at their own expense. I cannot but hope that the Government will not be disheartened at this circumstance, for some allowance is due to men who had worn their clothes to rags in the hard service they had undergone, and who had not for months seen any fare but their bare ration, or a town of any description.[1]

The force assembled at Mount Maunganui, and the nearby town of Tauranga was declared out of bounds.

Whitmore intended to march his men along the beach via Maketu to Matata, and they found plodding through soft sand in heavy marching order a poor start. They were joined by 400 Arawa who could not agree upon a chief of their own to lead them and chose Henry Tacy Clarke, a civil official. The latter took an instant dislike to the colonel, with whom he would have to work, describing his superior as 'a little, conceited, egotistical, self-sufficient ass'. He wrote of the journey along the shore:

> The poor European part of the Constabulary were ordered to march on to Matata — in vain they pleaded weariness and being foot-sore. The 'Brutes' must march, if they had to go on all fours. Officers were abused, and my heart sickened at the treatment they were getting.[2]

At Matata, the base for the expedition, the force was split into two columns. One, under St John with Fraser as his deputy, was sent by way of Whakatane to follow the course of the river of the same name to Ruatahuna. This force consisted of most of the Europeans, and was joined by 180 kupapa from the Whakatohea tribe at Opotiki.

The second, or right, column, was almost entirely made up of Arawa, of whom Clarke himself commented: 'No one knows better than myself that dealings with this people are trying to flesh and blood to a degree.' Major Roberts, in command, was only 28, and to lend him moral support Whitmore followed this route along the Rangitaiki River.

The first stage crossed the great Rangitaiki swamp, said to be the best wildfowl-shooting area in the country, but in due course two small redoubts were built as staging posts along the river and the force reached a spot known as Karamuramu. An advanced base was established here, and called Fort Galatea, after H.M.S. *Galatea* in which H.R.H. the Duke of Edinburgh was then making a royal tour to the Pacific.

The route taken by the right column was fairly circuitous, whereas by following the Whakatane River St John headed almost directly to his goal. The shorter journey was, however, far from the easier of the two, for after leaving the flat valley floor of Opouriao, the force had to struggle through gorges and sometimes to leave the river altogether when its bed became impassable.

Such country was custom-made for ambush, and at Paripari a ford faced a wooded terrace. A volley here shot and killed one of the guides, Lieutenant David White. He had to be buried while the action still raged, Major Mair reading the burial service under fire. At Hukanui Hill the men were compelled to cut footholds with tomahawks as they fought their way forward, but this was the last serious hurdle. Tahora and Orangikawa soon fell, opening the way to Ruatahuna.

A third column, commanded by Lieutenant-Colonel J. L. Herrick, came from the east coast to Lake Waikaremoana, the plan being to pass this prominent landmark and join up with the troops advancing from the north and west. It proved impossible to march around the shore because of 'the cliffs and bush, the depth of the bays, and the absence of all track'. It was therefore decided to build boats, but this proved to be such a slow job that the fighting was all over by the time the craft were ready. These were loaded down with rock and sunk to deny their use to the enemy, and have been found by divers in recent years.

On 5 May 1869 Whitmore splashed his way across the Rangitaiki River, here about 100 yards wide, to enter the narrow defile of its tributary, the Whirinaki. The initial wetting mattered little, for the force used this stream as a highway, crossing it no less than 55 times during the first day. No horses

The death of Lieutenant David White in the ambush at Te Paripari on the Whakatane River, 7 May 1869. A painting by S. Valda. From *With the Lost Legion in New Zealand*

were allowed beyond Fort Galatea, the colonel going on foot like everyone else.

The gorge was so shut in by the hills that scouting parties could not be sent out to cover the flanks against possible ambushes. An Arawa chief named Te Pokiha (Fox) took the post of honour (and danger) in the lead, but luckily it did not dawn upon the enemy that the column would attempt such a difficult route. They were watching an easier approach via Heruiwi.

Fox and Gilbert Mair started early next morning to encircle Ahikeruru (now Te Whaiti) to prevent the people in the pa from falling back on Ruatahuna. They were discovered before the move was completed, and the men made off, leaving their women and children behind. Their retreat was so precipitate that nobody was hurt. The Arawa chiefs carried the children on their backs and tried to cheer up the women. Clarke wrote to the husbands of the captives, offering safe conduct and the opportunity to settle in the Rotorua district.

The column survived an ambush, and on 9 May entered the valley in which Ruatahuna lay, the very heart of the Tuhoe territory. St John had arrived the day before, and the troops had done well to keep so closely to the plan after fighting their way through such rugged and largely unknown country.

A far more pressing problem than Te Kooti was the precarious food situation. Supplies captured at Ruatahuna were soon exhausted, and transport from the small exposed port of Matata could not keep up with requirements. The local horses were butchered, but it was evident that the force could not remain where it was much longer.

Pokiha Taranui (Major Fox), war chief of the friendly Arawa tribe. Pokiha took a prominent part in the fighting against the East Coast Maori at Maketu in 1864. He later led his men against the Hauhau and Te Kooti, being awarded Queen Victoria's presentation sword. *Alexander Turnbull Library*

Campaign dress. From left to right: Forest Rangers officer; New Zealand Armed Constabulary constable in 'shawl' dress; officer N.Z.A.C. in similar uniform. *Painting by F. Turton*

Whitmore wanted to push forward through the even more difficult country of the Huiarau Ranges to Lake Waikaremoana, but was vehemently opposed by the strong Arawa element. They pointed to the shortage of supplies and to the risk of the Te Kooti's bypassing the force to take vengeance on their undefended homes. Fox and his fellow chiefs flatly refused to go any farther, and the colonel had to take the unpalatable decision to fall back to Galatea. Major Mair was sent off with the wounded via the Horomanga Gorge, another difficult operation which was harassed by the enemy.

Whitmore himself had to be carried back on a litter, and wrote of the situation:

I find it difficult to say . . . how admirably our men have behaved throughout. Living on potatoes, labouring under heavy packs, with their clothes torn to rags, and their boots destroyed, their cheerfulness and ready obedience at all times cannot be too highly praised. Poor fellows who were bleeding in their feet, who have had hardly a day's rest since November last, and in spite of the quantity of clothes they have purchased since then can scarcely muster a sound garment amongst them, were yet ready and anxious to face the Huiarau snow-covered heights, and to risk possible starvation or a long retreat from the moment they heard of my wish to go to Waikare [Waikaremoana].[3]

Lieutenant-Colonel J. H. H. St John was an ex-Imperial officer of the 20th Regiment who had served with distinction in the Crimea. He joined the Waikato Militia as a captain in 1863, and later became an inspector in the Armed Constabulary. St John took an active part in the Waikato, Tauranga, Opotiki and Urewera campaigns. From *Defenders of New Zealand*

New Zealand Armed Constabulary garrison at Opepe. *Alexander Turnbull Library*

Whitmore was nonetheless far from being as optimistic as at the time of Ngatapa:

> The expedition has been most trying, and many men will never recover from its effects. I doubt for one if I shall completely.
>
> I don't say another attempt [to starve out Te Kooti] now is unpracticable [sic] by the secret track marked from Waikare to Tarawera. If you are anxious it shall be tried — but I can't go and except Roberts (and he doubtful) I am inclined to think that no senior officer will go pleasantly.[4]

The colonel left for Wellington to discuss a Taupo campaign and turned over command of the field force to Lieutenant-Colonel St John, with instructions to move further south to counter any break-out from the Urewera that Te Kooti might attempt. Even though the latter had not been captured, it was evident that the Urewera was no longer the sanctuary it had once been.

Grey (now no longer in office) had always maintained that Taupo was the strategic key to security in the North Island, and after a delay of three weeks St John finally left Galatea on a reconnaissance mission to gain information as to whether conditions would permit him to carry out his orders. He took with him a small escort from the Bay of Plenty Cavalry whose horses were still in fair condition. Lieutenant-Colonel Fraser was left in charge at Fort Galatea, and he could do little more than allow the men much-needed rest while awaiting the next move.

St John followed the Rangitaiki to its upper reaches before striking westward. The weather was wet, and in the sandy pumice of the Taupo desert (as the Kaingaroa Forest then was) the hoof prints of the little cavalcade showed not only that they had passed that way, but also how few of them there were. At last they reached a small isolated clump of trees with a few deserted whare comprising the settlement of Opepe.

Soon after they arrived, Captain J. C. St George came in from Tapuaeharuru, a pa lying on the opposite bank of the Waikato River from the present town of Taupo. St George was the Government agent there, and was dependent upon friendly local Maori. He told St John that all was quiet, and the party was so wet that the colonel decided to leave nearly all the men at Opepe to rest and dry out their clothes. Some were not happy to be left at a spot where Te Kooti might pass if he came south. St John laughed at their fears, assuring them that they were as safe as if in London and need not post sentries.

In the meantime Gilbert Mair had found that Te Kooti was on the move. Fraser at once sent two messengers after St John to warn him, but they fell foul of the Maori. The latter read the captured despatches, and on reaching Opepe posed as 'friendlies'. Their victims, bereft of clothes and weapons, fell quick victims to this stratagem, nine of the 13 men being killed.

Cornet Angus Smith, although wounded in the foot, managed to escape and tried to make his way to Tapuaeharuru to warn his chief. But on the way he was captured by the Maori, who stripped him and tied him to a tree with flax. It took Smith four days to free himself, and he then made his way as best he could to Fort Galatea, often on all fours because of his injured foot. When he finally reached his goal he had been without food or clothing for 10 days. There were some who criticised his being awarded the New Zealand Cross, but few recipients could have undergone greater privations.

Two brothers named Hallett came upon the bodies at Opepe when riding to Napier and returned to St John with the news. He and his remaining comrades searched for survivors, missing Smith, and went back to Galatea.

The ambush of Colonel Fraser's two despatch riders by Te Kooti's men near Opepe on 7 June 1869. One of the troopers was killed and the despatches captured. A painting by S. Valda. From *With the Lost Legion in New Zealand*

Captain John Chapman St George, killed at Te Porere 4 October 1869. *Alexander Turnbull Library*

Right: Captain (Sub-Inspector) Frederick Swindley, of Whitmore's élite Corps of Guides. This consisted of 12 scouts, all expert bushmen, who led the expedition into the unmapped wilderness. *Alexander Turnbull Library*

Below: Te Rangi-tahau, a chief of east Taupo, who was captured at Omarunui in 1866. Deported to the Chatham Islands, he escaped with Te Kooti, becoming one of his principal lieutenants. He was a ruthless warrior, and often acted as executioner with the sharp-edged stone club (patu) he holds in the photograph. *Hawke's Bay Art Gallery and Museum*

The memory of Opepe haunted St John until his early death. He soon had another problem on his hands. In an attempt to upgrade the track from Matata, the Armed Constabulary were put to work on preparing a road for bullock drays, so that the inefficient packhorses could be replaced. There were 56 men sick, and the rest maintained that the daily ration of a pound of biscuit and half a pound of bacon was insufficient when engaged on heavy labouring work. They downed tools, and although St John placed the N.C.O.s under arrest he could do nothing about the constables. He wrote to Haultain asking for additional supplies, and the rations were increased to one and a half pounds each of meat and biscuit.

While most of the troops accepted this solution, some were determined to get away from Fort Galatea and its satellite stations at any cost. On 16 June 12 of them deserted from Fort Clarke, and three were found on a ship about to leave Tauranga for Auckland. Lieutenant-Colonel Philip Harington reported:

> On being brought before me I asked them why they had deserted at a time when the country was in want of men, when they replied that they were thoroughly tired of serving in the force, and preferred the risk of very severe punishment to remaining. They complained that they were most insufficiently fed; that they did not receive their pay in accordance with the terms under which they enlisted; and they were therefore not in a position to buy clothes and extra food, that they were not well cared for when sick.[5]

Harington and St John believed that it would be impossible to keep troops at Taupo supplied via Matata and Fort Galatea. They therefore recommended that the road between Te Teko and Galatea be abandoned as useless for defence purposes. It was decided to follow this course. Clad in blankets and rags, the Armed Constabulary were withdrawn to Tauranga.

Lieutenant-Colonel Herrick, having abandoned the Waikaremoana enterprise, took his force south to Napier and then marched along the track leading over the ranges to Runanga. On a hill commanding the Waipunga and Runanga streams they built a redoubt, the first step in an effort to prevent Te Kooti from roaming at will between the Urewera and the King Country.

Captain (later Colonel) Thomas Porter, C.B., 1844–1920, poses at the right of the photograph with his Ngatai Maori auxiliaries outside the stockade and blockhouse at Gisborne. Porter started his career as a midshipman in the Royal navy, and on settling in New Zealand won a commission in the East Coast Hauhau campaigns. He was continuously on active service in 1868–71, and later commanded two New Zealand contingents in the Boer War. *Alexander Turnbull Library*

The interior of a blockhouse, showing the loopholed walls, which would be filled with gravel or sand to render them bulletproof. The weapons are, from left to right: two Adams revolvers, an Armed Constabulary sword bayonet, a Snider cavalry carbine, a Snider 2-band infantry rifle and two Snider artillery carbines. *N. Ogle, T. Ryan*

CHAPTER 24

BLOCKHOUSES, FORTS AND REDOUBTS

From the earliest days of colonisation, settlers erected fortified posts to defend their settlements. Such blockhouses and stockades were modelled on those built in the backwoods of Canada and the United States for protection against Indians.

Blockhouses were usually of two storeys, the upper projecting about three feet over the lower one all round. Houses were often strengthened and made bulletproof by packing sand between the outer walls and lining and loopholes were cut for return fire. These little forts frequently sheltered women and children at night up to the year 1873.

Country churches were turned into fortresses with loopholes and stockading. One correspondent of the period pompously described the Papakura church as being a 'visible transubstantiation of a bulwark of faith into a bulwark of earthly strength'. Such conversion of churches for warlike purposes only reinforced the Maori view that the clergy was no longer impartial, but were in fact actively supporting the Government. During the Waikato War, the little Presbyterian church at Pukekohe East was enclosed by a trench and a stockade of logs laid horizontally. It was successfully defended by 17 volunteers for six hours against a large Maori war party.

Large numbers of earthwork redoubts were raised by the British Army in frontier areas on confiscated and disputed land. In Taranaki and the Waikato, roads were safeguarded by chains of posts built within sight of one another

The Armed Constabulary post at Opunake, Taranaki. This fortification was a fine example of an earthwork redoubt, the walls being built entirely of sods of earth. *Alexander Turnbull Library*

The Waihi Redoubt, Taranaki, contained two large blockhouses at opposing angles and had a wooden stockade. Built in 1866, it later served as field headquarters during the struggle against Titokowaru. *Alexander Turnbull Library*

The Kaitake Redoubt, Taranaki, built in 1864. Outside the walls stands a signal mast, used to relay messages between military posts. *Alexander Turnbull Library*

and provided with signal masts for semaphore communication. Earth redoubts were formed of cut sods bound together with layers of fern, and were usually surrounded by a ditch or dry moat between six and 12 feet deep.

At first troops pitched their round bell tents within the redoubts, but as the fortifications became more permanent wooden barracks and blockhouses were often erected within the defences. Many New Zealand towns trace their origin to military posts which served as the nucleus around which settlements grew. By the early 1870s garrisons were linked by telegraph so that intelligence of the movements of guerrilla leaders such as Te Kooti could be swiftly relayed to headquarters.

An uneasy peace was imposed on the borders of pakeha-settled country after the end of the wars. Chains of blockhouses and redoubts guarded the pale between the farmers and the Kingites of the upper Waikato. One of the most important and strategic posts up to the 1880s was Taupo, on the shore of the great central lake.

There were also redoubts and stockades on either side of the Urewera country and along the Napier-Taupo road. Garrisons were supplied by the Armed Constabulary Field Force, who spent much of their time cutting roads, bridging rivers, erecting telegraph lines and patrolling the unsettled areas.

The Omata stockade was built early in 1860 entirely by settlers of the district, without the help of Imperial troops. It was situated on a commanding hill three and a half miles south of New Plymouth. This skilfully designed fort merits a detailed description:

The Omata Stockade, 1869. A painting by H. F. Rawson. *Taranaki Museum*

The Omata Stockade, Taranaki

It consisted of a strong blockhouse 62 ft long, 22 ft wide and 11 ft high, with two flanking towers each 22 ft high at the diagonally opposite angles, all loopholed with a surrounding ditch enfiladed by the towers. The figure of the post was oblong. The stockade was constructed of heavy timbers, some of which were as large as could be hauled up by a team of bullocks. They were either whole trunks of small trees or split parts of large ones, and were sunk 3 ft to 4 ft in the ground all round. The height of the solid timber wall so formed was 10 ft. The timbers were roughly trimmed with the axe to bring them as close together as possible and to remove any knots outside which might assist an enemy to scale the stockade. The small spaces left between the logs were covered inside with an upright row of thick slabs. The tops of the timbers were sawn off straight, and sawn battens, 6 in broad by 3 in thick, were laid along the top and fastened to the stockade with 7 in spike nails. The average thickness of the heavy timbers was about 12 in, and the whole was proof against musket-balls, and against rifle-balls except at very close range. A row of loopholes was cut all round about 5 ft above the inside floor, and there was a double row in the two small flanking bastions. These bastions were of two storeys each loopholed on all four sides. The lower part was a sleeping apartment; the upper was a post for sentries at night and in bad weather. The roof of each bastion was clear of the wall-plate, and was made to project about a foot beyond the wall of the building. This arrangement admitted of the sentries keeping a good lookout all round, and at the same time protecting them from the weather. It also allowed of firing through spaces between the roof and the wall-plate when more convenient to do so (as was often the case at long range) than through the loopholes. The roof of the sides and end of the main building within the walls projected about a foot beyond the stockade so as to make it practically impossible to scale. The deep and wide ditch was crossed by a drawbridge which had a span of 10 ft and worked on strong hinges; by ropes fastened to its front edge and running through blocks on top of the inner posts it was lifted up perpendicularly at night. The entrance gate was made of two thicknesses of timber, each 2½ in thick, the outer timbers running up and down, the inner diagonally, and strongly fastened with spike nails riveted. This formed a solid door 5 in thick. Around the inner walls were built the garrison's quarters, leaving an open courtyard in the middle of the stockade. The loopholes were cut at such an elevation as enabled the men to use their rifles clear of the roof, and also to cover any object down to the bottom of the ditch, as well as from the outer edge of the ditch down the glacis, and everywhere around the stockade. There was no 'dead ground' around the little fort; and, whatever the weather, the men were firing under cover. Outside, on the inner edge of the trench, stood the signal-staff, worked from within the building. It was a single tree, 60 ft long, sunk 6 ft in the ground, and secured by stays and guys.

Mr G. R. Burton, who designed the interior arrangements, was Captain in the Militia, and he received high praise for his amateur military engineering work from so competent an authority as Colonel (afterwards Major-General) Sir James E. Alexander, 14th Regt, who wrote in 1860 a report on the Omata stockade for the technical papers of the Royal Engineers' Institute, England.

This stockade was for some time occupied by 150 Imperial troops with two field guns. During this period a column of 250 men, with a howitzer (drawn by bullocks) was required to escort the provision carts from New Plymouth to the post.[6]

The Tarawera Redoubt, one of a chain built in 1869 to guard the line of communication between Napier and Taupo. The telegraph line enters the stockade. *Alexander Turnbull Library*

CHAPTER 25

THE END OF THE WARS

Although Te Kooti's genius as a will-o'-the wisp guerrilla enabled him to avoid the Government thrust into the Urewera, he realised that the support he commanded was far too small now that the Titokowaru diversion had been removed.

The appearance at Opepe was occasioned by his plans to gain a powerful ally, Rewi Maniapoto. Since Orakau the Waikato and Maniapoto people had cut off contact with the white man, Tawhiao's King Country being a state independent from the rest of the country. Wetere's bloody venture at White Cliffs did not have the blessing of his betters, who had no wish to be led into further rebellion which could well involve them in new losses.

Te Kooti now sought to enlist Rewi's help in carrying out a grandiose idea. He proposed returning to the East Coast to destroy the Ngati Porou and Arawa enemies, then to drive out the pakeha. He might have sounded more credible had his aims been more modest, but the former Waikato general came to see Te Kooti in action.

The Government had not been idle since Opepe. Following Herrick's advance along the Napier Taupo track, Major Roberts was sent with No. 6 Division to Tapuaeharuru. He released St George who, accompanied by Captain Preece, set out to look for Te Kooti with the kupapa chief Poihipi Tukairangi and the Taupo tribe.

Lieutenant-Colonel McDonnell was given an opportunity to redeem his reputation by taking command of a mixed force of kupapa and Herrick's Constabulary.

An Armed Constabulary patrol rest in a Maori settlement in Taranaki after the pursuit of Titokowaru. *Taranaki Museum*

A unit of the New Zealand Armed Constabulary seeking Te Kooti. Their loose shirts and rapaki, or waist-shawls, were excellent for work in the bush, where trousers were impractical because of the frequent crossing of creeks and rivers. *Alexander Turnbull Library*

Two small-scale engagements followed, at Tauranga-Taupo on the eastern shore of Lake Taupo, and at Te Pononga near Mount Pihanga. Both were indecisive, and Te Kooti hardly looked the leader who would drive the pakeha into the sea. Rewi Maniapoto decided that his people would do better to maintain an uneasy peace rather than join a forlorn hope.

McDonnell, bearing in mind his opponent's well-earned reputation for wiliness, was content to bide his time until he had firm news of Te Kooti's whereabouts. This was not long in coming. Te Kooti appeared to have learned nothing from his defeat at Ngatapa, for early in October word came that he was building a pa at Te Porere in the foothills of the Tongariro massif.

McDonnell moved at once to attack. His force was engaged by enemy skirmishers on its approach, but the Government men drove them off, overran the redoubt and inflicted heavy casualties. Te Kooti was wounded in the hand but, as ever, eluded capture. A sad feature of the day was the death in action of St George when in the forefront of the battle.

Te Kooti vanished without trace into the rugged country west of the lake. Donald McLean, who was Minister for both Defence and Native Affairs, decided on a new approach, and went to the King Country to open talks with Rewi and Tawhiao. His views had changed from earlier days of land deals:

Te Kooti Rikirangi Te Turuki, 1830–93, in old age. This painting by T. Ryan (no relation of the author) was based on a sketch from memory, as Te Kooti never allowed photographs or paintings of himself. *Alexander Turnbull Library*

The Imperial Government, to which the Colony is applying for assistance, is decidedly averse to a confiscation policy, and I believe the sooner it is abandoned in our dealings with the Natives of this Island the better for all parties concerned, as the loss of such acquisition, even on economic grounds, is always vastly greater than the gain.[1]

This was a complete turnabout from views expressed from Governor Grey downwards in 1863, and no doubt had much to do with the successful outcome of the new discussions. While the Kingites were not prepared to emerge from their self-imposed isolation to join in the life of the rest of New Zealand, Rewi promised to resist or capture Te Kooti if he entered the King Country. In return, the Government forces would not enter their territory when in pursuit.

Te Kooti had retired to the upper Wanganui district, where he solved his supply problem by raiding cattle and crops. By doing so he earned himself yet a third powerful Maori enemy, Kepa's Wanganui people. While Roberts and McDonnell blocked the north and south of Lake Taupo, Kepa came up from the south on the warpath.

In attempt to help Te Kooti out of his predicament, Tawhiao advised him 'to sheath his sword and live in peace'.[2] Privately the dissident was beginning to think this was a good idea, but he was in the hands of his more extreme followers such as Hakaraia and Kereopa. Putting on a brave face, Te Kooti scorned Tawhiao playing the king, and once again disappeared.

McDonnell and Roberts had other problems in addition to hunting Te Kooti. The food resources of the Taupo area were hardly sufficient to sustain the local Maori, so supplies had to be brought from Napier and Tauranga. The distances in both cases were long, and only pack animals could be used on the tracks. To cross the desert of pumice, the horses had also to carry their own forage.

A veteran of Te Kooti's campaigns, this old Maori warrior poses in war costume. *Alexander Turnbull Library*

Renata Kawepo, 1808–88, chief of the Ngati Kahungungu of Hawke's Bay, fought on the Government side at Omarunui. Renata went on several expeditions against Te Kooti, including the siege of Ngatapa. He lost an eye to one of Te Kooti's women followers at the Battle of Te Porere, Taupo. *Alexander Turnbull Library*

As the days dragged by with no news of Te Kooti, McDonnell had to send his kupapa home because they could not be fed at Tokaanu. New posts were established along the Napier road at Tarawera and Te Haroto, and manning these so seriously stretched personnel that the Armed Constabulary depot at Wellington sent up the last 60 available constables.

Te Kooti had little choice but to retreat northward along the corridor between the western shore of Lake Taupo and the eastern border of the King Country. The Government wished to end fighting if at all possible, and a meeting was arranged between Te Kooti and Mr J. C. Firth, a prominent settler, at Thompson's Monument, Matamata. The warrior admitted wanting to end hostilities, but would not agree to go to Auckland as a prisoner. Recalling the blood that had been spilt since he landed from the Chatham Islands, much of it by non-combatants, he doubtless expected an early trial and execution if the authorities got their hands on him.

McDonnell hurried in pursuit and overtook the Te Kooti's band at Patetere, about half-way between Tauranga and the Thames coast. The engagement was indecisive, Te Kooti slipping away towards the Bay of Plenty coast. Lieutenant-Colonel Fraser intercepted him at Paengaroa, but again lost this most elusive of men. Making for the shelter of the Urewera, Te Kooti decided to pay off an old score on the way by destroying the Arawa settlement at Rotorua. A naval deserter, Louis Baker, who had been captured, brought word to Gilbert Mair of the imminent attack, which threatened to develop into another massacre on the lines of Mohaka.

The Mair brothers never lacked bravery or initiative. It so happened that the captain had no more than a handful of Arawa warriors, but he pressed into service women and old men to give the appearance of additional defenders. Thus when Te Kooti approached he was surprised to find stronger opposition than he had expected.

Captain G. Mair (left) with a detachment of his Arawa Flying Column, N.Z.A.C., at his camp Kaiteriria on Lake Rotokakahi (Green Lake). Te Kooti's flag Te Wepu (The Whip), taken in battle on 7 February 1870, is shown at the right of the photograph. *Auckland Institute and Museum*

The hostile force sheered away towards Kaiteriria and then eastward for the Rangitaiki River. Determined not to let his enemies get away unscathed, Mair started in pursuit with such men as he had, and soon engaged the rearguard. He succeeded in killing Peka te Makarini (McLean), a notorious assassin of civilians. The Maori made for the deserted Fort Galatea, and despite their losses at Mair's hands reached the Urewera once again.

Mr J. D. Ormond, Superintendent of Hawke's Bay, wanted to mount another expedition from Taupo to go to Ruatahuna, as Whitmore had done from Tauranga, but the Government turned down the idea. In its place two of the most thrusting of the young officers in its service were authorised to raise flying columns of Arawa, Gilbert Mair operating from Kaiteriria on the southern tip of Rotokakahi (the Green Lake), and George Preece from his base at Te Teko.

The Tuhoe people were beginning to tire of their guest, and some surrendered. Mr F. E. Hamlin, leading an advance from Lake Waikaremoana, did reach Ruatahuna, but found only old men and women there. Ropata and Kepa scoured the Urewera, and steadily wore down the Tuhoe morale until Te Kooti was almost alone. Even then he escaped retribution, eluding all the hunters to reach sanctuary in the King Country. While Kereopa was taken and, after standing trial, paid for his crimes, Te Kooti was eventually pardoned under the Amnesty Act. The Government even gave him some land on the shore of Ohiwa Harbour, where he finally died as the result of an accident.

In 1872 hostilities thus came to an end. A decade later a civil disobedience movement in Taranaki, led by Te Whiti and Tohu, brought a serious confrontation at Parihaka. Thanks to Te Whiti's complete control of his large following, bloodshed was avoided. But neither war nor peaceful protest solved the intractable land problem, as we know today.

A file of 21 men of Mair's Arawa Flying Column. This photograph was taken in front of Kaiteriria Redoubt by Daniel Mundy of Dunedin on the day of Mair's return from the running fight with Te Kooti. *Alexander Turnbull Library*

Veteran officers of the New Zealand Armed Constabulary and Militia photographed at Parihaka in 1881. Back row (left to right): Captains W. E. Gudgeon, H. Morrison, Gordon, Taylor, Powell, Fortescue, S. Newall and Major A. Tuke. Front row (left to right): Captains Baker and Anderson, Lieutenant-Colonel J. M. Roberts, Captains G. Mair, H. W. Northcroft, W. B. Messenger and Major F. Y. Goring

Chronology of Events Relating to the Colonial Wars in New Zealand

22 January 1840	The first immigrant ship of the New Zealand Company arrives in Wellington.
6 February 1840	The Treaty of Waitangi is signed by 46 chiefs at the Bay of Islands.
3 May 1841	New Zealand becomes a Crown Colony, severing links with New South Wales.
17 June 1843	Captain Wakefield and 22 Europeans are killed at Tua Maruia, Wairau, after a dispute over land with Te Rauparaha.
8 July 1844	The flagstaff at Kororareka, Bay of Islands, is cut down at the instigation of Hone Heke.
10 January 1845	The flagstaff is cut down a second time.
19 January 1845	The flagstaff is cut down for a third time.
11 March 1845	The flagstaff is cut down for a fourth time and the town of Kororareka is sacked, with the loss of 10 soldiers and seamen dead.
30 April 1845	Otuihu Pa is burnt, and chief Pomare is arrested.
8 May 1845	An attack on Puketutu Pa by British troops is repulsed.
15 May 1845	Major Cyprian Bridge attacks Kapotai Pa at Waikare Inlet.
12 June 1845	Hone Heke is defeated at Pukenui by a loyal force under Tamati Waka Nene.
1 July 1845	British forces led by Colonel Despard are heavily repulsed while trying to storm Ohaeawai Pa.
11 January 1846	Ruapekapeka Pa is occupied by British troops, thus ending the war in the north.
3 March 1846	Te Rangihaeata's warriors begin to harass settlers in the Hutt Valley.
16 May 1846	The post at Boulcott's Farm in the Hutt Valley is attacked and seven soldiers are killed.
23 July 1846	Te Rauparaha is captured at Plimmerton by Governor Grey and taken to Auckland in H.M.S. *Calliope*.
29 July 1846	Pauatahanui Pa is evacuated by Te Rangihaeata after being attacked by British troops.
6 August 1846	Te Rangihaeata's pa at Horokiwi is attacked.
13 August 1846	The defence of Horokiwi is abandoned, thus ending the war at Wellington.
26 April 1847	Four Maori are executed at Wanganui for the murder of the Gilfillan family.
19 May 1847	The chief Topine te Mamaku attacks the settlement of Wanganui.
20 July 1847	The Battle of St John's Wood, Wanganui, ends indecisively.
21 February 1848	Governor Grey notifies peace with Te Mamaku at Wanganui.
5 November 1855	Four hundred New Plymouth settlers are called up for Militia service.
7 March 1859	Te Teira offers to sell the site at Waitara to Governor Gore Browne. Wiremu Kingi opposes this sale of land by his nephew.
27 February 1860	Surveyors are driven off at Waitara, Taranaki.
17 March 1860	Colonel Gold attacks the pa at Te Kohia, Waitara, which is evacuated the following day.
28 March 1860	Battle of Waireka, Taranaki.
27 June 1860	British troops are heavily defeated at Puketakauere Pa.
10 September 1860	General Pratt marches with a force of 1,400 men to the left bank of the Waitara River and burns four pa.
6 November 1860	The defeat of a Maori party at Mahoetahi.
18 January 1861	Huirangi Pa is attacked by General Pratt.
23 January 1861	Attack on No. 3 Redoubt, Huirangi.
2 February 1861	Pratt commences his sap at Te Arei Pa.
19 March 1861	Hapurona surrenders Te Arei Pa.
8 April 1861	Articles of Peace are signed, so ending the First Taranaki War.
1 April 1863	A final warning is given by the Maori that if the Government does not give up its claim to the Waitara Block, Tataraimaka would be attacked on 1 May.
4 May 1863	Hostilities in Taranaki are resumed when a detachment of troops is ambushed at Tataraimaka and nine men killed.
4 June 1863	The Katikara Pa, Tataraimaka, is captured by Colonel Warre.
12 July 1863	General Cameron's force crosses the Mangatawhiri River, the first definite act in the Waikato campaign.
17 July 1863	The Battle of Koheroa, Waikato.
12 August 1863	The gunboat *Avon* bombards Meremere Pa.
7 September 1863	The engagement at Camerontown, Waikato.
9 September 1863	The first engagement between Volunteers and Maori takes place at Mauku.
14 September 1863	Pukekohe East church is besieged by a large Maori war party.
25 September 1863	Mataitawa Pa, Taranaki, is attacked by Major Butler.
23 October 1863	A detachment is ambushed between Mauku and Drury, and eight soldiers killed.
1 November 1863	Meremere Pa, Waikato, is abandoned by its garrison.
20 November 1863	The repulse of three attacks on Rangiriri Pa, Waikato.
21 November 1863	The surrender of Rangiriri Pa.
8 December 1863	The British enter the Maori King's capital at Ngaruawahia.
21 February 1864	General Cameron captures Rangiaowhia, Waikato.
22 February 1864	The Maori are defeated at Hairini, near Rangiaowhia.
24 March 1864	Kaitake Pa, Taranaki, is stormed.
30 March 1864	Orakau Pa is surrounded by Cameron's forces.
2 April 1864	Rewi's warriors break out of Orakau Pa after an heroic resistance.

6 April 1864	The Hauhau wars commence in Taranaki, when a detachment from the 65th Regiment is ambushed at Te Ahuahu.
27 April 1864	The Tai Rawhiti are driven from Maketu, Bay of Plenty, by the Arawa.
29 April 1864	British troops are repulsed with heavy losses at the Gate Pa, Tauranga.
30 April 1864	A Hauhau attack on the redoubt at Sentry Hill, Taranaki, is repulsed with severe Maori casualties.
14 May 1864	Loyal Maori defeat Hauhau rebels at Moutoa Island in the Wanganui River.
21 June 1864	The defeat of the Maori at Te Ranga, Tauranga.
25 July 1864	The Tauranga tribes surrender to Colonel Greer.
10 September 1864	Te Arei Pa, Taranaki, is evacuated by the Maori.
17 December 1864	Maori land amounting to 1,200,000 acres is confiscated.
5 January 1865	General Cameron is ordered by Governor Grey to commence the Wanganui campaign.
24 January 1865	A surprise attack on the British camp at Nukumaru.
4 February 1865	Cameron's force crosses the Waitotara River.
2 March 1865	Rev. C. S. Volkner is killed by the Hauhau at Opotiki, Bay of Plenty.
7 April 1865	Cameron reaches the Waingongoro River, Taranaki.
27 May 1865	Wiremu Tamehana surrenders to General Carey at Tamahere, Waikato.
13 June 1865	Colonel Warre attacks villages inland from Warea, Taranaki.
19 July 1865	The siege of Pipiriki, on the Upper Wanganui River, commences and lasts until 30 July.
3 August 1865	Brevet-Major Fraser successfully attacks Pa-Kairomiromi on the Waiapu during his East Cape campaign.
3 August 1865	Carey destroys Okea Pa, Taranaki.
27 August 1865	Major General Trevor Chute, Commander of the Imperial forces in Australia and New Zealand, arrives to take over.
8 September 1865	A Colonial force lands at Opotiki to oppose the Hauhau on the East Coast.
20 October 1865	The Hauhau pa at Te Teko, Bay of Plenty, surrenders to Major W. G. Mair.
22 November 1865	Brevet-Major Fraser defeats the Maori at Waerenga-a-Hika Pa near Gisborne.
30 December 1865	Major General Chute sets out on his march from Wanganui to New Plymouth.
14 January 1866	Otapawa Pa, Taranaki, falls to Chute.
26 January 1866	British and Colonial troops arrive at New Plymouth after their successful march from Wanganui.
1 February 1866	Chute commences the return march to Wanganui.
9 February 1865	The force reaches Wanganui, after circling Mount Egmont and destroying seven fortified pa and 21 villages.
2 October 1866	Warre leads an attack on the Maori at Allen's Hill, Taranaki.
12 October 1866	The Hauhau are defeated at Omarunui and Petane, Hawke's Bay.
18 January 1867	The start of the Tauranga bush campaign.
4 February 1867	A combined attack is made on the Hauhau at Te Akeake.
17 March 1867	Arawa led by Captain G. Mair defeat the Maori at Te Koutu.
19 June 1867	Three sawyers are killed near Normanby, Taranaki, heralding the start of a rebellion led by the Maori chief Titokowaru.
4 July 1868	Te Kooti and his followers escape from the Chatham Islands.
12 July 1868	Turuturumokai Redoubt is attacked.
8 August 1868	Te Kooti drives off a large force under Colonel Whitmore at Ruakituri, Poverty Bay.
21 August 1868	The first attack on Te Ngutu-o-te-Manu Pa, Taranaki.
7 September 1868	Lieutenant-Colonel McDonnell's second attack at Te Ngutu-o-te-Manu is repulsed, and Major Von Tempsky is killed.
7 November 1868	Whitmore is defeated by Titokowaru at Moturoa, Taranaki.
10 November 1868	Te Kooti attacks Matawhero, Poverty Bay, and kills 70 Maori and European settlers.
5 January 1869	Te Kooti's pa at Ngatapa is stormed by a combined force of Europeans and friendly Maori.
2 February 1869	Titokowaru abandons his pa at Tauranga-ika, thus ending the South Taranaki campaign.
14 February 1869	Nine Europeans, including the Rev. J. Whiteley, are killed at White Cliffs (Pukearuhe) Taranaki. Taranaki.
9 March 1869	Te Kooti raids Whakatane, Bay of Plenty.
10 April 1869	Sixty Maori and Europeans are killed by Te Kooti at Mohaka, Hawke's Bay.
5 May 1869	Colonel Whitmore and Lieutenant-Colonel St John meet at Ruatahuna during their pursuit of Te Kooti in the Urewera.
7 June 1869	A detachment of cavalry is taken by surprise at Opepe, Taupo, and nine troopers are killed.
3 October 1869	Te Kooti is defeated at Te Porere, Taupo, by a Maori and European force commanded by Lieutenant-Colonel McDonnell.
7 February 1870	Captain Gilbert Mair and his Arawa Flying Column defeat Te Kooti at Earthquake Flat, Rotorua.
23 March 1870	Te Kooti is defeated at Maraetahi, Urewera, with the loss of 20 of his men.
17 April 1870	The Urewera tribes surrender to Captains Mair and Preece.
1 September 1871	Captain Porter's force defeats Te Kooti at Te Hapua, Urewera.
14 February 1872	Te Kooti is engaged for the last time, and the final shots of the war are fired at Mangaone, Urewera.
17 May 1872	Te Kooti finds sanctuary in the King Country.

The Victoria Cross

The Victoria Cross was instituted by Royal Warrant dated 29 January 1856 to recognise 'conspicuous gallantry in the presence of the enemy'. Fifteen medals were won during the New Zealand wars, and the following list of recipients, with details drawn from official rolls research by D. Corbett, is arranged alphabetically.

L.G. = *London Gazette*

Ensign John Thornton Down, 57th Regiment, L.G.22.9.64

'For his conduct on 2 October 1863 at Poutoko (Allan's Hill, New Plymouth) in rescuing a wounded comrade from the rebel Maori. Together with Drummer Stagpoole, they succeeded in bringing in the wounded man, who was lying at about fifty yards from the bush, although the enemy kept up a very heavy fire from the bush at close range, and also from fallen logs close at hand. The man had been wounded during an engagement with the rebel natives, and Ensign Down and Drummer Stagpoole responded to the call of the officer commanding the detachment of the regiment for volunteers to bring him in.'

Down died of fever in New Zealand in 1866, and is buried in Otahuhu Cemetery, Auckland. His name is on the brass tablet erected in St Paul's Cathedral to the memory of the officers of the 57th Regiment who fell in action or died during the New Zealand campaign.

Captain Charles Heaphy, Auckland Militia

The decoration won by Heaphy was an exception to the original rule that it be restricted to Imperial servicemen. In 1867, when the Victoria Cross was granted to Heaphy, it was held that because Colonel Sir Henry Havelock, V.C. had placed him in command of a detachment of British troops he became eligible as a person serving with 'our troops under the command of a general or other officer'. Heaphy's V.C. was the first to be awarded to a member of a colonial force and to a non-Regular serviceman.

At Waiari, on 11 February 1864, two men were killed while trying to rescue a wounded corporal. Heaphy then went out to the man and dressed his wounds while the enemy continued to fire at him. With the help of some soldiers, the casualty was brought in. Although he had been hit five times and wounded twice, Heaphy insisted upon remaining on duty until the end of the action.

After his arrival in 1840 as the New Zealand Company's draughtsman in the *Tory*, Heaphy explored in the South Island, and became one of the country's foremost early artists. He spent most of his life as a land commissioner and surveyor, dying at Brisbane, Australia, in 1881.

Colour-Sergeant John Lucas, 40th Regiment, L.G.19.7.61

'On 18 March 1861 Colour-Sergeant Lucas acted as sergeant of a party of the 40th Regiment employed as skirmishers to the right of No. 7 Redoubt and close to the Huirangi Bush, facing the left of the positions occupied by the natives. At about 4 p.m. a very heavy and well-directed fire was suddenly opened upon them from the bush and the high ground on the left. Three men being wounded simultaneously, two of them mortally, assistance was called for in order to have them carried to the rear; a file was immediately sent, but had scarcely arrived when one of them fell, and Lieutenant Rees was wounded at the same time. Colour-Sergeant Lucas, under a very heavy fire from the rebels who were not more than thirty yards distant, immediately ran up to the assistance of this officer and sent one man with him to the rear. He then took charge of the arms belonging to the killed and wounded men and maintained his position until the arrival of supports under Lieutenants Gibson and Whelan.'

Lucas was promoted to Sergeant-Major. He died in Dublin, Ireland, on 29 February 1892.

Above: Ensign J. Down and Drummer Stagpoole rescuing a wounded comrade, 1864. From *Navy and Army Illustrated. Above Centre:* Colour-Sergeant J. Lucas defending his position against the Maoris. *D. Corbett. Above Right:* Colour-Sergeant E. McKenna takes command after the death of Captain Smith. *D. Corbett. Right:* Captain Charles Heaphy, Auckland Militia. *Alexander Turnbull Library*

Colour-Sergeant Edward McKenna, 65th Regiment, L.G.16.1.64

'For gallant conduct at the engagement near Cameron Town on 7 September 1863 after both his officers, Captain Smith and Lieutenant Butler, had been shot, in charging through the position of an enemy heavily outnumbering him, and drawing off his small force, consisting of two sergeants, one bugler and 35 men through a broken and rugged country with the loss of one man killed and another missing. Lieut-General Cameron C.B. commanding Her Majesty's forces in that Colony, reports that in Colour-Sergeant McKenna the detachment found a commander whose coolness, intrepidity and judgement justified the confidence placed in him by the soldiers brought so suddenly under his command.'

McKenna was promoted to Ensign on 8 September 1863, and after his death his widow presented his Victoria Cross, medals and a revolver given to him by his wounded officer to the Auckland Museum in 1912.

Lieutenant-Colonel John Carstairs M'Neill, 107th Regiment, L.G.16.7.64

'For valour and presence of mind which he displayed in New Zealand on 30 March 1864 which is thus described by Private Vosper of the Colonial Defence Force. Private Vosper states that he was sent on duty on that date with Private Gibson of the same force as an escort to Major (now Lieut-Colonel) M'Neill, Aide-de-Camp to Lieut-General Sir Duncan Cameron. Lieut-Colonel M'Neill was proceeding to Te Awamutu on duty at the time. On returning from that place and about a mile on this side of Ohaupo, this officer having seen a body of the enemy in front, sent Private Gibson back to bring up infantry from Ohaupo, and he and Private Vosper proceeded leisurely to the top of a rise to watch the enemy. Suddenly they were attacked by about fifty natives who were concealed in the fern close at hand. Their only chance of escape was by riding for their lives, and as they turned to gallop Private Vosper's horse fell and threw him. The natives thereupon rushed forward to seize him but Lieut-Colonel M'Neill, on perceiving that Private Vosper was not following him, returned, caught his horse and helped him to mount. The natives were firing sharply at them and were so near that according to Private Vosper's statement, it was only by galloping as hard as they could that they escaped. He says that he owes his life entirely to Lieut-Colonel M'Neill's assistance, for he could not have caught his horse alone, and in a few minutes must have been killed.'

Major-General Sir John Carstairs M'Neill, V.C., G.C.V.O., K.C.B., K.C.M.G., died at St James's Palace on 25 April 1904.

Assistant-Surgeon William George Nicholas Manley, Royal Artillery, L.G.22.9.64

'For his conduct during the assault on the rebel pa near Tauranga on 29 April 1864, in most nobly risking his own life, according to the testimony of Commodore Sir William Wiseman C.B., in his endeavour to save the life of the late Commander Hay of the Royal Navy, and others. Having volunteered to accompany the storming party into the pa, he attended on that officer when he was carried away mortally wounded, and then volunteered to return in order to see if he could find any more wounded. It is stated that he was one of the last officers to leave the pa.'

Manley gained the Royal Humane Society's medal for saving a man of the Royal Artillery who had fallen overboard in the Waitotara River on 21 July 1865. He was promoted to Surgeon-General, and created C.B. in 1884. Manley died on 16 November 1891.

Samuel Mitchell, Captain of the Foretop, Royal Navy, L.G.26.7.64

'For his gallant conduct at the attack at Te Papa (the Gate Pa) on 29 April 1864, in entering the pa with Commander Hay and when that officer was mortally wounded, bringing him out, although ordered by Commander Hay to leave him and seek his own safety. This man was at the time Captain of the Foretop of the *Harrier* doing his duty as Captain's Coxswain, and Commodore Sir William Wiseman brings his name to special notice for this act of gallantry.'

Mitchell was drowned on 16 March 1894 in the Mikonui River, South Westland, and is buried in Hokitika Cemetery.

Sergeant John Murray, 68th Regiment, L.G.4.11.64

'For his distinguished conduct during the engagement at Tauranga on 21 June 1864 when the enemy's position was being stormed, in running up to a rifle-pit containing from eight to ten of the enemy, and, without any assistance, killing and wounding every one of them. He is stated to have afterwards proceeded up the works fighting desperately and still continuing to bayonet the enemy.'

Murray died on 7 November 1911.

Leading Seaman William Odgers, Royal Navy, L.G.3.8.60

'William Odgers, Leading Seaman of Her Majesty's Ship *Niger* on 28 March 1860 displayed conspicuous gallantry at the storming of a pa at Waireka, New Plymouth during operations against the rebel natives in New Zealand, having been the first to enter it under heavy fire and having assisted in hauling down the enemy's colours.'

Odgers died on 20 December 1873.

Lieutenant Arthur Frederick Pickard, Royal Artillery, L.G.22.9.64

'For gallant conduct during the assault on the enemy's position at Rangiriri on 20 November 1863 in exposing his life to imminent danger in crossing the entrance of the Maori keep at a point upon which the enemy had concentrated their fire, with a view to rendering assistance to the wounded, and more especially to the late Captain Mercer, R.A. Lieutenant Pickard crossed and recrossed the parapet to procure water for the wounded when none of the men could be induced to perform this service, the space over which he traversed being exposed to a cross-fire, and testimony is borne to the coolness displayed by him and Assistant-Surgeon Temple under the trying circumstances to which they were exposed.'

Colonel Pickard, C.B. became Equerry to Queen Victoria. He died of tuberculosis at Cannes, France, early in the 1890s.

Left: Leading Seaman William Odgers at the storming of Kaipopo Pa, Waireka, Taranaki. *From Navy and Army Illustrated. Far Left:* Captain of the Foretop Samuel Mitchell carries the mortally wounded Commander Hay. From *Picturesque Atlas of Australasia. Lower Left:* The incident at Te Ranga when Sergeant John Murray of the 68th Regiment killed a Maori about to tomahawk a corporal of the 43rd Regiment. A painting by Major G. F. Von Tempsky. *Auckland Institute and Museum*

Lance-Corporal John Ryan, 65th Regiment, L.G.16.1.64

'For gallant conduct at the engagement near Cameron Town on 7 September 1863. This non-commissioned officer, with Privates Bulford and Talbot, of the same regiment, who have been recommended for the Medal for Distinguished Conduct in the field for their behaviour on the same occasion, removed the body of the late Captain Smith from the field of action after he had been mortally wounded, and remained with it all night in the bush surrounded by the enemy.'

Ryan was drowned near Tuakau on 29 December 1863, while trying to rescue a comrade.

Captain Hugh Shaw, 18th Regiment, L.G.28.11.65

'For his gallant conduct at the skirmish near Nukumaru on 24 January 1865 in proceeding under a very heavy fire with four privates of the regiment who volunteered to accompany him, to within thirty yards of the bush occupied by the rebels in order to carry off a comrade who was badly wounded. On the afternoon of that day, Captain Shaw was ordered to occupy a position about half a mile from the camp. He advanced in skirmishing order and when about thirty yards from the bush he deemed it prudent to retire to a palisade about sixty yards from the bush as two of his party had been wounded. Finding that one of them was unable to move, he called for volunteers to advance to the front, to carry the man to the rear and the four privates referred to accompanied him under heavy fire to the place where the wounded man was lying and they succeeded in bringing him to the rear.'

Major-General Hugh Shaw, C.B. died in September 1904.

Captain Frederick Augustus Smith, 43rd Regiment, L.G.4.11.64

'For his distinguished conduct during the engagement at Tauranga on 21 June 1864. He is stated to have led his company in the most gallant manner at the attack on the Maori's position and although wounded previously to reaching the rifle-pits, to have jumped down into them when he commenced a hand-to-hand encounter with the enemy, thereby giving his men great encouragement and setting them a fine example.'

Lieutenant-Colonel Smith died on 22 July 1887.

Drummer Dudley Stagpoole, 57th Regiment, L.G.22.9.64

'For his conduct on 2 October 1863 at Poutoko in rescuing a wounded comrade from the rebel Maori. Together with Ensign Down, they succeeded in bringing in the wounded man who was lying at about fifty yards from the bush, although the enemy kept up a very heavy fire from the bush at short range and also from behind fallen logs close at hand. The man had been wounded during an engagement with the rebel natives, and Ensign Down and Drummer Stagpoole responded to the call of the officer commanding the detachment of the regiment for volunteers to bring him in. The Medal for Distinguished Conduct in the field has already been conferred on Drummer Stagpoole for the energy and devotion which he displayed on 25 September 1863 at the affair near Kaipakopako in having, though wounded in the head, twice volunteered and brought in wounded men.'

Stagpoole died on 1 August 1911, and is buried at Hendon Park.

Captain Hugh Shaw, 18th Royal Irish Regiment. *Hawke's Bay Art Gallery and Museum*

Assistant-Surgeon William Temple, L.G.22.9.64

'For gallant conduct during the assault of the enemy's position at Rangiriri on 20 November 1863 when he and Lieut A. F. Pickard R.A. exposed their lives to imminent danger in crossing the entrance of the Maori Keep at a point upon which the enemy had concentrated their fire, with a view to render assistance to the wounded and more especially to the late Captain Mercer R.A. Lieut Pickard it is said, crossed and recrossed the parapet to procure water for the wounded when none of the men could be induced to perform this service, the space over which he traversed being exposed to a cross-fire and testimony is borne to the calmness displayed by him and Assistant-Surgeon Temple under the trying circumstances to which they were exposed.'

Lieutenant-Colonel Temple died on 13 February 1919.

The Distinguished Conduct Medal

Private John Hennigan

Prior to the Crimean War, no recognised gallantry medal existed for other ranks of the British Army. Unofficial regimental awards had been made. The Meritorious Service Medal and the Long Service Medal already existed, but both were associated with good conduct in quarters rather than with distinguished conduct in the field.

On 4 December 1854, a Royal Warrant was issued to meet the need for an official gallantry medal to be awarded to other ranks (private soldiers) for 'distinguished service and gallant conduct in the field'.

Citations for the Distinguished Conduct Medal before 1914 are comparatively rare, therefore the following list of recipients from the Official Register for service in New Zealand records only the name and rank of the soldier, and the date and place of the action in which he won the award.

Royal Artillery	Sergeant-Major J. Hamilton	Rangiriri	20.11.63
18th Regiment	Private John Brandon	Nukumaru	24.1.65
	Private George Clampitt	Nukumaru	24.1.65
	Private John Graham	Nukumaru	24.1.65
	Private James Kearnes	Nukumaru	24.1.65
	Private James Acton	Papoia	18.10.66
	Private John Hennigan	Papoia	18.10.66
43rd Regiment	Colour-Sergeant W. B. Garland	Gate Pa	28.4.64
57th Regiment	Private T. Bishop		1864
	Private J. Donaghy	Kaitakara	4.6.63
	Sergeant D. O'Connor	Kakaramea	13.3.65
	Drummer D. Stagpoole	Kaipakopako	25.9.63
65th Regiment	Sergeant John Bracegirdle	Camerontown	7.9.63
	Private W. Bulford	Camerontown	7.9.63
	Private J. Cole	Camerontown	7.9.63
	Private J. Talbot	Camerontown	7.9.63
	Private B. Thomas	Camerontown	7.9.63
	Sergeant W. Meare		1863
68th Regiment	Corporal J. Byrne	Te Ranga	21.6.64
	Sergeant-Major John Tudor	Te Ranga	21.6.64
	Lance-Sergeant J. Castles	Kakaramea	13.3.65
70th Regiment	Private G. Dowling	Orakau	2.4.64

The New Zealand Cross

The New Zealand Cross was adopted as a decoration which would rank next to the Victoria Cross for members of Militia, Volunteer and Armed Constabulary units who 'when serving in the presence of the enemy, shall have performed some single act of valour or devotion to duty'.

The medal was instituted by the Governor of New Zealand, Sir George Bowen, by an order in council dated 10 March 1869, and met an urgent need for some equivalent to the Victoria Cross for which locally raised forces were then ineligible. At the time of its inception it was known by a variety of names before settling on its present title: New Zealand Cross of Valour, Cross of New Zealand, Silver Cross, Colonial Cross, Order of the Southern Cross, Order of Valour, Order of Merit, Colonial Order of Merit and Southern Cross.

Governor Bowen conferred five decorations before notifying London and was officially rebuked for overstepping the limits of the authority vested in him by the Queen. Because the awards had already been made, however, Queen Victoria had little option but to ratify the order in council.

Only 23 New Zealand Crosses were bestowed during the New Zealand wars, and none has been awarded since, making it one of the rarest of decorations. The recipients are listed in the order in which their names appear in the Roll of the New Zealand Cross.

Constable Henare Kepa Te Ahururu, No. 1 Division A.C.

'For his gallant conduct during the attack on the enemy's position at Moturoa on 7 November 1868.

The storming party, failing to find an entrance, passed round to the rear of the work. Conceiving an entrance to the pa was desired, Constable Kepa climbed the palisades of the fortification alone; in doing which he was shot through the lungs, but nevertheless walked out of action and brought his arms into camp.'

Constable Solomon Black, No. 1 Division A.C.

'For his gallant conduct at the siege of Ngatapa in January 1869.

The rear of the enemy's position was assigned to the attack under Major Fraser, consisting of Nos. 1 and 3 Divisions A.C. and Hotene's Ngatiporou. The extreme right, on a scarped stony ridge, was commanded from the enemy's rifle-pits and works, and a lodgment was only effected by cutting out standing room with a pickaxe. The enemy made several determined sorties against this point, and it became extremely difficult to maintain the position, which was essential to the success of the operation. A party of twelve volunteers were at length placed there, and they succeeded, with some loss, in holding the position till the end of the siege, and in repelling several resolute attacks. One of the most conspicuous for his bravery was Constable Black.'

Constable Benjamin Biddle, No. 1 Division A.C.

The citation for Constable Biddle is identical to that of his comrade, Constable Black.

Trooper William Lingard. From *Defenders of New Zealand*

Trooper William Lingard, Kai-Iwi Cavalry Volunteers

'For his gallant conduct before the enemy on 28 December 1868.

While the Kai-Iwi and Wanganui Troops of the Cavalry Volunteers were reconnoitring the enemy's position at Taurangaika, a portion of the Force galloped in close to the palisades of the pa, receiving the enemy's fire at the distance of a few yards, several men becoming dismounted through having their horses shot. Trooper Lingard rode past the pa, at the distance of about forty yards, and cut with his sword the tether line of a horse belonging to the enemy, brought it to one of his comrades whose horse was shot, and assisted him to mount thereon.'

Sergeant George Hill, No. 1 Division A.C.

'On 10 April 1869, Constable (now Sergeant) George Hill, of No. 1 Division Armed Constabulary, accompanied the Wairoa Natives who, under Ihaka Whanga, proceeded to relieve Mohaka, then being attacked by Te Kooti. A party volunteered to run the gauntlet of the enemy's fire, and to dash into the Jerusalem Pa, then sorely pressed. This was a dangerous service, and it was in great measure due to the example set by Constable Hill, who led the party, that it was successfully carried out. During the subsequent portion of the siege, Constable Hill animated the defenders by his exertions and contributed greatly to the repulse of Te Kooti, and his conduct is spoken of with admiration by the Natives themselves.'

Cornet Angus Smith, Bay of Plenty Cavalry Volunteers

'On 7 June 1869, when the party of Cavalry in the charge of Cornet Smith was surprised at Opepe by Te Kooti's band, and 9 men out of 13 were killed, Cornet Smith, though suffering from a desperate wound in his foot, set out with the object of finding the tracks of his Commanding Officer, and apprising him and the party with him of their danger, when a less brave or thoughtful man would have proceeded straight to Fort Galatea, which post he would no doubt have reached in 48 hours, with comparatively little risk, and with the certainty of getting immediate medical assistance for himself. On his road, Cornet Smith was captured by the rebels, tied up to a tree, and stripped of all his clothing and Crimean medals. He was in this position for four days without food or water, when he managed to release himself, and proceeded to Fort Galatea, which he reached on 17 June, having been ten days without food or clothing. On account of his wounds he had to go for a considerable distance on his hands and knees, and to risk his life twice by swimming rivers.'

Sergeant Arthur Wakefield Carkeek, A.C.

'On 7 February 1870, while the force under the command of Lt-Col McDonnell was serving in the Patetere country, Te Kooti with his force came out of the bush on the further side of the ranges and attacked Ohinemutu, where Captain Mair, with some Arawas, were posted. It was of the utmost importance that immediate notice should be sent to Lt-Col McDonnell of the whereabouts of the enemy, and Sergeant Carkeek, who was then at Ohinemutu, used every exertion to get Natives to convey a note to him at Tapapa, through the bush, but no one could be induced to incur the risk. Sergeant Carkeek then determined to take the information himself; and, having found a Native who agreed to accompany him, started at daylight on the 8th, and arrived at Tapapa at about 3 p.m., having come upwards of thirty miles through dense bush known to be haunted by the enemy, and in danger of being surprised by them at any moment, when certain death would have been his fate.'

Dr Isaac Earl Featherston, volunteer on the staff of Major-General Chute, C.B.

Extract from the recommendation by Major-General Chute:

'As I have already acknowledged in my despatches the eminent services rendered to me by Dr Featherston throughout the Campaign, I now consider it my duty to recommend this Officer in the strongest terms for the Distinctive Decoration of the New Zealand Cross, in recognition of his meritorious and intrepid services during the period referred to, and more particularly at the storming of that formidable Pa Otapawa, where, I must in truth say, Dr Featherston so exposed himself in the service of his Queen and Country as to become, as it were, a target for the enemy's fire, thus by his noble example stimulating the courage of the Native Allies.'

Inspector John Mackintosh Roberts, A.C.

'This gallant officer was awarded the New Zealand Cross, by his excellency the Governor, Sir George Grey, for his resolute bearing on 6 September 1868, at Te Ngutu o te Manu, where owing to a miscarriage of order issued by Colonel McDonnell to retire, he and his men were left behind, and eventually had to fight their way back through standing bush closely pursued by the enemy. To his coolness and determination on this occasion may be attributed the saving of the force under his command.

And for the courage and judgement displayed by him at the Battle of Moturoa, on 7 November 1868, when having only arrived during the night, he with his young and newly raised division succeeded in covering the retreat of Colonel Whitmore's force, though greatly outnumbered, and at one time nearly surrounded.

To his fortitude as a soldier and the confidence he inspired, was mainly due the discipline of his men who kept their ranks in a dense bush in spite of the repeated efforts of the enemy to close with them, and so enable the force, encumbered with the wounded to draw off in good order.'

Lieutenant-Colonel Roberts served for many years as a magistrate, and at his death in 1928 was the last surviving officer of the colonial forces to have served during the wars of the nineteenth century.

Above Left: Cornet (later Captain) Angus Smith. *National Museum*
Above Right: Sergeant Arthur W. Carkeek. *National Museum*

Major Kepa Rangihiwinui, N.Z.M., Native Contingent

'For devoted and chivalrous conduct at Moturoa on 7 November 1868, when at the head of a very small portion of his tribe, with which he covered a flank of the retreat, and assisted in the removal of the wounded, although exposed to a very heavy fire at a close range. And for the personal gallantry and constancy shown by him in conducting the pursuit of Titokowaru's followers after their defeat at Otauto on 13 March 1869, hanging on their rear, and constantly harassing them during several days in dense bush. His force on this occasion was composed entirely of volunteers, several officers and many men of the Armed Constabulary having volunteered to follow this distinguished chief, besides the members of his own tribe.'

Major Ropata Wahawaha, Native Contingent
'For personal gallantry and loyal devotion on the occasion both of the first and last attack on Ngatapa, and more especially for the courage he showed on the first occasion, at the head of only 70 men, when all the rest of the Native Contingent had retreated, and left him without support. Major Ropata then pushed his way close to the entrenchments, and held a position at pistol-shot distance all day, and until, under cover of night, he was compelled by want of ammunition to retire, having sustained heavy losses.'

Top Left: Major Ropata Wahawaha. *Alexander Turnbull Library. Top Centre:* Captain Francis J. Mace. From *Defenders of New Zealand. Right:* Sergeant Christopher Maling. *Taranaki Museum. Above Left:* Captain (Sub-Inspector) George Preece. From *Defenders of New Zealand. Above Centre:* Assistant-Surgeon Samuel Walker. From *Defenders of New Zealand*

Far Left: Dr Isaac E. Featherston. From *Defenders of New Zealand Centre. Left:* Inspector John M. Roberts. *Alexander Turnbull Library. Left:* Major Kepa Rangihiwinui. *Alexander Turnbull Library*

Captain Francis Joseph Mace, Taranaki Militia
'For conspicuous bravery in the performance of his duty throughout the Taranaki war; for most valuable and efficient services in conveying despatches through the enemy's country, and in acting as a guide upon many important expeditions. Notably his conduct at the Katikara River, on 4 June 1863; at Kaitake, on 11 March 1864, and at Warea, on 20 October 1865.

Captain Mace's services were publicly noted by General Pratt, Colonel Warre, and other officers, upon several occasions; and he personally received the thanks of Governors Gore Browne and Grey.'

Frank Mace was mentioned eight times in despatches, and after all his hazardous exploits lived to be 90 years of age.

Sub-Inspector George Preece, A.C.
'For personal bravery (when Interpreter to the Native Contingent, and attached to Major Ropata) on the occasion of the first attack on Ngatapa. Mr Preece's behaviour was so brilliant as to attract the admiration of Major Ropata, who recommended him for special reward to the Colonel Commanding the following day, with the very complimentary remark that, with two or three more like him, he would have been able to break into the pa, at that time not fully completed.'

Preece was the son of a pioneer missionary, and lived until 1928.

Assistant-Surgeon Samuel Walker, A.C.
'For conspicuous gallantry in the performance of his duties as Assistant-Surgeon on many occasions during the campaign of 1868–69, and notably at the successful attack upon the position and encampment of Titokowaru at Otautu, on 13 March 1869, where he was exposed to a very heavy fire, and bore himself with great courage.'

Sergeant Christopher Maling, Corps of Guides
'For most valuable and efficient services as Sergeant of the Corps of Guides on many occasions, and especially in going out to scout in advance with three men (two of whom were shot on the morning of 20 February 1869) by which an intended ambuscade was discovered, and many lives saved. And for a long reconnaissance with two men of the Corps of Guides (which lasted two nights and days) in advance, to ascertain the direction of Titokowaru's retreat after he had evacuated Tauranga-ika. This service was a most daring one, and of the utmost importance to the force, as intelligence was thus obtained which in no other way could have been procured.'

Sergeant Richard Shepherd, A.C.
'For distinguished bravery at Otautu, on 13 March 1869, while holding the ground close to the encampment, and enabling a close reconnaissance to be made by Major Kepa and the Colonel Commanding. Sergeant Shepherd was dangerously wounded on this occasion.'

Sergeant Samuel Austin, Wanganui Volunteer Contingent
'For gallant and distinguished conduct on 7 January 1866, when, at the capture of the Putahi Pa, Lieutenant-Colonel McDonnell was severely wounded, and Sergeant Austin carried him during a great part of the engagement under a raking fire, and finally off the field, which action was witnessed by General Chute, who then thanked him for his fearless and heroic conduct, not only in this instance, but on all occasions during the campaign on the West Coast.

Also on 17 October 1866, at the capture of the village of Keteonetea. Captain William McDonnell, leading a small advance guard of Maoris, came upon an ambush, and fell severely wounded; his men leaving him, retired on the main body, who commenced to retreat, when Sergeant Austin, assisted by another man (since dead) returned to where Captain McDonnell lay, on the point of being tomahawked by the enemy, and at all risks carried him off under a heavy fire.'

Trooper Antonio Rodriguez, Taranaki Mounted Volunteers

'For noble and daring conduct in assisting and carrying wounded men from the field under fire, on several occasions, notably on 2 October 1863, at Poutoko, and 11 March 1864 at Kaitake, upon which latter occasion he was particularly mentioned in garrison orders after the engagement. Rodriguez's conduct was repeatedly mentioned by Colonel Warre and other officers in their despatches.'

Private Thomas Adamson, Corps of Guides

'For good and gallant services as a scout and guide throughout the campaign of 1868–69, continually undertaking hazardous and laborious reconnoitring expeditions almost alone in advance of the force. And for personal gallantry when attached, with other guides, in advance of the column beyond Ahikeruru, on 7 May 1869, where they unmasked an ambuscade, and Adamson, with others, was severely wounded, and the guide Hemi killed.'

Lieutenant-Colonel Thomas McDonnell, N.Z.M.

'In October 1863 Sub-Inspector McDonnell, Colonial Defence Force, volunteered to accompany the late Major Von Tempsky to reconnoitre the enemy's position and works at Paparata, 14 miles distant from General Cameron's advance post at Whangamarino, which was surrounded by rebel Native outlying parties and scouts. The only track known was in the hands of the enemy and constantly used by them in moving from their stronghold at Meremere to Paparata. This undertaking was successfully carried out by Major Von Tempsky and Sub-Inspector McDonnell, who ran extreme danger from scouting parties of the Natives, and having had to conceal themselves in a swamp close to Paparata during part of the night and the whole of the next day.

During the campaign of 1866, on the West Coast of the North Island, Major McDonnell was serving with the Imperial troops in command of a Native Contingent, and distinguished himself by frequent acts of bravery, more especially at the capture of Putahi Pa, when, although severely wounded in the foot, he insisted on leading his men till the close of the engagement.

The late General Chute has on more than one occasion pressed the claims of Lieutenant-Colonel McDonnell upon the Colonial Government for the distinction of the New Zealand Cross.'

McDonnell, like others, was long denied the Cross under the contention that it could not be given retrospectively for acts of bravery performed before the award was instituted. McDonnell also suffered from unpopularity with certain powerful figures in Wellington, notably his old rival Whitmore and Sir Donald McLean.

Captain Gilbert Mair, N.Z.M.

'In February 1870, after Te Kooti had succeeded in escaping from the pursuing column under Lieutenant-Colonel McDonnell, at Patetere, and engaged and repulsed that under Lieutenant-Colonel Fraser from Tauranga he turned to his right, to regain the protection of the Urewera Mountains by way of the friendly settlement of Rotorua, which he purposed destroying on his march. Captain Mair was at Rotorua, with no troops except a handful of Arawa Natives, when one Baker, a deserter from Her Majesty's navy, who had been residing among

the Maoris, brought him intelligence of Te Kooti's intentions. Captain Mair thereupon made every possible preparation, creating a fictitious appearance of force by employing old men and women to show themselves to represent troops. Te Kooti, finding the settlement apparently so strong, turned towards Kaitiriria, and made off towards the Rangitaiki River. Captain Mair thereupon boldly assumed the offensive with such young men as he could get, and pursued Te Kooti's force, inflicting heavy loss, closing with the rear-guard, and not returning till after dark, when he was almost alone, and had driven the enemy down to Fort Galatea, on the Rangitaiki River, which was, unfortunately, unoccupied by troops. During this spirited engagement, which lasted many hours, Captain Mair, by personal example and devoted gallantry, inspired his men to come to hand-to-hand conflict with Te Kooti's rearguard, himself killing the notorious Peka McLean, and driving the rest before him in disorder.'

Lieutenant-Colonel Thomas McDonnell. From *Defenders of New Zealand*

Captain Gilbert Mair. From *Defenders of New Zealand*

Ensign Henry W. Northcroft. From *Defenders of New Zealand*

Cornet Harry Charles William Wrigg, Bay of Plenty Cavalry Volunteers

'In consideration of his having on 29 June 1867 (with Trooper McDonald), voluntarily carried despatches from Lieutenant-Colonel John H. H. St John, then at Opotiki, to Lieutenant-Colonel Philip Harington at Tauranga, through country infested by the Native tribes then at war with the British.'

Ensign Henry William Northcroft, Patea Rangers

'In consideration of his having performed the undermentioned services:

On 2 October 1866 at the attack on Pungarehu, West Coast; Ensign Northcroft rescued from the enemy with great bravery and at the risk of his own life Sergeant-Major Duff who was mortally wounded and helpless.

At the attack upon Tirotiro Moana in November 1866, Ensign Northcroft bravely held his position until help arrived, and thus prevented the mutilation of the body of Private Economedes by the enemy, and the capture of the carbine and revolver belonging to the deceased.'

Henry Northcroft did not receive the New Zealand Cross until 27 June 1910, nearly 44 years after these events, and his was the final award to be made.

The New Zealand War Medal

Sergeant Charles Bullot, of the Taranaki Mounted Volunteers. *Taranaki Museum*

This decoration was not authorised until 1 March 1869, and was then issued to men of the Imperial Army for services in the New Zealand wars of 1845–47 and 1860–66. On 3 March it was extended to include the Royal Navy and Royal Marines. By order of the House of Representatives the award of the medal was then extended to cover the Colonial forces on 1 September 1869.

On the reverse of the medal, within the laurel wreath, there may appear the dates between which the recipient served in New Zealand for most of the Colonial units, however, no date at all is given.

In the case of the Imperial troops, the medal was granted to all who served in any capacity, irrespective of whether they were engaged in actual combat. The issue to local men was much more restricted, and those entitled to receive it were:

1. Those who had been under fire in any engagement between the years 1845–47 and 1860–66, and from 1866 until the cessation of hostilities.
2. The next of kin of any officers and men of the Colonial units who were killed in action or who died of wounds.
3. Those who performed conspicuous or distinguished service in the field, though not actually under fire.

No campaign or battle clasps were approved for this medal, but many men had special clasps which they wore unofficially.

An Old Campaigner

Sergeant George (Rowley) Hill (1837–1930) had a fighting career of extraordinary variety and adventure. He was born in the Devonshire town of Dawlish, and joined the Royal Navy in 1851. He saw over 10 years' service as a bluejacket. He was in H.M.S. *Leopard* at the bombardment of Sebastopol, and on returning to England from the Black Sea he joined H.M.S. *Shannon* which was bound for the China station. *Shannon* was ordered to Calcutta when the Indian Mutiny broke out.

Hill was part of Captain Peel's famous Naval Brigade, which took a battery of 32 pounders to the heart of India. He fought at the taking of Lucknow, where he was slightly wounded, at Delhi and in the desperate battles at Cawnpore under Sir Colin Campbell. In 1860 he was in the Mediterranean in H.M.S. *Hannibal,* and took French leave at Palermo to enlist, like many other British sailors, in Garibaldi's Army of Liberation. After the campaign in Italy, where he was wounded, he rejoined his ship, and the desertion was overlooked as English sympathy with Garibaldi was running high. He later served in H.M.S. *Euryalus.*

On coming to New Zealand in 1863 he joined No. 2 Company of Von Tempsky's Forest Rangers and fought in the Waikato, Taranaki and the Hauhau campaigns on the East Coast. Later he was in Major Fraser's No. 1 Company of Military Settlers in Hawke's Bay. He then joined No. 1 Division of the Armed Constabulary, and received the rare decoration of the New Zealand Cross for his part in the defence of Hiruharama Pa, Mohaka.

When the defence forces were reorganised in 1886, Hill joined the Submarine Mining Section of the Permanent Force at Auckland. His last attempt at military service came at the end of the century, when he volunteered to serve against the Boers in South Africa, but the authorities considered his age (63) too advanced. He settled in Devonport, Auckland, where he lived to his death at the age of 93.[1]

This photograph of Rowley Hill, taken about the turn of the century, shows his ten medals. From the left, bottom row: two from the Royal Humane Society, Empire Veterans Association Cross, Baltic Medal (1854–55), Turkish Medal for the Crimea (1854–56), Crimea Medal with bar for Sebastopol (1854–56), Indian Mutiny Medal with bars for Lucknow and the Relief of Lucknow (1857–58); top row: New Zealand War Medal (1860–66), New Zealand Cross, New Zealand Long Service and Good Conduct Medal.

[1] *(The New Zealand Wars and Pioneering Period)*

Bibliography

Alexander, Sir J. E., *Bush Fighting,* London, Sampson Low, Marston, Low & Searle, 1873
Alexander, Sir J. E., *Incidents of the Maori War,* London, R. Bentley, 1863
Barthorp, M., *To face the Daring Maories,* London, Hodder & Stoughton, 1979
Barton, L. L., *Australians in the Waikato War,* Sydney, Library of Australian History, 1979
Beer & Gascoigne, *Plough of the Pakeha,* Cambridge, Cambridge Independent, 1975
Best, E., *The Pa Maori,* Wellington, Government Printer, 1927
Buick, T. L., *New Zealand's First War,* Wellington, Government Printer, 1926
Claridge, J. H., *75 Years in New Zealand,* Auckland, J. H. Claridge, 1938
Clark, P., *Hauhau,* Auckland, Oxford University Press, 1975
Corbett, D. A., *Regimental Badges of New Zealand, Auckland, Ray Richards, 1980*
Cowan, J., *Settlers and Pioneers,* Wellington, Department of Internal Affairs, 1940
Cowan, J., *Sir Donald MacLean,* Wellington, A.H. & A.W. Reed, 1940
Cowan, J., *The Adventures of Kimble Bent,* Wellington, Whitcombe & Tombs, 1911
Cowan, J., *The Old Frontier,* Te Awamutu, Waipa Post Printing & Publishing Co., 1922
Cowan, J., *The History of the New Zealand Wars and the Pioneering Period,* Wellington, Government Printer, 1955
Dalton, B. J., *War and Politics in New Zealand 1855–1870,* Sydney, Sydney University Press, 1967
Dominion Archives, *Archives of the Army Dept,* Wellington, 1953
Featherston, D., *Weapons and Equipment of the Victorian Soldier,* Poole, Blandford Press, 1978
Fortescue, Sir J., *The History of the British Army,* London, Macmillan, 1927
Fox, Sir W., *The War in New Zealand,* London, Smith, Elder & Co., 1866
Gascoyne, F. J. W., *Soldiering in New Zealand,* London, T. J. S. Guilford & Co. Ltd, 1916
Gorton, E., *Some Home Truths re the Maori War 1863 to 1869,* London, Greening & Co. Ltd, 1901
Gretton, G. le M., *The Campaigns and History of the Royal Irish Regiment,* London, Published by the regiment, 1902
Gudgeon, T. W., *Defenders of New Zealand,* Auckland, H. Brett, 1887
Gudgeon, T. W., *Reminiscences of the War in New Zealand,* London, Marston, Searle & Rivington, 1879
Hattaway, R., *Reminiscences of the Northern War,* Auckland, New Zealand Herald, 1899
Houston, J., *Maori Life in Old Taranaki,* Wellington, A.H. & A.W. Reed, 1965
Hughes, B. P., *British Smooth Bore Artillery,* London, Arms & Armour Press, 1974
Lovegrove, C. L., *Wairoa-Military History of Waverley,* Patea, Historical Society, 1969
Mair, G., *Reminiscences and Maori Stories,* Auckland, Brett Printing & Publishing, 1923
Maning, F. E., *Old New Zealand,* London, R. J. Creighton & A. Scales, 1863
McDonnell, T., *Incidents of the War,* Auckland, H. Brett, 1887
McKillop, H. F., *Reminiscences of 12 Months' Service in New Zealand,* London, Richard Bentley, 1849
McLintock, A. H., *Crown Colony Government in New Zealand,* Wellington, Government Printer, 1958
McLintock, A. H., *Encyclopaedia of New Zealand,* Wellington, Government Printer, 1966
Maxwell, E., *Recollections and Reflections of Old New Zealand,* Dunedin, A.H. & A.W. Reed, 1935
Miller, W. G., *Race Conflict in New Zealand 1814–65,* Auckland, Blackwood Paul, 1966
Montague, R., *Dress and Insignia of the British Army in Australia and New Zealand 1770-1870,* Sydney, Library of Australian History, 1981
Morris, N., *Early Days in Franklin,* Auckland, Franklin County Council, 1965
Parham, W. T., *John Roberts NZC — A Man in his Time, Whakatane, Whakatane & District Historical Society, 1983*
Parham, W. T., *Von Tempsky — Adventurer,* Auckland, Hodder & Stoughton, 1969
Picard, A. F., *Minutes of the Proceedings of the Royal Artillery Institution,* Volume IV, Woolwich, Royal Artillery Institution, 1865
Power, W. T., *Sketches in New Zealand,* London, Longman, Brown, Green & Longmans, 1849
Reed, A. W., *Two Hundred Years of NZ History,* Wellington, A.H. & A.W. Reed, 1979
Rickard, L. S., *Tamihana the Kingmaker,* Wellington, A.H. & A.W. Reed, 1964
Robley, H. G., *Moko or Maori Tattooing,* London, Chapman & Hall, 1896
Rolleston, R., *The Master — J. D. Ormond of Wallingford,* Wellington, A.H. & A.W. Reed, 1980
Ruffell, W. L., *Weaponry and Tactics in the Taranaki Wars,* Vol. VIII, Nos. 2/3, 1981, N.Z. Military Historical Society's Journal *The Volunteers*
Ruffell, W. L., *The Armstrong Gun,* Vol. VI, Nos. 2/3/4, 1979; Vol. VII, Nos. 1/2/3, 1980, *The Volunteers* as above
Rusden, G. W., *History of New Zealand,* London, Chapman & Hall, 1883
St John, J. H. H., *Pakeha Rambles in Maori Lands,* Wellington, R. Burrett, 1873
Scholefield, G. N., *Dictionary of New Zealand Biography,* Wellington, Department of Internal Affairs, 1940
Sinclair, K., *A History of New Zealand,* Wellington, Penguin Books, 1959
Stafford, D. M., *Te Arawa,* Wellington, A.H. & A.W. Reed, 1967
Trollope, A., *Australia and New Zealand,* London, Chapman & Hall, 1873
Vennell, C. W., *Such Things Were,* Dunedin, Waikato Independent, 1939
Vennell, C. W., *The Brown Frontier,* Wellington, A.H. & A.W. Reed, 1967
Waikato Art Museum, *Gustavus Ferdinand Von Tempsky — The Man and the Artist,* Hamilton, 1978
Wards, I., *The Shadow of the Land,* Wellington, Department of Internal Affairs, 1968
Whitmore, G. S., *The Last Maori War in New Zealand,* London, Sampson Low, Marston & Co., 1902
Williams, J. A., *Politics of the New Zealand Maori,* Auckland, Oxford University Press, 1969

Manuscript Sources
Belich, J., *Titokowaru's War and its place in NZ History,* 1979
Bridge, C., *Journal of Events on an Expedition to New Zealand commencing 4 April 1845,* Alexander Turnbull Library
Whisker, A., *Memorandum Book,* Auckland Institute & Museum

Text References

Introduction
1. Crosby, R.D., *The Musket Wars*, 1999, p.17.
2. Belich James., television series, *The New Zealand Wars*, Landmark Productions, 1998.
3. Maxwell, Peter., *Frontier*, 2000

The Maori warrior and warfare
1. Manning. F.E., *Old New Zealand*, 1876, p.347.
2. *Monthly Review*, 1889.
3. Gudgeon. T.W., *Defenders of New Zealand*, 1887, p.517.
4. Fortescue. Sir J., *The History of the British Army*, Vol 13, 1927.
5. Manning., *ibid*, p.48.
6. Alexander. Sir J.E., *Incidents of the Maori War*, 1863, p.187.

Hone Heke's challenge
1. Bridge. Maj. C., *Journal of Events on Expedition to New Zealand, commencing 4 April 1845*.
2. *ibid*.
3. *ibid*.
4. Buick, T.L., *New Zealand's First War*, 1926, p.118.
5. Bridge, Maj. C., *Ibid*.
6. Hattaway., Robert., Reminiscence of the Northern War, *New Zealand Herald*, 1899.
7. Taylor, Rev. Richard., diary entry for 12 March 1847, conversation with Lieut. Page of the 58ᵗʰ Regt, who was present at Ruapekapeka. Alexander Turnbull Library.
8. Burrows. Robert., *Journal*, Church Missionary Society Archives, London.
9. Pugsley, Chris., *Walking Heke's War*, New Zealand Defence Quarterly, No 4, 1994.
10. Kawharu, Freda., on Hone Heke Pokai, *Dictionary of New Zealand Biography*, Vol 1, 1990.

British campaign dress in New Zealand in the 1840's
1. Buick T.L., *New Zealand's First War*, 1926, p 14.
2. Hattaway. R., *Reminiscences of the Northern War*, 1899, p.6.

Trouble moves south
1. Hinton, Joseph., *Told From The Ranks*, edited by E. Milton. Small, London, 1901.

The Taranaki saga begins.
1. Eyre-Kenny, Capt. H., *New Zealand Military Journal*, July 1913.
2. Webb. E.A.H., *The History of the 12ᵗʰ (Suffolk) Regiment*, 1865-1913.

The advance on Rangiriri
1. Cowan. James., *The History of the New Zealand Wars and The Pioneering Period*, 1955, p.233.
2. Correspondence G15, Appendices to Journal of the House of Representatives, 1871.
3. *ibid*.
4. Cowan, James., *ibid*, Vol. 1, p.268.
5. *Daily Southern Cross*, August 1863.
6. Von Tempsky, Maj. G.F., *Memoranda of the New Zealand Campaign in 1863 and 1864*.
7. McDonnell, Lieut. Col. Thomas., Manuscript, Auckland Public Library.

British artillery in New Zealand
1. Minutes of the Proceedings of the Royal Artillery Institution 1865.

Courage is not enough
1. Von Tempsky, Maj. G.F., *Memoranda of the New Zealand Campaign in 1863 and 1864*, p.26.
2. McDonnell, Maj. T., *Incidents of the War*, 1887, p.571.
3. Cowan. James., *The History of the New Zealand Wars and the Pioneering Period 1955*, Vol 1, p.359.
4. *Auckland Star*, 15 October 1928.
5. Von Tempsky, G.F., *ibid*, p.83.
6. Cowan, J., *ibid*, Vol 1, p.391.
7. *ibid*, Vol 1, p.391.
8. *ibid*, Vol 1, p.401.

The Maori Pa
1. Pugsley, Chris., *The Maori did not Invent Trench Warfare*, NZ Defence Quarterly, No 22, 1998.

The Lame Seagull's March
1. Gamble, Lieut Gen. D.J., *Journal of 1861-55*., WO 33/16 PRO.
2. Von Tempsky, Maj. G.F., *Letter* to Frederick Weld, 21 July 1865.
3. Cameron. Sir. Duncan., *Letter* to Lieut. T. McDonnell., 20 October 1863.
4. Belich, James., entry on General Cameron in *The Dictionary of New Zealand Biography*, Vol 1, 1990.
5. *The Weekly News*, 30 January 1864.
6. Tedder. Corp. Edward., *Memorandum Book* for 1863-64, collection of P. Horne.

Fighting in the east
1. Hope. Capt. C.W., *Dispatch*, 12 September 1865.
2. *Daily Southern Cross*, 23 September 1865.

A march around Mt Egmont
1. Von Tempsky, Maj. G.F., *A Campaign on the West Coast of New Zealand*, January and February 1866. p.12.
2. *ibid*, p.13.
3. *ibid*, p.15
4. Chute, Maj. Gen. Trevor., *Dispatch*, 8 January 1866.
5. Von Tempsky, G.F., *ibid*, p.19.
6. Chute, Maj. gen. Trevor., *Dispatch*, 12 February 1866.
7. Von Tempsky, G.F., *ibid*, p.25.
8. *ibid*, p.27.
9. *ibid*, p.32.

New Zealand Armed Constabulary in the field
1. Parham. W.T., *John Roberts NZC – A Man in His Time*, 1983, p.34.
2. McDonnell. Maj. Thomas., *Dispatch*, 22 August 1868.
3. Cowan. James., *The History of the New Zealand Wars and the Pioneering Period*, 1955, Vol. II, p.213.
4. Cowan, James., *ibid*, Vol II, p.213.
5. *ibid*, Vol II, p.214.
6. Featherston, Dr. Isaac., *Letter* 27, 17 September 1868, T. McDonnell papers.
7. Haultain, Col. Theodore., *Report file*, mw5011, series 32, National Archives.
8. Whitmore, Lieut. Col. George., *Letter* to Col. Haultain, 2 November 1868.

Whitmore takes command
1. Whitmore, Lieut. Col. George., *Dispatch*, 30 December 1868.
2. Whitmore, Lieut. Col. George., *Dispatch*, 8 January 1869.
3. Rusden. G., *The Groans of the Maoris*, London, 1888.
4. Whitmore, Lieut. Col. George., *Dispatch*, 3 February 1869.

The Urewera expedition
1. Whitmore, Lieut. Col. George., *Letter*, to Col. Haultain, 23 April 1869.
2. *Historical Review*, Whakatane, December 1962, p.132.
3. Whitmore, Lieut. Col. George., *Dispatch*, 18 May 1869.
4. Whitmore, Lieut. Col. George., undated *Letter* to Col Haultain.
5. Harrington, Lieut. Col. Phillip., *Letter* to Col Haultain, 16 July 1869.
6. Cowan, James., *The History of the New Zealand Wars and the Pioneering Period*, 1955, Vol. 1, p.169.

Blockhouses forts and redoubts
1. Cowan, James., *The History of the New Zealand Wars and the Pioneering Period*, 1955, Vol 1, p.169.

The end of the wars
1. Ormond, John., *Letter*, 27 October 1869.
2. Parham, W.T., *John Roberts NZC – A Man in his Time*, 1983.

The New Zealand Cross
1. Cowan, James., *The History of the New Zealand Wars and the Pioneering Period*, 1955, Vol II, p.536.

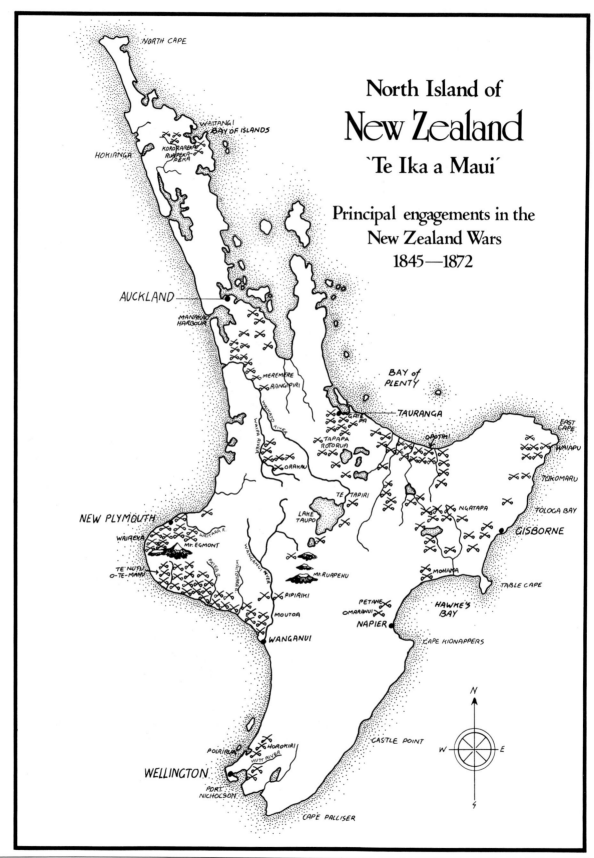

North Island of
New Zealand
`Te Ika a Maui´

Principal engagements in the
New Zealand Wars
1845—1872

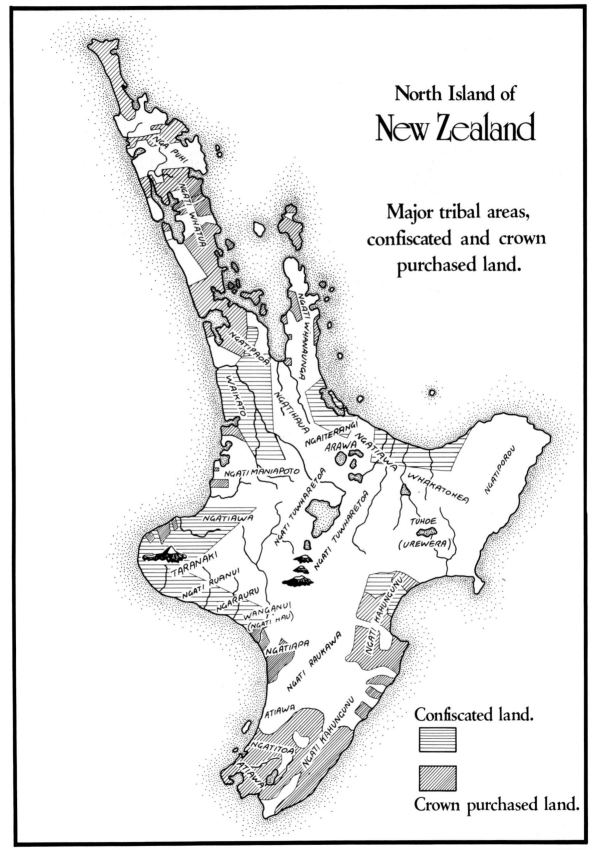

North Island of

New Zealand

Major tribal areas, confiscated and crown purchased land.

Confiscated land.

Crown purchased land.

Index

Other Grantham House Illustrated Histories

TARAWERA — THE DESTRUCTION OF THE PINK AND WHITE TERRACES
Geoff Conly

The Tarawera eruption of 1886 was New Zealand's worst volcanic disaster of recorded times with a death toll of 153. The Pink and White Terraces were acclaimed as the eighth wonder of the world.

Colour plates include paintings by Blomfield, Barraud, Heaphy, Hoyte and Watkins.

THE HARBOUR FERRIES OF AUCKLAND *David Balderston*

A former ferry master writes with knowledge and affection about the special delight of a ferry trip on Auckland Harbour. From the grand old Victorian and Edwardian ladies of the Devonport Steam Ferry Company to the vessels used today.

A SERVANT OF THE CITY — THE WELLINGTON CITY MISSION 1904-1984
Janette A. Gosnell

An important social history of Wellington which spans 80 years. It is about people of all ages in an urban environment and gives an insight into the changing social conditions of each decade.

WHEN TRAMS WERE TRUMPS IN NEW ZEALAND *Graham Stewart*

Suburban travel before the motorcar. New Zealanders rode them to school, to work, to sports and many to fame. A pictorial parade of these classic vehicles through the changing facades of streets in our cities, spanning more than 100 years.